THE NEW WORLD ECONOMIC ORDER

How Will It Affect You?

ISSUES FOR THE 21ST CENTURY

Dr. Elliot O. Douglin

THE NEW WORLD ECONOMIC ORDER
How Will It Affect You?
ISSUES FOR THE 21ST CENTURY

Dr. Elliot O. Douglin
1997 Camp Meeting

Truth for the Final Generation
P.O. Box 725
Bridgetown, Barbados, W.I.
Tel/Fax (246) 421-7297
email: truth@sunbeach.net

Truth for the Final Generation
P.O. Box 216 Caldwell, Idaho 83606
email: info@TruthInJesus.org

Visit us on the web at http://www.TruthInJesus.org

International Standard Book Number: 0-9741841-4-4

Printed in the United States of America   2 3 4 5 6 7 8 9 10
First Printing: November 2004

Cover design and book design by Sawtooth Graphics, Caldwell, ID, USA

CONTENTS

Introduction   v

The Passing of a Century and a Millennium   1

A New World Economic Order Coming Soon   11

Looking Back On Two Centuries of Freedom   19

Freedom, Open-Market Economy and the New World Order   33

The History of Sunday Laws   39

The American Paradox   57

The 1961 Douglas Dissent   65

Is the Constitution Right?   79

The Limits of Civil Authority   93

The Genius of the First Amendment   107

Opposition to the First Amendment   115

A Morally Renewed America   127

Doubly UnProtestant   141

Is the Charge Valid?   147

America In Prophecy   165

Absolute Principles Involved   181

Utopia or Disaster?   191

The Survivors   209

Introduction

A new world economic order is ahead of us. It will usher in sweeping changes to our accustomed way of life, especially affecting the liberties which we have progressively enjoyed over the past two centuries.

This book, *The New World Economic Order — How Will It Affect You?*, presents an in-depth analysis of the key issues involved in the establishment of the new world system, which will be implemented in the near future, and whose ground work has already been laid.

The analysis includes a comprehensive study of the principles of liberty of conscience, and the First Amendment to the U.S. Constitution, which has served as a model for countries, which have embraced the principles of liberty.

This book also presents the history, the law, and the theology which form the basis of the rights and liberties of conscience, which are guaranteed under the constitutions, or by the governments, of most countries.

But this book goes further and examines the absolute issues at stake and the far-reaching consequences of the new world economic order. You, the reader, will be most definitely affected, and for this reason, if no other, this book is necessary reading for you.

Dr. E. Douglin

The Passing of a Century and a Millennium

*W*E ARE LIVING IN THE MOST EXCITING and, at the same time, the most perilous period of the history of our world. Calamities by air, sea and land, the unsettled state of society, the alarms of war, the decline in the stability of the natural environment are all portentous. They forecast approaching events of the greatest magnitude. Great changes are soon to take place in our world and the final movements toward a New World Economic Order, with its consequences for our planet, will be rapid ones. As we approach the turn of yet another century we do so with both a sense of expectation and foreboding.

The passing of a century produces a sense of awe and a power to move the human spirit. But the passing of ten centuries or 1000 years triggers an awareness of destiny and provokes apprehension of the future. This present 1000 year period started in 1001 A.D. and will end in 2000 A.D. Some of our elderly folk may encompass a century or most of it in their life span. But a thousand year period stretches the limit of our ability to reckon time. As the world approaches, reaches and passes the year 2000 A.D. we shall be closing off the twentieth century (1901-2000) and the second millennium since Christ (1001-2000). For those who live through the transition period of the last few years of the 20th Century, the year 2000 itself, and the first few years of the 21st Century, i.e. the beginning of the third millennium, it will be a time of tremendous challenge, and unprecedented global change.

As we enter the third millennium we carry into it the most phenomenal advances in science and technology the world has yet seen. Just imagine that at the start of this century, in the years 1900-1901, radio, television, telephone, air transport and the computer were either unknown or in their embryonic scientific form. Now, as we approach 2000 A.D. we have super technologies which this generation takes for granted which, were our great-great-grand parents resurrected to see them, they would not believe their eyes!

Nuclear power, space exploration, supersonic aircraft, facsimile transmissions, computer and information technology, the Internet, satellite and global communication, open-heart surgery, transplant surgery — and the list could go on and on — all are examples of the tremendous advances in science and technology which have characterized the 20th Century.

But, at the same time, we are also carrying into the 21st Century unprecedented levels of violent crime, lawlessness, and the criminal potential to counterfeit and abuse almost all financial systems and many other things besides.

We are carrying into the "third millennium" unrivalled levels of drug abuse and new disease patterns. The chronic degenerative diseases, such as heart attack, cancer, diabetes, and hypertension continue to kill millions yearly. New viral illnesses such as H.I.V., Ebola and others, and the resurgence of old infectious diseases, such as T.B., pose massive threats to global health and economy.

The resurgence of old infections, which were thought to have been conquered, is especially alarming. The following report from a professional periodical, The Economist, reveals some interesting economic facts:

> "The problem humans have with germs is that they work by rules that humans find hard to deal with, rules so different that before Pasteur no one knew what they were. Germs are quick; humans are slow. Germs have no thought for the future; humans plan. Germs have no technologies; humans are consummate users of tools. Most important, germs never give up. Humans do so all too readily.

> "For centuries staphylococcus bacteria made trivial wounds fatal injuries. Then science came up with a tool to use against them: penicillin. In 1952 staphylococcus bacteria were almost 100%

susceptible to penicillin, and the scourge became an irritant. By 1982 90% of the strains had become resistant to the drug. Clever humans, not unduly worried, changed tools. The germs developed resistance to the new ones. Now, only one safe drug can be relied upon to fight staphylococcus: vancomycin. Other bugs are already resistant to it; their relevant know-how, bits of information encoded in DNA, may be all too easily transferred. Then the game will be back to square one—except that far more people undergo surgery now than before antibiotics made it safe. In 1992 4% of Americans who underwent surgery became infected. Most of those 920,000 people were infected with staphylococcus.

"In late 18th century Europe, tuberculosis killed perhaps one in five. Careful use of antibiotics gradually put paid to it. After a while, the world decided that the fight was over; but no one told the tuberculosis bacillus. In New York city, spending on tuberculosis fell from $40m in 1968 to $2m in 1989. The cuts hit outpatient work, so no one was there to ensure that the sick—often homeless drug addicts—took their medicine properly. That let resistance bloom. By the beginning of 1991 almost half of New York's new cases of tuberculosis were resistant to the main drugs previously used, and the costs of hospitalizing people with tuberculosis in the city had reached $50m a year.

"Many problems fail to yield to public spending. Tuberculosis in America is not one of them. National surveillance worked well until the 1970's. When, against expert advice, responsibility for this work was given to the states, the programme fell apart. In 1986, just as the comeback was getting underway, the multi-drug resistance unit at the Centres for Disease Control in Atlanta was closed. All told, cuts in tuberculosis programmes during the 1980s saved America perhaps $200m. According to one estimate, America spent more than $1 billion on multi-drug-resistant tuberculosis in the five years up to 1994.

"America stands out only because it is rich enough and knowledgeable enough to lack excuse. But similar stories, and worse, have unfolded around the world. In developing countries, most cases of tuberculosis could be cured with drugs that cost as little as $13 a patient. Yet, worldwide, less than 50% of the detected cases are being cured. There seems no fundamental reason why the world should not achieve a success rate of at least 85%. Clinics in Somalia already do. The World Health Organization, itself in dire need of reform, estimates that cheap, systematic interventions might save 12 million of the 30 million likely to die from tuberculosis in the next ten years." The Economist, May 20, 1995, pp. 14, 15.

Pre-Millennial Tension

As we approach, reach and pass the year 2000 A.D. most people will experience an increasing sense of expectation and/or apprehension. Sociologists call it "pre-millennial tension." Again from *The Economist*:

"Sociologists of religion, not often known for their humour, came up with a good turn of phrase a few years ago to describe this phenomenon of nervous expectation. They diagnosed PMT, 'pre-millennial tension.' PMT is already credited with influencing events as diverse as the rise of cults and necromancers in the former Soviet Union, the Waco and Solar Temple bloodbaths, the international vogue for New Age lifestyles, and the susceptibility of American and British public opinion to tales of Satanic ritual child-abuse.

"Perhaps it is PMT which lies behind the fear that life on earth could be destroyed any year now by a celestial-body collision; which makes people read reports of apparently novel reminders of mortality such as the Ebola virus with a special sense of terror; and which gives added weight to the predictions of ecological doomsayers who insist that the greenhouse effect is about to bring terminal catastrophe. When 2000 has safely come and gone, assuming that it does, the world may find itself possessed by a corresponding sense of optimism, a reassured conviction that humanity has now entered upon a new beginning. But, for the moment, most people are far from convinced." The Economist, January 4, 1997, p. 83.

Some History on the Passing of a Century

It seems that the end of a century has generally produced emotional agitation and either a sense of excitement or apprehension, or both, in the human spirit. We can perhaps cast a backward glance at the turn of the eighteenth century and the turn of the nineteenth century and learn from history a little of the sense of foreboding that impacts on the popular psyche at such times. From *The Economist*, January 4 1997:

> "Admittedly the sense of foreboding is sometimes set off by social and economic factors—natural disasters, the collapse of political systems, the displacement of populations. But even where these are not present, the end of a calendar era is liable to bring on the symptoms of PMT: disorientation, loss of faith in institutions, a rising sense of unfocused excitement, and visions of an apocalyptic or utopian future.

> "The drama of real events largely explains what went through people's minds in the 1790's. The physical and psychological violence of the French revolution had ensured that this would be a period of great emotion. Not for the first time, it became hard to distinguish religious from political mystics. In England, the government suppressed prophets who welcomed events in France as a fulfillment of biblical eschatology. The fact that a century's end was approaching was probably not a major factor. At the end of the 18th century, the anno-domini century did not loom as large in popular consciousness as it does today: in Britain, people were as likely to think of themselves as living in the 40th year of the reign of King George III as in the year 1799.

> "Awareness of the ticking clock, rather than omens of disaster, may have played a bigger role in the mood of the 1890's. Then, a combination of bewildering technological advance and political change had made most people think that the 20th century would be a time of peace, stability and universal good health. The turn of the century gave birth to the concept of *fin de siecle* (the title of a play that opened in Paris in April 1888) as well as the idea that the time could define a cultural climate: the Naughty Nineties were the first decade in the history of the world to bear a nickname.

> "But the optimism was not shared by everyone. The philosopher George Steiner speaks of a 'great ennui' which fastened on

images of destruction: 'Whether the psychic mechanisms involved were universal or historically localized, one thing is plain: by about 1900 there was a terrible readiness, indeed a thirst, for what Yeats called 'the blood-dimmed tide.' A gloomy minority of Europeans correctly (as it turned out) conjured up images of catastrophe; and some Americans found in the pains of their country's industrialization a similar fascination with prophecies of doom.'

"And the prospect in the evening of the 1990's? You might think that the closing years of a century which has seen the defeat of the fascist and communist monsters, and the end of a millennium which has discovered the means of achieving religious liberty, political democracy and economic abundance, would be a moment of quiet gratitude and cheerful self-confidence. Instead, in much of the world—even in the apparently victorious democracies—people are worrying about racial violence, new clashes of power, nasty economic surprises, novel kinds of disease. Truly, at such turning points of the calendar, the clump of time's boots seems to make men shiver."

Indeed, a sense of foreboding springs up in the human mind at the turn of a century or the passing of a millennium. People are wondering what the 21st century will have in store for mankind. Will the wonderful scientific and technological advances of the 20th century furnish the problem-solving tools we need? Or, will the present critical problems intensify and be joined by other, as yet unknown, problems which will threaten us all with extinction?

A Sense of Foreboding, But of What?

We go about our ordinary duties day by day as ordinary citizens oblivious to changes occurring behind the scenes of overt human activity. Our daily routine does not suggest that there will be any radical change to our accustomed way of life, at least for the foreseeable future.

But unknown to the teeming millions of human persons on our planet there are already well advanced plans for a new geopolitical system called the New World Economic Order.

The idea of a geopolitical new world order is not new. What is new is that for the first time in modern history concrete plans for the establishment of such a system are well advanced.

As a reader of this book you may or may not have heard of words like *globalists*, *transnationalists*, or *geopolitea*. These words describe the concept of a global government which will replace the present *national* system. The present world is a world of many nations, each with its own national system of administrative, executive and judicial authorities. But the proposed new geopolitical system will transcend and unify the present national systems which we all know so well.

Although many organizations have global outreach plans only three modern day organizations, the Papacy, the Capitalist West and Soviet Communism have had a geopolitical agenda for a long time.

These three powers were locked in competition for victory in the struggle for world dominance. This competition intensified in the decades of the seventies and eighties.

Soviet and Eastern European Communism has since then collapsed, leaving the other two contenders to continue the struggle. But in this struggle there can be only one winner. As a matter of fact the forces of Western Capitalism will eventually allow a religio-political event to occur which will open the door for Papal administrative, executive, moral and judicial control of a new global system.

The blueprints for global control are now well documented. Professor Malachi Martin, expert on Papal policy and a Vatican insider, has written a book entitled *The Keys of This Blood* in which he reveals some stunning geopolitical plans.

Writing in the eighties (before the collapse of communism) for his book which was published in 1990, Malachi Martin wrote:

> "Willing or not, ready or not, we are all involved in an all-out, no-holds-barred, three-way global competition. Most of us are not competitors, however. We are the stakes. For the competition is about who will establish the first one-world system of government that has ever existed in the society of nations. It is about who will hold and wield the dual power of authority and control over each of us as individuals and over all of us together as a community; over the entire six billion people expected by demographers to inhabit the earth by early in the third millennium.
>
> "The competition is all-out because, now that it has started, there is no way it can be reversed or called off.

"No holds are barred because, once the competition has been decided, the world and all that's in it — our way of life as individuals and as citizens of the nations; our families and our jobs; our trade and commerce and money; our educational systems and our religions and our cultures; even the badges of our national identity, which most of us have always taken for granted — all will have been powerfully and radically altered forever. No one can be exempted from its effects. No sector of our lives will remain untouched.

"The competition began and continues as a three-way affair because that is the number of rivals with sufficient resources to establish and maintain a new world order.

"Nobody who is acquainted with the plans of these three rivals has any doubt but that only one of them can win. Each expects the other two to be overwhelmed and swallowed up in the coming maelstrom of change. That being the case, it would appear inescapable that their competition will end up as a confrontation.

"As to the time factor involved, those of us who are under seventy will see at least the basic structures of the new world government installed. Those of us under forty will surely live under its legislative, executive and judiciary authority and control. Indeed, the three rivals themselves — and many more besides as time goes on — speak about this new world order not as something around a distant corner of time, but as something that is imminent. As a system that will be introduced and installed in our midst by the end of this final decade of the second millennium.

"What these competitors are talking about, then, is the most profound and widespread modification of international, national and local life that the world has seen in a thousand years. And the competition they are engaged in can be described simply enough as the millennium endgame.

"Ten years before this competition became manifest to the world at large, the man who was destined to become the first, the most unexpected and, for some at least, the most unwelcome competitor of all in this millennium endgame spoke openly about what he saw down the road even then.

"Toward the end of an extended visit to America in 1976, an obscure Polish archbishop from Krakow by the name of Karol Wojtyla stood before an audience in New York City and made one of the most prophetic speeches ever given.

"We are now standing in the face of the greatest historical confrontation humanity has gone through,' he said, '...a test of two thousand years of culture and Christian civilization, with all its consequences for human dignity, individual rights and rights of nations. But,' he chided his listeners on that September day, 'wide circles of American society and wide circles of the Christian community do not realize this fully...'

"Perhaps the world was still too immersed in the old system of nation-states, and in all the old international balance-of-power arrangements, to hear what Wojtyla was saying. Or perhaps Wojtyla himself was reckoned as no more than an isolated figure hailing from an isolated country that had long since been pointedly written out of the global power equation. Or perhaps, after the industrial slaughter of millions of human beings in two world wars and in 180 local wars, and after the endless terrors of nuclear brinksmanship that have marked the progress of the twentieth century, the feeling was simply that one confrontation more or less wasn't going to make much difference.

"Whatever the reason, it would seem that no one who heard or later read what Karol Wojtyla said that day had any idea that he was pointing to a competition he already saw on the horizon: a competition between the world's only three internationally based power structures for truly global hegemony.

"An isolated figure Karol Wojtyla may have been in the fall of 1976—at least for many Westerners. But two years later, in October of 1978, when he emerged from the Sistine Chapel in Rome as Pope John Paul II, the 264th successor to Peter the Apostle, he was himself the head of the most extensive and deeply experienced of the three global powers that would within a short time, set about ending the nation system of world politics that has defined human society for over a thousand years.

"It is not too much to say, in fact, that the chosen purpose of John Paul's pontificate — the engine that drives his papal grand policy and that determines his day-to-day, year-by-year strategies — is to be the victor in that competition, now well under way. For the fact is that the stakes John Paul has placed in the arena of geopolitical contention include everything — himself; his papal persona; the age-old Petrine Office he now embodies; and his entire Church Universal, both as an institutional organization unparalleled in the world and as a body of believers united by a bond of mystical communion." Malachi Martin, The Keys of This Blood, pp. 15-17. SIMON and SCHUSTER, 1990

The "Millennium endgame," as Professor Martin puts it, is well under way. Very soon from now there will begin the discussions and agitations of the very first step in the establishment of the New World Order. It will be a religio-political step to be taken by the West which will be the signal for the start of global change and global crisis.

Indeed the new century and the new millennium will bring us face to face with the new geopolitical system, man's first modern attempt to solve world problems by a new religio-economic order.

A New World Economic Order Coming Soon

*P*LANS ARE AFOOT TO ESTABLISH a new world economic order: a global system of political-economic-judicial control aimed at making the world a safer, better place in which to live. Unknown and unnoticed by the vast majority of people, the world is moving towards a global geopolitical system of international control of human activity. Our world is faced with terribly malignant problems. The list is terrifying:

- The rapid rise in the level of crime, violence and general lawlessness throughout the world and especially in all the world's major cities.
- Ongoing problems between capital and labour, i.e. between big business enterprises and their employees.
- Problems plaguing world economy; recession; inflation; third world poverty and debt.
- International trafficking of illegal drugs.
- International terrorism.
- The threat of water and food shortages as the world population increases.
- The global "green-house" effect caused by industrial production of certain gases. This will cause global atmospheric temperatures to rise, producing melting of more ice at the poles and therefore a rise in ocean tides and an increase in the frequency and severity of hurricanes, cyclones and floods.

- New patterns of infectious disease (HIV, Ebola, etc.)
- Increasing levels of environmental pollution by industrial, nuclear and domestic wastes.
- The progressive abuse of freedom by every succeeding generation during the twentieth century.
- Fanatical Cult leaders that mislead, delude and destroy many.

All of these problems are on the increase and international authorities are seeking for some global system which will solve or control such potentially destructive problems. Many experts and authorities strongly believe that the very survival of mankind will be under serious threat if these problems are not dealt with adequately and urgently.

A Global System of Control

The proposed global system will be one in which all people are registered, numbered and monitored and will be allowed to engage in economic activity only if they are obedient to the rules of the system. It is proposed that no one will be allowed to buy or sell unless that person accepts the terms of the system and obeys its rules.

People who disobey the system will be subjected to civil penalties in the courts of law. Those countries with the greatest technology, such as the United States of America (USA) and the European Union, will be the first to implement the system.

But, you may ask, why would such drastic measures be needed? It will be argued that surely something has to be done to stop the alarming increase in crime, terrorism, disease and poverty. And, surely something should be done to ensure that everyone be fed, clothed and housed at the basic acceptable level of human dignity.

It will be proposed that the problems facing the world must be solved at any cost. And therefore the people should be prepared to accept strict laws and severe penalties, all in the interest of making the world a better place in which to live.

Most people will gladly accept a system aimed at making the world a safer and better place in which to live, even if civil penalties have to be more severe than before.

A Confederacy of Systems

In order for the new world economic order to succeed there will have to be the cooperation of politicians, religionists, economists, scientists, technologists and legal experts. Also involved will be the commercial sector, trade unions and law enforcement agencies.

This new geopolitical system will seek to establish a favorable balance between work and recreation. It is being suggested by many psychologists and family life experts that the intensity of the demands of work, such as long hours every day of the week, has eroded the foundations of family life and, therefore, of society.

Trade unions will insist that workers' rights be respected and that workers be allowed one rest day per week. Surveys have indicated that productivity improves when workers are allowed one rest day per week rather than requiring them to work everyday of the week.

The popular Christian churches will be united in calling for Sunday to be the universal day of rest and family togetherness and worship. But because many businesses may think more of the dollar than of the day of rest, Sunday rest will eventually be enforced by legislation.

Church-State Union

Religious leaders will eventually persuade the masses that compulsory Sunday rest should be enforced by legislation. And politicians will eventually pass legislation to enforce Sunday rest because of popular demand.

There will therefore be a church-state union in which worship on a particular day, Sunday, will be part of the law of the land, with civil penalties attached to the Sunday law.

Supernatural Support for the System

It will also be declared that messages from the spiritual realms endorse the Sunday laws as a vital part of the new world economic order. Miraculous and sensational occurrences will strengthen the opinion that the new world economic order, with its Sunday laws, has the stamp of divine approval placed upon it.

The overwhelming majority of earth's population will not only support the system but will become increasingly intolerant of anyone or any group that does not fall into line with the terms and rules of the system.

Massive Support From the People

Philosophical reasoning, religious persuasion, supernatural miracles and the intensity of the problems facing mankind will eventually produce massive support for the new system. All will believe that it is the only way forward for each nation of the world, and for the world as a whole. There will be pronouncements that the system will produce lasting peace, safety and prosperity while reducing crime and improving productivity. Religionists will assert, with adamance, that the Sunday rest will ensure the return of the blessings of the Lord upon the world. It will seem to all that the new world political-religious economic system is the answer to world problems.

Individual Freedom or World Survival?

Right now (at the time of writing in 1997) we enjoy the basic human rights of freedom of opinion, freedom of expression, freedom of conscience in matters of religion and philosophy; but, in the new world economic order, soon to come, there will be the removal of at least some of these individual freedoms.

The argument will run like this: The survival of the world is more important than the rights of an individual. And the individual must be prepared to sacrifice some individual freedoms for the overall common good of all.

And, remember, precedents have already been set, in recent history, that in matters of national or global emergencies, the rights of the individual are negated by the need to ensure the survival of the majority.

For example, during the Second World War, after Japan bombed Pearl Harbor on December 7, 1941 and destroyed America's Pacific Fleet, approximately 120,000 Japanese Americans, born in the U.S.A. and loyal to her flag, were suddenly arrested and placed in concentration camps without "due process of law."

Scholars Alfred A. Kelly and Winfred Harbison in their book, *The American Constitution: Its Origins and Development* (New York: W.W. Norton, 1955), p. 841, wrote:

> "In future wars no person belonging to a racial, religious, cultural or political minority can be assured that community prejudice and bigotry will not express itself in a program of suppression justified as 'military necessity', with the resulting destruction of his basic rights as a member of a free society. Bills of Rights are written in large part to protect society against precisely such a possibility, and insofar as they fail to do so they lose their meaning."

When the new world economic order is fully established, each individual will have to comply with the terms and rules of the system or be subjected to civil penalties in the courts of law.

Compulsory Sunday laws will be a central component of the new global system. Those individuals or groups who have a different persuasion of which day is the day of rest and worship, will not be tolerated. They will be arrested and charged with violation of the Sunday laws and will be fined, imprisoned and subjected to economic boycott. Those who, for example, believe that Saturday is the true day of rest and worship will be progressively pressurized under the new global system.

As a matter of fact, acceptance of, and compliance with the Sunday laws will be a necessary prerequisite for receiving licence and registration documents and business numbers for participating in any economic activity in the new world economic order.

Euro-American Control

With the fall of communism in eastern Europe and central Asia, the USA has rapidly emerged not only as the sole super power, but also as the nation which is taking the lead in establishing the new world economic order. Throughout the world the USA is quietly but powerfully flexing the muscles of its economic, military and technological might and leadership.

In the USA there are already, and will continue to be, increasing calls for a national Sunday Law as part of a new economic and moral America. Indeed, almost all States in the USA already have ancient Sunday "blue" laws written in their law books, but these have been rendered dormant by the amendment to the USA Constitution allowing for liberty of conscience in religious matters.

Calls for strict Sunday laws will come mainly from what are called the fundamental (Sunday keeping) evangelical Christian denominations. They will put forward the claim that America's moral healing and future prosperity depends on the strict observance of Sunday as the Lord's Day.

Meanwhile in Europe the Papacy is moving forward steadily with its plan for a closer European unity based not merely on economic and technological policies but also on Europe's historic religion—the Christianity of the Church of Rome.

Malachi Martin, expert on Vatican affairs and expositor of papal policies, in his book *"The Keys of This Blood"* reveals the principal objectives of the papacy for Europe, and indeed the world.

The papacy strongly believes that lasting economic prosperity and peace in Europe cannot be realized unless the historic European Church be allowed what is regarded as its rightful role of once more controlling and directing the spiritual and moral affairs of Europe in close alliance with the political directorate of the European Union.

The USA followed by Europe, will lead the way in establishing the new world economic order. A superstrong USA and a superstrong European Union will be able to exert the necessary economic, technological and military power to persuade or, should we say, to put enough pressure on other nations to accept the terms of the new world economic order.

When Will This New Geopolitical System Be Established??

Well, if the Vatican's plans succeed as scheduled, the system should be in place somewhere around the year 2000, or soon thereafter.

Malachi Martin in his book *The Keys of This Blood* (published in 1990) reminds us of the Papal plan:

> "Those of us who are under seventy will see at least the basic structures of the new world government installed. Those of us under forty will surely live under its legislative, executive and judiciary authority and control. Indeed, the three rivals themselves — and many more besides as time goes on — speak about this new world order not as something around a distant corner of time, but as something that is imminent. As a system that will be introduced and installed in our midst by the end of this final decade of the second millennium.(sic)" The Keys of This Blood, (Simon & Schuster, September, 1990) pp. 15, 16.

The Papacy intends that the new global system be established by the year 2000. Whether or not it turns out to be so will depend on the speed with which the U.S.A. proceeds with its plans.

Though the U.S.A. is taking the leading role in establishing the new world order, the Papacy, according to Mr. Martin, intends to take the leading role in the executive and judicial administration of the geopolitical new world economic order.

A global geopolitical economic system is around the corner. It will be a confederacy of all the various aspects of modern civilization. But its main and most peculiar characteristic will be religious-political or church-state union.

The church-state union will resemble the church-state union of the Middle Ages, when the Roman Church wielded an ecclesiastical-political dominance over Europe, and Sunday laws will be the mark of the ecclesiastical authority of the New World Economic Order.

Constitutional Changes

The soon-to-come New World Economic Order will be accompanied by sweeping changes in the constitutions of the nations. The change will first be made in the Constitution of the USA.

The US constitution guarantees liberty of conscience in matters of faith and worship. It further declares that no law shall be passed to prohibit the free exercise of the individual's religious preference.

Therefore, in order for the US Congress to pass legislation to enforce a national Sunday Law, the amendment to the U.S. Constitution guaranteeing the free exercise of one's religious preference would have to be repealed or interpreted differently.

Similar changes will take place in all the other nations of the world. It will be argued that the progressive abuse of freedom by every succeeding generation during the last two centuries has brought the world to the brink of chaos. It will be further asserted that individual liberties must be curtailed for the common good of the entire world.

Religious authorities in the USA and Europe are already claiming that disrespect for Sunday as the Lord's Day is an important factor in the rapid decline in law and order in modern western societies. They are adamant in their belief that proper observance of Sunday is linked with the moral and economic renewal of the USA and Europe.

This argument will be generally accepted, and, the necessary changes to the constitutions will be made in order to enforce the terms and laws of the New World Order as the only way to save our planet.

Vast changes will soon sweep across the socio-economic, political and religious landscapes of our world — changes which will permanently alter our way of life on this planet. Yet so few people understand what is really happening or how they will be affected.

Not All Will Comply

History has made it abundantly clear that there is never one hundred per cent compliance with any system of national or international control. Some minority groups will raise their voices in protest against the system. But philosophical persuasion, legislative pressure and inexplicable "miraculous" phenomena will silence most of the objecting minorities.

Those who oppose for religious reasons will not give in either to the arguments or to the legal pressure and their protest will bring matters to crisis proportions.

Harsh penalties will be administered to those who oppose the system but this will not silence them. Even the threat of the death penalty will not deter them in their protest. The world will thereby be brought to the greatest crisis in the history of mankind.

Those who refuse to comply will give historical and scriptural evidence to prove that no imperial or global system can succeed by trampling on the rights of the individual in matters of conscience and faith.

Yes, reader, a new world religious-political economic order is coming soon, and with it will come the greatest crisis in history.

Why? Will there be more to the new world order than meets the eye? What far reaching issues and absolute principles of human rights will be involved in such a crisis? Will the new system be successful or will it usher in something ghastly? We must examine the issues.

Looking Back On Two Centuries Of Freedom

*T*HE HISTORY OF THE STRUGGLE FOR FREEDOM is perhaps as long as the history of recorded civilization. The history of freedom itself is no more than 6% of the history of recorded civilization.

Certainly, in our common era of 2000 years after Christ, civil and religious liberty, as we now know it, has only been widely enjoyed over the past 200 years. And even so, such freedom has had to be developed through many a struggle before and during those 200 years.

In the period of ancient history before Christ, imperial autocratic governments prevailed. Liberty of conscience in civil and religious matters, and freedom of choice in electing a government were privileges largely unknown to the peoples who lived at that time.

The great empires of antiquity such as Egypt, Assyria and then Babylon, Medo-Persia, Greece and Rome were totalitarian in nature and tolerated no individual deviation from the national religion or national political system. Greece was perhaps the most liberal of the ancient empires. In some of the ancient Greek city states (at least in Athens) officials were elected, hence the word *demokratia*, whence comes *democracy*.

In our common Christian era, during the so-called "Dark-Ages," the Medieval Church dominated Europe for over a millennium during which time European Governments were in the form of Kingdoms. Religious liberty was unknown to the masses of people in Europe.

There were two distinct movements in Europe which laid the foundations for the modern development of civil and religious liberty.

The Protestant Reformation

Firstly, and most importantly, there was the Protestant Reformation centered in Germany. The Reformation was a religious movement which laid the foundation of modern religious liberty. During the Middle Ages any individual who dared to differ with the doctrines or traditions of the Roman Catholic Church, and who refused to recant, was executed by the civil government of his own country under the direction of the Papacy. The Papal Church employed the civil governments or states of Europe to punish any individual deviation from the doctrines or traditions of the Roman Church.

The Reformation, led by Martin Luther, asserted that neither Church nor state has the right to force any person to obey or practice any doctrine or tradition which he or she does not conscientiously believe. In other words, the Protestant Reformation defended the basic human freedom of liberty of conscience in matters of faith and worship.

Indeed one of the noblest testimonies ever uttered for the Reformation, and for human individual liberty, was the Protest offered by the Reformed Princes of Germany at the *Diet of Spires* in 1529. The courage, faith and firmness of the Princes gained for succeeding ages the liberty of thought and conscience. Their Protest gave to the reformed church the name of Protestant; its principles are the very essence of Protestantism and the very essence of the Constitutions of all free nations.

The historian D'Aubigné has left on record a summary of the principles of the Protest of the Reformed Princes of Germany:

> "The principles contained in this celebrated Protest...constitute the very essence of Protestantism. Now this Protest opposes two abuses of man in matters of faith: the first is the intrusion of the civil magistrate, and the second the arbitrary authority of the church. Instead of these abuses, Protestantism sets the power of conscience above the magistrate, and the authority of the word of God above the visible church. In the first place, it rejects the civil power in divine things, and says with the prophets and apostles, 'We must obey God rather than man.' In presence of the crown of Charles the Fifth, it uplifts the crown of Jesus Christ. But it goes farther: it lays down the principle that all human teaching should be subordinate to the oracles of God."
> D'Aubigné, p. 13

The protesters had moreover affirmed their right to utter freely their convictions of truth. They would not only believe and obey, but teach what they believed to be truth. And they denied the right of priest or .magistrate to interfere with either their freedom to obey or their freedom to teach their beliefs. The Protest of Spires was a solemn witness against religious intolerance, and an assertion of the right of all men to worship God according to the dictates of their own consciences without interference by any church or by any political legislation.

The Protestant Reformation clearly exposed the Roman Catholic doctrine, that God has committed to the Church the right to control the conscience, and to define and punish heresy, as one of the most deeply rooted of Papal errors.

Notwithstanding the wonderful work (in the sixteenth century) of the Reformation in restoring the right of the individual to freedom of conscience in matters of faith and worship, the spirit of intolerance persisted throughout Europe for two more centuries and only slowly gave way to the Reformation spirit of liberty of conscience.

In England, during the sixteenth and seventeenth centuries the Anglican Church, which was the state church, being supported by the civil authority, would permit no dissent from her traditions. Attendance upon her service was required by law, and unauthorized assemblies for religious worship were prohibited, under penalty of imprisonment, exile and death. Such religious intolerance in England paradoxically paved the way for the development of liberty in America.

In Pursuit of Freedom

Those English Christians who disagreed with the doctrines and traditions of the formal English church were called Puritans and suffered much persecution until they were forced to flee from England.

At the opening of the seventeenth century the monarch who had just ascended the throne of England declared his determination to make the Puritans "conform, or harry them out of the land, or else worse." George Bancroft, *History of the United States of America*, pt 1, ch. 12, par. 6.

Hunted, persecuted, and imprisoned, they could discern in the future no promise of better days, and many yielded to the conviction that for such as would serve God according to the dictates of their conscience.

"England was ceasing forever to be a habitable place." J.G. Palfrey, History of New England, ch. 3, par. 43.

Some at last determined to seek refuge in Holland. Difficulties, losses, and imprisonment were encountered. Their purposes were thwarted, and they were betrayed into the hands of their enemies. But steadfast perseverance finally conquered, and they found shelter on the friendly shores of the Dutch Republic.

In their flight they had left their houses, their goods, and their means of livelihood. They were strangers in a strange land, among a people of different language and customs. They were forced to resort to new and untried occupations to earn their bread. Middle-aged men, who had spent their lives in tilling the soil, had now to learn mechanical trades. But they cheerfully accepted the situation, and lost no time in idleness or repining. Though often pinched with poverty, they thanked God for the blessings which were still granted them, and found their joy in unmolested spiritual communion.

> "They knew they were pilgrims, and looked not much on those things, but lifted up their eyes to Heaven, their dearest country, and quieted their spirits." Bancroft, pt. 1, ch. 12, par. 15.

When first constrained to separate from the English church, the Puritans had joined themselves together by a solemn covenant, as the Lord's free people, "to walk in all his ways, made known or to be made known to them." Here was the true spirit of reform, the vital principle of Protestantism. It was with this purpose that the Pilgrims departed from Holland to find a home in the New World.

The Protestant pilgrims had fled from England to Holland. They then journeyed across the Atlantic to America. They sought a country without a king and a church without a pope. That mysterious phenomenon, the irrepressible desire for liberty of mind and conscience, drove them across the ocean to a new land.

In Early America Freedom Developed Slowly at First

It was the desire for liberty of conscience that inspired the Pilgrims to brave the perils of the long journey across the sea, to endure the hardships and dangers of the wilderness, and with God's blessing to lay, on the shores of America, the foundation of a mighty nation. Yet honest and God-fearing as they were, the Pilgrims did not yet comprehend the great principle of religious toleration. The freedom which they sacrificed so much to secure for themselves, they were not equally ready to grant to others.

> "Very few, even of the foremost thinkers and moralists of the seventeenth century, had any just conception of that grand principle, the outgrowth of the New Testament, which acknowledges God as the sole judge of human faith." Martyn, vol. 5, pp. 70, 71.

The doctrine that God has committed to the church the right to control the conscience and to define and punish heresy is one of the most deeply rooted of papal errors. While the reformers rejected the creed of Rome, they were not entirely free from her spirit of intolerance. The dense darkness in which, through the long ages of her rule, popery had enveloped all Christendom had not even yet been wholly dissipated. Said one of the leading ministers in the colony of Massachusetts Bay, "It was toleration that made the world anti-Christian; and the church never took harm by the punishment of heretics." Ibid., vol. 5, p. 335. The regulation was adopted by the colonists, that only church-members should have a voice in the civil government. A kind of State church was formed, all the people being required to contribute to the support of the clergy, and the magistrates being authorized to suppress heresy. Thus the secular power was in the hands of the church. It was not long before these measures led to the inevitable result—persecution.

In the sixteenth and seventeenth centuries the struggle for freedom continued in America. It took the courage and the bold unflinching persistence of great men of foresight to continue the struggle for complete liberation of the human conscience in matters of faith and worship.

The Work of Roger Williams (1603-1684)

In 1631, eleven years after the planting of the first colony, Roger Williams came to the New World. Like the early Pilgrims, he came to enjoy religious freedom; but unlike them, he saw—what so few in his time had yet seen—that this freedom was the inalienable right of all, whatever might be their creed. He was an earnest seeker for truth, holding it impossible that all the light from God's Word had yet been received. Williams "was the first person in modern Christendom to assert, in its plenitude, the doctrine of the liberty of conscience, the equality of opinions before the law." He declared it to be the duty of the magistrate to restrain crime, but never to control the conscience.

> "The public or the magistrates may decide," he said, "what is due from men to men, but when they attempt to prescribe a man's duty to God, they are out of place, and there can be no safety;

for it is clear that if the magistrate has the power, he may decree one set of opinions or beliefs today and another tomorrow; as has been done in England by different kings and queens, and by the different popes and councils in the Roman Church; so that belief would become a heap of confusion." Martyn, vol. 5, p. 340.

Attendance at the services of the established church was required under a penalty of fine or imprisonment.

"Williams reprobated the law; the worst statute of the English code was that which did but enforce attendance upon the parish church. To compel men to unite with those of a different creed, he regarded as an open violation of their natural rights; to drag to public worship the irreligious and the unwilling, seemed like requiring hypocrisy. 'No one,' he said, 'should be forced to worship, or to maintain a worship, against his own consent.' 'What!' exclaimed his antagonist, amazed at his tenets, 'is not the laborer worthy of his hire?' 'Yes,' replied he, 'from those who hire him." Bancroft, pt. 1, ch. 15, par. 2.

Roger Williams was respected and beloved as a faithful minister, a man of rare gifts, of unbending integrity and true benevolence; yet his steadfast denial of the right of civil magistrates to authority over the church, and his demand for religious liberty, could not be tolerated. The application of this new doctrine, it was urged, would "subvert the fundamental state and government of the country." Ibid., pt. 1, ch. 15, par 10. In 1635 he was sentenced to banishment from the colonies, and finally, to avoid arrest, he was forced to flee, amid the cold and storms of winter, into the unbroken forest.

"For fourteen weeks," he says, "I was sorely tossed in a bitter season, not knowing what bread or bed did mean." "But the ravens fed me in the wilderness;" and a hollow tree often served him for a shelter.—Martyn, vol. 5, pp. 349, 350. Thus he continued his painful flight through the snow and the trackless forest, until he found refuge with an Indian tribe whose confidence and affection he had won while endeavoring to teach them the truths of the gospel.

Making his way at last, after months of change and wandering, to the shores of Narragansett Bay, he there laid the foundation of the first State of modern times that in the fullest sense recognized the right of religious freedom. The fundamental principle of Roger Williams' colony was "that every man should have the right to worship God according to the light of his own conscience." Ibid.,5, p. 354. His little State, Rhode Island, became the asylum of the oppressed, and it increased and prospered until its foundation principles—civil and religious liberty—became the cornerstones of the American Republic. (Williams died in 1684).

Building On Roger Williams' Foundation

Thomas Jefferson (1743-1826), the third president of the USA, was one of the great architects of modern civil and religious liberty. He was zealously and passionately committed to the concepts of natural law, of inviolable rights, and of government by consent. In September 1776 he embarked upon legislative reforms unprecedented in human history. By 1786 his bill on the complete separation of church and state was at last fully adopted.

James Madison (1751-1838), the fourth president of the U.S.A., was also one of the chief architects of the U.S. Constitution. He was elected to the Virginian Constitution Convention in 1776 and appointed to the committee to prepare a declaration of rights and to draft a plan for state government. There for the first time he met Thomas Jefferson and began a friendship that was to last for half a century. There he also proposed an amendment to separate church and state in Virginia. This proposal was defeated at the time but adopted later.

Both Jefferson and Madison advocated those principles of individual liberty and human rights which were to become enshrined in the U.S. bill of rights—the Declaration of Independence.

The Declaration of Independence was drafted by a committee including Benjamin Franklin, John Adams, Robert Livingstone and Roger Sherman, with Thomas Jefferson as chairman.

Thus, at last, the struggles for freedom during the sixteenth and seventeenth centuries gave birth to the Declaration of Independence and the US Constitution. The foundations had been laid for freedom to surge on progressively from victory to victory during the nineteenth and twentieth centuries. As it did, the effects of the principles concretized in America were increasingly felt around the world.

Indeed, we can say that the two hundred years from 1800 - 2000 have been the two centuries of the greatest enjoyment of liberty in the history of mankind. But we must always remember that the liberty enjoyed in the last two centuries was won by the sweat and blood of brave men down the previous centuries, especially from 1526-1776.

The U.S. Declaration of Independence and the U.S. Constitution

In that grand old document, which the American forefathers set forth in 1776 as their bill of rights, (the Declaration of Independence), they declared: "We hold these truths to be self-evident, that all men are created equal; that they are endowed by their Creator with certain unalienable rights; that among these are life, liberty, and the pursuit of happiness." And the Constitution guarantees, in the most explicit terms, the inviolability of conscience: "No religious test shall ever be required as a qualification to any office of public trust under the United States." "Congress shall make no law respecting an establishment of religion, or prohibiting the free exercise thereof."

> "The framers of the Constitution recognized the eternal principle that man's relation to his God is above human legislation and his right of conscience inalienable. Reasoning was not necessary to establish this truth; we are conscious of it in our own bosom. It is this consciousness, which, in defiance of human laws, has sustained so many martyrs in tortures and flames. They felt that their duty to God was superior to human enactments, and that man could exercise no authority over their consciences. It is an inborn principle which nothing can eradicate." Congressional Documents, (USA) Serial No. 200, Document No. 271.

As the tidings spread through the countries of Europe, of a land where every man might enjoy the fruit of his own labor, and obey the convictions of his conscience, thousands flocked to the shores of the New World. Colonies rapidly multiplied. "Massachusetts, by special law, offered free welcome and aid, at the public cost, to Christians of any nationality who might sail beyond the Atlantic 'to escape from wars or famine, or the oppression of their persecutors.' Thus the fugitive and the downtrodden were, by statute, made the guests of the commonwealth." Martyn, vol. 5, p. 417. In twenty years from the first landing at Plymouth, as many thousand Pilgrims were settled in New England.

To secure the object which they sought,

> "they were content to earn a bare subsistence by a life of frugality and toil. They asked nothing from the soil but the reasonable returns of their own labor. No golden vision threw a deceitful halo around their path. . . . They were content with the slow but steady progress of their social polity. They patiently endured the

privations of the wilderness, watering the tree of liberty with their tears, and with the sweat of their brow, till it took deep root in the land." Ibid.

A Lesson For All the World:
The Early American Struggle for Liberty of Conscience

W.L. Johns in his book, *Dateline Sunday, U.S.A.*, summarizes the birth of U.S. religious liberties thus:

> "Writing to Edward Livingstone from his Montpelier home in the summer of 1822, ex-president James Madison declared: 'We are teaching the world the great truth that Governments do better without kings and nobles than with them. The merit will be doubled by the other lesson that Religion flourishes in greater purity, without than with the aid of government.'

> "Madison regretted that in some states disestablishment still had not been achieved. He felt that any alliance or coalition between government and religion imperiled the success of both. He argued that 'religion and Government will both exist in greater purity, the less they are mixed together,' and he supported his theory by citing the example of Virginia, 'where it is impossible to deny that religion prevails with more zeal and a more exemplary priesthood than it ever did when established and patronized by public authority.'

> "From its inception the Federal Government had no established religion or church tradition. Free of establishments, the new republic was consequently free of religious laws, such as Sunday laws, on a national level. James Madison liked it that way.

> "Madison approved of executive proclamation of fasts and festivals, providing they were merely 'recommendatory', not obligatory. Government has 'a right to *appoint* particular days for religious worship throughout the state, without any penal sanction *enforcing* the worship.'

> "Madison's attitude was based upon commitment to individual property rights as well as independence of church and state. Among property rights, Madison included 'time.'

"If there be a government, then, which prides itself on maintaining the inviolability of property; which provides that none shall be taken directly, even for public use, without indemnification to the owner, and yet directly violate the property which individuals have in their opinions, their religion, their persons, and their faculties;—nay more, *which indirectly* violates their property, in their actual possessions, in the labor that acquires their daily subsistence, and in the hallowed remnant of time which ought to relieve their fatigues and soothe their cares, the inference will have been anticipated, that such a government is not a pattern for the United States." Letters and Other Writings of James Madison (1865 Vol. 3 pp. 273 In American State Papers, page 158.) W.L. Johns, Dateline Sunday, USA, pp. 33, 34.

Actually, it was back in 1791, November 3rd, that the first ten amendments to the US constitution became a part of the supreme law of the land. James Madison offered the first amendment in its original form to Congress in 1789. The first sentence of the first amendment rejected centuries of precedent, guaranteeing that religion was to be neither the slave nor the master of the state.

Thomas Jefferson observed,

"I contemplate with sovereign reverence that act of the whole American people which declares that their legislature should 'make no law respecting an establishment of religion or prohibiting the free exercise thereof', thus building a wall of separation between church and state." W.L. Johns, Dateline Sunday, USA, p. 21.

The French Revolution

The second distinct European movement which contributed to the development of modern civil liberty was the French Revolution which occurred in the late 1700's, reaching its peak of intensity between 1793 and 1796.

For the first time in the history of Christian Europe, a nation threw the papacy out of the Ecclesiastical-political office of church-state control it had unquestioningly held for over a millennium.

Protestantism had non-violently freed Germany from Papal control in the sixteenth century, but atheism and secularism violently freed France of Papal control in the late eighteenth century.

In 1798 Pope Pius was taken captive by Napoleon's General Berthier thereby officially setting European states free of Papal control. Protestantism and secularism had expelled the Papacy from church-state control in Europe.

Brief Summary Of Events Leading Up To The Start Of The Nineteenth Century And A New Era Of Freedom:

1526	Protestant reformation started in Germany
1529	The Protest of the Princes in Germany
1620's	English Puritans cross the Atlantic to America to plant first colony in USA.
1635 - 1684	Roger Williams establishes a colony, Rhode Island, recognizing full rights of individual in matters of faith
1776 - 1786	The Jefferson liberty reforms leading to the US declaration of independence and constitution
1780 - 1796	French revolution
1798	Pope Pius taken prisoner
1800	Freedom of individual conscience fully established

When one remembers that millions of people were executed for their beliefs during the more than 1000 years of Papal dominance in Europe, one can perhaps better appreciate the tremendous and triumphant struggles for freedom leading up to 1800.

More Victories Still Had To Be Won

The onward march of freedom turned its attention next to slavery. Slavery is one of the worst forms of violation of human rights. It reduces the human person to a level beneath the animals, and crushes the human spirit and conscience into a blasphemous subservience which is morally and criminally inhuman.

The same concepts which led to the development of liberty of conscience in matters of faith, worship and thought, led to the call for the abolition of slavery.

First, the slave trade was abolished in the early nineteenth century, in 1807 by Britain, in 1808 by the USA and by 1813 in most other European countries. Afterwards slavery itself was abolished by the middle of the nineteenth century, (1863 in the USA), although some South American countries continued slavery until late into the nineteenth century (e.g. Brazil eventually abolished slavery in 1888).

But although the Negro slaves were freed, they were considered second class citizens, and were not allowed the same civil rights as white people. This was especially so in the USA. Then that irrepressible desire in the human spirit for liberty became activated again.

In December 1955 a black woman, Rosa Parks, was arrested for refusing to move to the back of a public bus in Montgomery, Alabama. Blacks in Montgomery responded with a year long boycott, which Martin Luther King (1929-1968) helped to lead. There followed much racial violence by whites against blacks until the US Supreme Court ruled in 1956, in a similar case, that segregation in public transportation was illegal.

King continued his non-violent struggles and protests against racial inequality well into the 1960's. He was often jailed and subjected to slanderous attacks by his opposition.

As a result of the Civil Rights Movement, President John F. Kennedy sent a Civil Rights Bill to Congress. On August 28, 1963, a quarter million protesters marched on Washington for jobs and liberty. King delivered his electrifying speech "I have a Dream". In 1964 Congress passed the Civil Rights Act, and in 1965 Congress passed the Voting Rights Act. Both Acts together gave to blacks the same civil rights that had always been enjoyed by whites. Freedom had won another significant victory.

But there were more victories to come. Racial prejudice had become concentrated to its most heinous and inhuman form in the Apartheid system of South Africa. Thousands were being killed annually in order to maintain that wicked system.

But, again, there was a man of liberty—Nelson Mandela. Though he and other freedom-fighters were outlawed and jailed, their protest and struggle was continued in the face of bitter persecution.

At last, the then white President, F.W. De Klerk saw the light, and freed Mandela in February 1990. The rest is history. Freedom came to South African blacks as it had come to Zimbabwean blacks in 1980.

In the meantime, Communism, a system of state dictatorship which seeks to impose an iron grip (and total control) over every aspect of life (and is therefore one of the greatest scourges of liberty in the 20th

Century) had collapsed in Eastern Europe. It still lives on, however, in China and one or two other countries.

Human Rights Soar To The Heights

Today, even the basic rights of criminals are guaranteed. Recently, the British Privy Council ruled that it was inhuman to keep a condemned murderer on death row for more than five years. More than two murderers have had their death sentences commuted to life imprisonment because of this ruling. (Pratt and Morgan case, Jamaica, West Indies.)

We have come a long way from the days when the human rights of a good man were denied him if he believed differently from the Pope, to the days when even the rights of criminals are guaranteed.

Indeed, the plant of freedom has fully matured and blossomed into all the modern liberties we enjoy today. The seeds sown in the sixteenth century grew slowly in the seventeenth and eighteenth centuries, and more rapidly in the nineteenth and twentieth centuries, into the mature and sturdy plant of modern liberty and human rights.

Dangers On The Horizon

"The price of liberty," Jefferson said, "is eternal vigilance. And those who stand vigil must have the wisdom to discern the earliest signs of any movement against liberty of conscience."

The generation of human beings entering the twenty-first century will be a generation, by and large, that was born free and that has become complacent about freedom, even taking it for granted.

There is perhaps no greater threat to freedom than complacency.

We now have a generation of people who know very little, if anything, about the severe struggles endured and the high price paid, in blood, to gain the freedoms which we now take for granted.

And so, another threat now raises its ominous head.

The generation entering the twenty-first century will be the freest in the history of our world. But not only that, they will also be the greatest abusers of freedom in the history of our world.

When a people who have forgotten the price of freedom begin to abuse it, there will be those among them who will suggest that the only way to curtail the abuse of freedom is to restrict it. It is an argument that sounds good but only at the superficial level. It is an argument that sounds compelling to those who are in a panic over the increasing crime, lawlessness and corruption now rampant in society. And it is an argument which gives an easy way out for those who fail to see how people can be changed for the better without coercion of conscience.

In summation, then, as we enter the third millennium, we do so with two enemies to freedom. The first, is the reality of our taking freedom for granted; the second, is our abuse of freedom.

It will be an easy matter for most people to accept a restriction of liberty of conscience if they are persuaded that it will make the world a safer place. But will it? Or, can it?

Freedom, Open-Market Economy and the New World Order

FREEDOM'S TRIUMPHANT ADVANCE has not only liberated the human conscience but is also opening up markets on a global scale. The principle of open market economy is similar to the principle of open-conscience religion. The First Amendment to the U.S. Constitution emphatically declares that no religion should be especially favored or disfavored by the state:

> "Congress shall make no law respecting an establishment of religion or prohibiting the free exercise thereof."

The constitutions of all free nations are similar in this respect. In applying this principle to the market place we can clearly and logically conclude that governments should not favor or give any advantage to any one producer, or any group of producers, or any set of goods or services over another producer and his set of goods or services.

Where this principle operates it means that the economic behavior of a product or service will depend entirely on the competitive ebb and flow of all the factors which determine successful marketing. This means that success or failure would depend on quality and quantity of goods, and quality of marketing techniques, rather than on special favors or concessions being granted by the state.

The consumer, therefore, becomes the most important single factor in determining whether a particular product succeeds economically or not. All of the various marketing strategies and techniques are aimed at persuading the consumer to choose to purchase a particular product.

The two basic factors would be cost and quality of the product but many other factors also impact on the consumer's choice.

At the international level the operation of this principle would mean that no nation should expect any special favors or concessions from any other nation or from the global market. The products of any nation would be allowed to freely enter any international market and compete with other products from other nations. Thus, the competition would be based on cost, quality, marketing strategies and techniques, consumer needs and spending patterns. In other words, the basic determinant would be the free choice of the consumer and the factors influencing that choice.

Free Global Trade

Experts agree that developing countries should not isolate themselves from the global economy. Rather they should freely and fully enter the global market participating fully in world trade, seeking to take advantage of the possibilities for international trade, international investment and capital flows.

Open economy with its open market trading is regarded by the experts to be best for the overall global economy and also for developing countries. Developing nations may complain that they are not able to stand up to the competition from industrial nations in the global market. The cost of importing certain basic materials for production enterprises and the lack of technology are cited as crucial factors in affecting the real purchasing value of the currency of developing nations. The real purchasing power of their currency will affect the quality and quantity of their produce, the quality and quantity of their marketing strategies and techniques, and subsequently their ability to compete successfully in the global market.

Economic Shocks

But there is another problem of even greater significance. By connecting itself to the global, open-market economy, a nation also exposes itself to what economists call external shocks.

By external shock is meant economic disturbances that originate in certain phenomena outside a nation but which impact negatively on that nation's economy.

We will not in this book go into the complex economic details of the mechanisms of economic external shock, but we shall touch on some important points which are relevant to our study of the imminent new world order. Let us look at some of the economic phenomena which can occur in industrial nations and which can produce external shock to the economies of developing countries.

The nature of global business and economy tends to be cyclical. Sometimes global business and economy are functioning at levels of high performance. At other times they fall to very low functioning levels called recessions. Global recession may have terrible effects on the economic performance of a developing country.

The fall in prices of some key export commodities can impact negatively on developing nations dependent on earnings from such export commodities. There are the factors of:

- cost and constraints on borrowing
- changes in the real interest rate globally

Experts agree that the global economic environment has been very unstable and uncertain since 1970. As a matter of fact, two major, very deep, recessions have been experienced by industrial nations since 1970.

The sharp rise in oil prices in 1973-74 triggered a recession in industrial countries that spelt disaster for many Third World economies. Oil prices rose again in 1979-80 thereby triggering another recession in the early 1980s.

External shocks usually cause a severe drain on a nation's foreign reserves by way of both export and import shocks. By export shock we mean reduced earnings from export commodities. By import shock we mean increasing costs of certain key imports such as oil.

Many developing countries have responded to unfavorable economic shock by borrowing from official lenders such as the International Monetary Fund (IMF). The IMF usually requires stringent adjustments in the economic structure of the borrowing nations. These remedial adjustments have produced severe socio-economic dislocation of the populations in many developing countries, with many of these countries having to devalue their currency.

What has been given so far in this chapter is a very simplified overview of some of the factors which can cause economic disaster in developing countries and economic strain in industrial countries.

This brings us to a very important conclusion:

> Open-market economy should work very well so long as the global economic environment remains stable and behaves in a uniform way.

But we have seen that, (especially during the twentieth century and more particularly since 1970), global business, global trade and global economy have all been adversely affected, and unexpectedly so, by a number of complex global phenomena.

The increasing frequency and severity of natural disasters; the vulnerability of open economies to international crime and corruption; the possibility of unexpected declines in productivity; high interest rates, and other factors beyond our control, all indicate that the economic predictions of the experts can go either way.

Religio-economic Concepts

There are many religionists and economic experts in the USA who believe that the USA was, and is, a nation blessed of God. But they believe that America is moving away from the channel of divine blessing.

In recent years increasing numbers of natural disasters have been experienced in the USA. Coupled with this phenomenon of increasing natural disasters is the fact of increasing levels of very serious crimes, making city life progressively more unsafe. And, as if this is not enough, the USA is by far the largest world market for illegal, mind-destroying, addictive drugs.

Because of all these negative factors, many religionists, and other authorities are suggesting, and rightly so, that America's departure from God is the root cause of her moral and socio-economic problems. They are suggesting that greater respect for, and reverence of, the Sunday Lord's day will go a long way towards making America a safer, better, more productive place in which to live and do business.

On the other hand, in the European Union, the Papacy believes and is spreading abroad its idea that,

> "...just as no system of politics is viable unless it is based on the spirituality of genuine religious belief in God and Christ, so no religious belief is viable unless it is deeply involved in political systems." The Keys of This Blood, 492.

Protestant religious leaders in the USA and Papal leaders in Europe are in agreement that Sunday laws must be a central component of any viable open-market world economic order.

An unstable world environment can adversely affect the economies of both industrial and developing nations. And the complex, and sometimes mysterious, phenomena which can destabilize global economy are usually unpredictable and difficult to analyze in terms of cause and effect. For all these reasons and more, authorities are proposing a new world economic order in which tighter controls and careful international monitoring of economic indicators will be an absolute necessity.

In addition, Sunday rest will be intricately interwoven with the mechanisms for global productivity and trade. The USA will be the first industrialized nation to enforce Sunday rest and worship by civil law, and to link such legislation to socio-economic performance. The European Union will follow the US example fairly quickly. This will mean that the most influential economic powers of the free western world will be united in establishing the religio-economic Sunday rest legislation as part of the new world economic order.

The masses of population will be convinced that economic prosperity must be linked to moral stability and respect for the "Lord's Day." Moreover, the occurrence of strange phenomena, even more mysterious than the factors which trigger global recessions, will further convince almost everyone that moral and economic renewal can only be successful if Sunday rest is enforced by civil law. This line of argument will be advocated most adamantly by American religious leaders.

A Century Of Amazing Changes And Unstable Conditions

There is no doubt that the twentieth century has seen unprecedented global emergencies. Scarcely had the century gotten underway when the First World War struck—unexpectedly.

Scarcely had the world recovered from the alarming trauma of that first global war, when, notwithstanding the implementation of the League of Nations, the Second World War struck it again and even more unexpectedly.

In between the two world wars there was the deep recession of the 1930s. Also, just at the end of the first global war, Communism was born in the 1917 Russian Revolution and by the end of the Second World War, had spread and developed to include many eastern European states. The development of Communism triggered the "Cold War" during which tremendous sums of money were spent on the amassing and development of lethal nuclear weapons.

Then came the "oil price crisis" of the early 1970s and the economic climate of the world was altered suddenly and permanently; that crisis was also unexpected.

In the early eighties another deep recession struck the global economy thereby worsening the economic malaise that had started in the seventies for many developing nations.

The decade of the eighties was indeed an amazing one, and especially so because towards the end of that decade the foundation was laid for the collapse of Russian Communism. This trend continued into the early nineties with the progressive collapse of Eastern European Communism and the dismantling of the Berlin Wall which had separated East and West Germany.

In the early eighties a new killer virus struck the world like lightning, the HIV virus. The disease now affects millions of humans across the globe and demands a considerable portion of the economic resources for medical treatment and research. The HIV epidemic is even more significant because it indicates a link between human moral behavior and changes in the natural environment. In addition it shows that we have no way of knowing whether or not sudden unexpected disasters will occur. Or rather, we now know, for sure, that such disastrous changes in the natural biological systems around us will occur with increasing frequency and severity.

As we entered the decade of the nineties weather patterns continued to change, with severe flooding of major US cities and an increasing potential for more dangerous storms.

With such actual and potential instability all around us there is the increasing demand for a new global economic order including some unifying symbol or mark which will tie moral healing to economic prosperity and help to slow down, if not stop, the alarming increase in global instability. What this unifying symbol or mark will be is clearly revealed by history and will be the subject of our next chapter.

The History of Sunday Laws

*I*T IS A FACT OF HISTORY that the most specific and accurate indicator of the degree of separation between church and state and of the degree of civil and religious liberty, in any nation in Christendom, is the presence or absence of legislation concerning Sunday. No other legislation has been as involved in the whole matter of civil and religious freedom and liberty of conscience as Sunday laws have been.

A study of the history of Sunday laws shows a remarkable similarity between the reasons put forward for the first Sunday laws in the fourth century and the reasons suggested for the passing and enforcement of Sunday laws in modern times.

Over two centuries before the Papacy had achieved full political-ecclesiastical control in Europe, (538 A.D.), a Sunday law had been passed and had been progressively enforced in the Christianized Roman Empire.

The Historical Background of the First Successful Sunday Law

During the fourth and fifth centuries the Roman Empire had begun to decline rapidly in political unity and socio-economic strength. Barbarian hordes threatened invasion. The iron monarchy was slowly rusting.

At the same time the antagonism between Roman paganism and the growing Christian religion created severe difficulties between church authorities and imperial political leaders. Progressively increasing numbers of pagans became Christian converts and the simple Christianity of the New Testament became less simple and less pure as it became diluted by Roman paganism.

The popularity and influence of the bishops at Rome grew steadily as the people were taught more and more to depend on priests for salvation.

Eventually, by the fourth century A.D. the bishops had evolved a theocratic theory of government in which they would use the power of the state for the furtherance of their aims.

The historian Neander left on record this important information for us:

> "There had in fact arisen in the church a false theocratical theory, originating not in the essence of the gospel, but in the confusion of the religious constitutions of the Old and New Testaments, which...brought along with it an unchristian opposition of the spiritual to the secular power, and which might easily result in the formation of a sacerdotal State, subordinating the secular to itself in a false and outward way.

> "This theocratical theory was already the prevailing one in the time of Constantine; and...the bishops voluntarily made themselves dependent on him by their disputes, *and by their determination to make use of the power of the State for the furtherance of their aims.*" Torrey's Neander, Boston, 1852, p. 132.

Political turbulence and unrest greeted Constantine when he ascended the imperial throne. The throne itself was shaky enough; in fact, the Roman Empire was in crisis. But until his death in 337 A.D. Constantine attempted in every way possible to restore stability and strength.

Paganism predominated. Nonetheless, Christians were a vocal and influential minority which held a special appeal for Constantine. He became influenced not merely by the Christian religion itself, but by the theocratic theory of the Christian bishops of Rome, yet retained many of his pagan beliefs and customs.

According to the historian Philip Schaff, Constantine was "the first representative of the imposing idea of a Christian theocracy, or of that system of policy which assumes all subjects to be Christians, connects civil and religious rights, and regards church and state as the two arms of one and the same divine government on earth...Christianity appeared to him, as it proved in fact, the only efficient power for the political reformation of the empire, from which the ancient spirit of Rome was fast departing." Philip Schaff, History of the Christian Church, 5th Edition, (Revised), Vol. 3, pp. 15,16.

Moreover, Neander pointed out that Constantine's efforts to stabilize the Empire and to reconcile Christians and pagans were "not so much for the cause of God, as for the gratification of his own ambition and love of power." Neander, Vol. 3, p. 31 (Torrey's Translation).

The bishops desired to use the power of the state for the furtherance of their aims, and Constantine desired the support of the bishops in his quest for power and authority.

The bishops desired the establishment of their idea of a Christian theocracy with church and state as the two arms of one and the same divine government on earth, and Constantine desired greater unity and harmony in the Empire, especially between pagans and Christians.

The Roman Empire was in a serious crisis, and Christianity was threatened by paganism.

Constantine's first act on the behalf of the Christians was his Edict of Toleration, A.D. 313, which granted "to Christians, and to all, the free choice to follow that mode of worship which they may wish." Eusebius, Ecclesiastical History, Book 10, Ch. 5.

Indeed a new day had dawned for a dedicated religious minority in the Roman Empire. But as soon as religious liberty had been given to the bishops of Rome, they, through their so-called theocratic theory, had sought to control the whole Empire, and to make all people Christians by using the power of the state for the furtherance of their aims of making their Christianity the controlling religion of the Roman Empire.

The Venerable Day Of The Sun

We quote now from W.L. Johns' *Dateline Sunday, U.S.A*:

> "In a quest for additional devices of unity, Constantine noted the significance attached to the first day of the week by Christian and pagan alike. Many Christians had for a long time attached the 'Lord's Day' label to the first day of the week and marked it for a weekly festival in celebration of Christ's resurrection. The Mithraists worshiped the sun as a deity, so the day of the sun was sacred to them also. Constantine found it politically expedient, therefore, to please these two diverse segments of his realm by honoring the 'venerable day of the sun' through governmental edict in which 'he expressed himself, perhaps with reference at once to the sun-god, Apollo, and to Christ, the true Sun of Righteousness, to his pagan and his Christian subjects.' Philip Schaff, Vol. 3, pp. 15, 16.

"The retention of the old pagan name of 'Dies Solis,' or 'Sunday,' for the weekly Christian festival is, in a great measure, owing to the union of Pagan and Christian sentiment with which the first day of the week was recommended by Constantine to his subjects, Pagan and Christian alike, as the 'venerable day of the Sun.' His celebrated decree has been justly called 'a new era in the history of the Lord's Day.' It was his mode of harmonizing the Christian and Pagan elements of the Empire under one common institution." A.P. Stanley, Lectures on the History of the Eastern Church, p. 227.

"At a time when forces were already at work which would tear the empire into shreds, the first Sunday law did provide a common denominator of unity." Dateline Sunday, USA by W.L. Johns (1967), pp. 238-239.

The First Successful Sunday Law

It is clear then, that the bishops of Rome held strongly to their theory of establishing a theocratic government in the Empire. It is equally clear that Constantine was greatly influenced by this theory and saw it as a means of holding the disintegrating Empire together. The question may now be asked, what means did the bishops employ to secure control of the power of the state? Answer — the means of Sunday laws. They secured from Constantine the following Sunday law:

"The Emperor Constantine to Helpidius"

"On the venerable day of the sun, let the magistrates and people living in the towns, rest, and let all work-shops be closed. Nevertheless, in the country, those engaged in the cultivation of land may freely and lawfully work, because it often happens that another day is not so well fitted for sowing grain and planting vines; lest by neglect of the best time, the bounty provided by Heaven should be lost. Given the seventh day of March, Crispus and Constantine being consuls, both for the second time." [A.D. 321.] Code of Justinian, Book 16, Title 10, Law 1. (In Codex Theodosianus col. 1611). (See also Neander, Ibid. 300).

Indeed, as W. L. Johns stated in the earlier quotation, the first Sunday law was enforced by church and state to provide a common denominator of unity at a time of crisis in the Roman Empire and at a time when the Roman Church wished to implement her theory of theocratic government.

The Purpose Of The Early Sunday Laws

An American historian, theologian, religious liberty expert, liberty of conscience activist, and reformer of the 19th century, A.T. Jones, has left on record a masterful analysis of the significance of the history of the development of Sunday legislation in the fourth century. From his book *Civil Government and Religion*:

> "This was not the very first Sunday law that they secured; the first one has not survived. But although the first one has not survived, the reason for it has. Sozomen says that it was 'that the day might be devoted with less interruption to the purposes of devotion.' And this statement of Sozomen's is endorsed by Neander ('Church History,' vol. 2, p. 298). This reason given by Sozomen reveals the secret of the legislation; it shows that it was in behalf of the church, and to please the church.

> "By reading the above edict, it is seen that they started out quite moderately. They did not stop all work; only judges, townspeople, and mechanics were required to rest, while people in the country might freely and lawfully work.

> "This Sunday law of A.D. 321 continued until A.D. 386 when— 'Those older changes effected by the Emperor Constantine were more rigorously enforced, and, in general, civil transactions of every kind on Sunday were strictly forbidden. Whoever transgressed was to be considered, in fact, as guilty of sacrilege.'—Neander, Id., p. 30.

> "Then as the people were not allowed to do any manner of work, they would play, and as the natural consequence, the circuses and the theaters throughout the empire were crowded every Sunday. But the object of the law, from the first one that was issued, was that the day might be used for the purposes of devotion, and the people might go to church. Consequently, that this object might be met, there was another step to take, and it was taken. At a church convention held at Carthage in 401, the bishops passed a resolution to send up a petition to the emperor,

praying—'That the public shows might be transferred from the Christian Sunday, and from feast days, to some other days of the week.'— Id.

"And the reason given in support of the petition was:-'The people congregate more to the circus than to the church.'—Id., note 5.

"In the circuses and the theaters large numbers of men were employed, among whom many were church-members. But, rather than to give up their jobs, they would work on Sunday. The bishops complained that these were compelled to work: they pronounced it persecution, and asked for a law to protect those persons from such 'persecution.' The church had become filled with a mass of people, unconverted, who cared vastly more for worldly interests and pleasures than they did for religion. And as the government was now a government of God, it was considered proper that the civil power should be used to cause all to show respect for God, whether or not they had any respect for him. But as long as they could make something by working on Sunday, they would work rather than go to church. A law was secured forbidding all manner of Sunday work. Then they would crowd the circuses and the theaters, instead of going to church. But this was not what the bishops wanted; this was not that for which all work had been forbidden. All work was forbidden in order that the people might go to church; but instead of that, they crowded to the circus and the theater, and the audiences of the bishops were rather slim. This was not at all satisfying to their pride; therefore the next step, and a logical one, too, was, as the petition prayed, to have the exhibitions of the circuses and the theaters transferred to some other days of the week, so that the churches and the theaters should not be open at the same time. For if both were open, the Christians (?), as well as others, not being able to go to both places at once, would go to the circus or the theater instead of to the church. Neander says:

'Owing to the prevailing passion at that time, especially in the large cities, to run after the various public shows, it so happened that when these spectacles fell on the same days which had been consecrated by the church to some religious festival, they proved a great hindrance to the devotion of

Christians, though chiefly, it must be allowed, to those whose Christianity was the least an affair of the life and of the heart.'—Id.

"Assuredly! An open circus or theater will always prove a great hindrance to the devotion of those Christians whose Christianity is the least an affair of the life and of the heart. In other words, an open circus or theater will always be a great hindrance to the devotion of those who have not religion enough to keep them from going to it, but who only want to use the profession of religion to maintain their popularity, and to promote their selfish interests. On the other hand, to the devotion of those whose Christianity is really an affair of the life and of the heart, an open circus or theater will never be a particle of hindrance, whether open at church time or all the time. But those people had not enough religion or love of right, to do what they thought to be right; therefore they wanted the State to take away from them all opportunity to do wrong, so that they could all be Christians. Satan himself could be made that kind of Christian in that way; but he would be Satan still.

"Says Neander again:

> 'Church teachers . . . were in truth often forced to complain that in such competitions the theater was vastly more frequented than the church.'—Id.

"And the church could not then stand competition; she wanted a monopoly. And she got it.

"This petition of the Carthage Convention could not be granted at once, but in A.D. 425 the desired law was secured; and to this also there was attached the reason that was given for the first Sunday law that ever was made; namely,—'In order that the devotion of the faithful might be free from all disturbance.'—Id., p. 301.

"It must constantly be borne in mind, however, that the only way in which 'the devotion of the faithful' was 'disturbed' by these things, was that when the circus or the theater was open at the same time that the church was open, the 'faithful' would go to the circus or the theater instead of to church, and therefore their 'devotion' was 'disturbed.' And of course the only way in which the 'devotion' of such 'faithful' ones could be freed from all disturbance, was to close the circuses and the theaters at church time.

"In the logic of this theocratical scheme, there was one more step to be taken. It came about in this way: First the church had all work on Sunday forbidden, in order that the people might attend to things divine. But the people went to the circus and the theater instead of to church. Then the church had laws enacted closing the circuses and the theaters, in order that the people might attend to things divine. But even then the people would not be devoted, nor attend to things divine; for they had no real religion. The next step to be taken, therefore, in the logic of the situation, was to compel them to be devoted—to compel them to attend to things divine. This was the next step logically to be taken, and it was taken. The theocratical bishops were equal to the occasion. They were ready with a theory that exactly met the demands of the case; and the great Catholic Church Father and Catholic saint, Augustine, was the father of this Catholic saintly theory. He wrote:

> 'It is indeed better that men should be brought to serve God by instruction than by fear of punishment, or by pain. But because the former means are better, the latter must not therefore be neglected. ...Many must often be brought back to their Lord, like wicked servants, by the rod of temporal suffering, before they attain to the highest grade of religious development.'—Schaff's Church History, vol. 2, sec. 27.

"Of this theory Neander remarks:-

> 'It was by Augustine, then, that a theory was proposed and founded, which... contained the germ of that whole system of spiritual despotism of intolerance and persecution, which ended in the tribunals of the Inquisition.'— Church History, p. 217.

"The history of the Inquisition is only the history of the carrying out of this infamous theory of Augustine's. But this theory is only the logical sequence of the theory upon which the whole series of Sunday laws was founded.

"Then says Neander:-

'In this way the church received help from the State for the furtherance of her ends.'

"This statement is correct. Constantine did many things to favor the bishops. He gave them money and political preference. He made their decisions in disputed cases final, as the decision of Jesus Christ. But in nothing that he did for them did he give them power over those who did not belong to the church, to compel them to act as though they did, except in that one thing of the Sunday law. Their decisions, which he decreed to be final, were binding only on those who voluntarily chose that tribunal, and affected none others. Before this time, if any who had repaired to the tribunal of the bishops were dissatisfied with the decision, they could appeal to the civil magistrate. This edict cut off that source of appeal, yet affected none but those who voluntarily chose the arbitration of the bishops. But in the Sunday law, power was given to the church to compel those who did not belong to the church, and who were not subject to the jurisdiction of the church, to obey the commands of the church. In the Sunday law there was given to the church control of the civil power, that by it she could compel those who did not belong to the church to act as if they did. The history of Constantine's time may be searched through and through, and it will be found 'that in nothing did he give to the church any such power, except in this one thing—the Sunday law.' Neander's statement is literally correct, that it was 'in this way the church received help from the State for the furtherance of her ends." A.T. Jones, Civil Government and Religion, pp. 85-90.

Sunday Laws In Medieval Europe

Sunday sacredness was progressively endorsed and enforced by Church councils all the way down through the Middle Ages. Civil penalties of increasing severity were attached to the Sunday legislation. In all the various nations of Europe Sunday laws were enforced with civil penalties of increasing severity. Here are some examples from early European history.

The earliest mention of Sunday in an English law is the following:

> "I, Ine (A.D. 688-726), king of the West Saxons, with the advice of Cenred, my father, and Hedde and Erkenwald, my bishops, with all my aldermen and most distinguished sages, and also with a large assembly of God's servants, considering of the health of our souls and the stability of our realm,...made several enactments, of which this is the third: If a bondman work on Sunday by his lord's command, let him be free; and let the lord pay thirty shillings' fine (wite); but if the bondman went to work without his knowledge, let him suffer in his hide, or pay a ransom. But if a freeman work on that day without his lord's command, let him forfeit his freedom, or sixty shillings; if he be a priest, double." Haddan and Stubbs, Councils, etc., Oxford, 1871, p. 214.

The seventeenth canon of King Ethelred's synod, called at Enmha in 1009, reads:

> "The festival of the day of the sun is to be kept zealously as is becoming, and they should abstain diligently from trading and from conventions of the people and from hunting and secular works on the holy days." Cancian. 4, 297.

After Hungary had embraced Christianity, King Stephen issued a Sunday law (A.D. 1016), which was adopted with a few additions at the national council in Szaboles (A.D. 1092). We append its substance as given by Hefele:

> "Whoever neglects to attend his parish church on Sunday or high festivals, shall be scourged. If a lay member hunts on that day, he shall lose a horse, which he may redeem with an ox. If any one of the clergy goes hunting, he shall be deposed until he renders satisfaction. If he neglects to attend church or carries on a trade, he shall lose a horse. If he erects a stall in which to trade, he has either to tear it down or pay fifty-five pounds. If a Jew works on Sunday, he shall lose the tool wherewith he labors." Hefele, 5, 205, 206, sec. 590.

Sunday Laws in the USA in the 17th and 18th Centuries
Not only were strict Sunday laws characteristic of the church-dominated states of Europe during the middle ages, they were even

more characteristic of the early history of the USA before the principle of liberty of conscience was fully established. Religious intolerance flourished in America in the 17th and 18th centuries. We quote again from W.L. Johns:

"It comes as no surprise that Sunday blue laws blossomed in this fertile soil of intolerance, where clergy dominated church and state. In 1629 the Massachusetts Bay Colony decreed: 'To the end the Saboth may bee celebrated in a religious manner, we appoint, that all that inhabite the plantacon, both for the generall and pticuler imployments, may surcease their labor every Satterday throughout the yeire at 3 of the clock in the afternoone, and that they spend the rest of that day in catechising and preparacion for the Saboth as the minister shall direct.' Records of the Governor, Vol. 1, p. 395.

"In November of the following year, John Baker was whipped for 'shooteiny att fowle on the Sabboth day.' Ibid., p. 82.

"The Virginia Sunday law of 1610 prohibited Sunday 'gambling' and required attendance at 'diuine seruice' in the morning and 'in the afternoon to diuine seruice, and Catechising, upon paine for the first fault to lose their provision, and allowance for the whole weeke following, for the second to lose the said allowance, and also to be whipt, and for the third to suffer death.' Peter Force, Tracts Relating To The Colonies In North America, Vol. 3, No. 2, pp. 10, 11. (Washington D.C. 1844, Published by Peter Smith, Gloucester, Mass. 1963.)

"Sunday traveling on horseback, on foot, or by boat to an out-of-town meeting or assembly not specifically provided for by law was illegal. Tradesmen, artificers, and laborers could not conduct business or perform work on land or water. Games, sports, play, and recreation were taboo, 'works of necessity and charity only excepted.'

"In Plymouth Colony church attendance was required, and 'such as sleep or play about the meetinghouse in times of the public worship of God on the Lord's day' could expect to have the constable report their names to the court. Violent riding was banned, as was smoking tobacco." The Compact With the Charter and Laws of the Colony of New Plymouth (Boston 1836), pp. 93, 157, 158.

"The cage, the stocks, heavy fines, and whipping customarily recompensed violators. A man named Birdseye from Milford, Connecticut, was reportedly sentenced to the whipping post for scandalously kissing his wife on Sunday.' Ralph Nader, "Blue Law Causes Examined," Harvard Law Review, Nov. 25, 1959.

"According to Mrs. Alice Morse Earle's history, "The Sabbath in Puritan New England", one of the leading characters in the enforcement of the Puritan Sunday "was the 'tithing man,'...who entered private houses to assure himself that no one stayed at home on the 'Sabbath' [Sunday] and hustled up any loiterers....He was empowered to stop all Sunday work.' In fact, tithing man was always busy on Sunday doing sleuth work, spying out other people's liberties, and haling them before the civil magistrate for neglect of religious duties.

"In 1670 'two lovers, John Lewis and Sarah Chapman, were accused and tried for 'sitting together on the Lord's day under an apple tree in Goodman Chapman's orchard." "A Dunstable soldier, for 'wetting a piece of old hat to put in his shoe to protect his foot—for doing this heavy work on the Lord's day, was fined, and paid forty shillings." "Captain Kemble, of Boston, was in 1656 set for two hours in the public stocks, for his 'lewd and unseemly behavior,' which consisted in kissing his wife 'publicquely' on the Sabbath day, upon the doorsteps of his house," on his return from a three years' voyage. An English sea captain was "soundly whipped" for a like offense. A man, who had fallen into the water and absented himself from church to dry his only suit of clothes, was found guilty and "publicly whipped." Smoking on Sunday was forbidden. To stay away from church meant "cumulative mulct" Other equally foolish and drastic laws prohibited the people from walking, driving, or riding horseback on Sunday, unless they went to church or to the cemetery." "The Blue Laws of New Eng-land," Liberty, Vol. 58 (1963), No. 1, pp. 18, 19.

"The iron fist of the clergy-dominated state was an everyday fact of colonial life. Stringent Sunday laws were a weekly reminder of this union. Freedom of individual conscience had a long way to go." W.L. Johns, Dateline Sunday, U.S.A., pp. 4-7.

The years leading up to 1798 were the remarkably memorable years as far as the development of human rights and liberty of conscience were concerned. The history of that period clearly shows, that only as the principles of religious liberty and separation of church and state were established in the USA, was the enforcement of Sunday laws relaxed.

Mason, Jefferson And Madison Built 'The Wall Of Separation'

We shall now look at the history of the development of religious liberty in the USA. Our source material is the book *Dateline Sunday, USA* by lawyer and constitutional expert, W. L. Johns.

> "With the Baptists, Quakers, and Presbyterians moving into the South, the time had come to consider more carefully the establishment of religion in a political context. These minorities were present in Virginia, a colony dominated in its religious affairs by the Church of England and the home of some of the most astute political leadership of the Revolution, George Mason, James Madison, and Albermarle County's Thomas Jefferson.

> "Jefferson believed that complete personal freedom of conscience was inseparable from 'the principle of majority rule.' This principle 'depended on the premise of a well-informed public, each member of which could choose among, moral or political alternatives with absolute freedom from mental coercion.' This is the key to Jefferson's lifelong insistence on complete separation of church and state." E. M. Halliday, Nature's God and the Founding Fathers, American Heritage, Vol. 14 (1963), No. 6, p. 7.

> "The Virginia House of Burgesses, meeting in Williamsburg, was a forum for issues affecting civil and religious liberty. Here constant demands were heard for the recognition of basic human rights. A steady stream of petitions and requests to protect these rights flowed to the legislature from Virginia citizens. By 1776, the year that James Madison of Port Conway arrived as a delegate, the House of Burgesses was reviewing the entire structure of Virginia government.

> "Madison served on a committee to draw up a bill of rights which would provide the philosophical base for the new government. The great George Mason of Gunston Hall was chief author of the articles in this bill, which was to become the prototype for similar

manifestos in other states as well as, eventually, for the Bill of Rights of the United States Constitution." E. M. Halliday, Nature's God and the Founding Fathers, American Heritage, Vol. 14 (1963), No. 6, p. 100.

"The last of a sixteen-section 'Declaration of Rights', adopted by the House of Burgesses on June 12, 1776, reflected the thoughts of Jefferson, and its final draft carried the influence of Madison's thinking as well. It declared: 'That religion, or the duty which we owe to our Creator, and the manner of discharging it, can be directed only by reason and conviction, not by force or violence; and therefore all men are equally entitled to the free exercise of religion, according, to the dictates of conscience.' American Archives, Fourth Series, Vol. 6, pp. 1561, 1562.

"Patrick Henry penned the original draft of this article, which included a reference to 'the fullest toleration in the exercise of religion.' Madison was committed to nothing short of 'free exercise' and succeeded in having 'toleration' dropped from the final draft. He reasoned that a state which could 'tolerate' could also prohibit.

"The Anglican Church still remained the established religion of the Virginia colony. 'Government salaries for Anglican ministers had been suspended.... [But] it was impossible to be legally married...unless the ceremony was performed by an Anglican clergyman, and heresy against the Christian faith was still a crime.' Halliday, Op. cit., p. 101.

"Presbyterians pushed for abolition of the establishment. In October, 1776, just after the Declaration of Independence had been signed, the Presbytery of Hanover presented a memorial to Virginia's General Assembly asking for the removal of 'every species of religious as well as civil bondage,' and noting that 'every argument for civil liberty gains additional strength when applied in the concerns of religion.' Then they added this statement:

'We ask no ecclesiastical establishment for ourselves, neither can we approve of them and grant it to others....We are induced earnestly to entreat that all laws now in force in this commonwealth which countenance religious domination may be speedily repealed,—that all of every religious sect may be protected in the full exercise of their several modes of worship, and exempted from all taxes for the support of any church whatsoever, further than what may be agreeable to their own private choice or voluntary obligation.' Dissenters Petition, 1776," from Bishop Meade, Old Churches, Ministers, and Families of Virginia, Vol. 2, Appendix, pp. 440-443. In American State Papers, pp. 73, 74.

"When Patrick Henry championed a general tax labeled 'A Bill Establishing a Provision for Teachers of the Christian Faith' in 1784, Madison denounced it as 'chiefly obnoxious on account of its dishonorable principle and dangerous tendency.' Writings of James Madison, Vol. 1, pp. 130, 131. In American State Papers, page 99.

"Madison opposed any concept which gave Christianity a legal preference over other religious persuasions and which was in any way short of absolute separation of church and state.

"In response to a suggestion from George and Wilson Cary Nicholas, members of the General Assembly, Madison took his pen in hand to arouse a public which already had freedom on its mind. In 'A Memorial and Remonstrance,' which was printed and circulated for signatures in 1785, he warned, 'It is proper to take alarm at the first experiment on our liberties.' He cited the free men all over America who refused to wait until usurped power had strengthened itself through exercise. Then he applied this logic to the religious freedom issue at hand, asking:

'Who does not see that the same authority which can establish Christianity, in exclusion of all other Religions, may establish with the same ease any particular sect of Christians, in exclusion of all other sects? that the same authority which can force a citizen to contribute three pence only of his property for the support of any one establishment, may force him to conform to any other establishment in all cases whatsoever?' Ibid., pp. 84, 85.

"The impact of Madison's precise logic created a public reaction so intense that proponents of the 'Provision for Teachers of the Christian Religion' measure conceded defeat. The memorial had been signed by several different religious sects, even including a considerable number of the old hierarchy.

"Madison seized this moment to push for the adoption of an 'Act for Establishing Religious Freedom,' written by Jefferson in 1779 but shelved at that time for lack of support. So prized was the content of this document that Jefferson chose it, coupled with his authorship of the Declaration of Independence and his founding of the University of Virginia, as the outstanding achievements of his life which were to be carved on his tombstone.

"But the mood of 1785 contrasted with the mood of 1774. Seasoned by a hard-fought and costly conflict with Great Britain, political reformers were prepared to make religious liberty as absolute as the desired political freedom which the people sought. The act was passed by the Assembly in December of 1785:

> 'No man shall be compelled to frequent or support any religious worship, place, or ministry whatsoever, nor shall be enforced, restrained, molested, or burthened in his body or goods, nor shall otherwise suffer on account of his religious opinions or belief; but that all men shall be free to profess and by argument to maintain their opinions in matters of religion, and that the same shall in no wise diminish, enlarge or affect their civil capacities.' Writings of Thomas Jefferson, In Norman Cousins, In God We Trust (New York: Harper & Brothers Publishers, 1958), pages 126, 127.

"Church-state separation had achieved legal status in Virginia!

"The Virginia act of disestablishment was published widely, even in foreign countries. But when Jefferson urged New England political leaders to move for disestablishment in their colonies, he received little encouragement. John Adams reported the mood of some: 'I knew they might as well turn the heavenly bodies out of their annual and diurnal courses, as the people of Massachusetts at the present day from their meetinghouse and Sunday laws.' Diary of John Adams." In American State Papers, page 101.

"The time was ripe for Federal intervention. Men of philosophical orientation like Jefferson sensed that this was the moment to establish 'every essential right.' The voice from Monticello cautioned:

'The spirit of the times may alter, will alter. Our rulers will become corrupt, our people careless. A single zealot may commence persecution, and better men be his victims. It can never be too often repeated, that the time for fixing every essential right on a legal basis is while our rulers are honest, and ourselves united. From the conclusion of this war we shall be going downhill. It will not then be necessary to resort every moment to the people for support. They will be forgotten, therefore, and their rights disregarded. They will forget themselves, but in the sole faculty of making money, and will never think of uniting to effect a due respect for their rights. The shackles, therefore, which shall not be knocked off at the conclusion of this war, will remain on us long, will be made heavier and heavier, till our rights shall revive or expire in a convulsion.' Thomas Jefferson, Notes on Virginia, Query XVII. In American State Papers, page 101.

"When the Federal Constitutional Convention adjourned on September 17, 1787, it had produced an impressive document. It guaranteed that there would be no religious test for holding public office in the new government. But the Constitution had no bill of rights and no positive guarantees of church-state separation. George Mason was so distraught at this shortcoming that he refused to sign or approve the work of the convention. When Jefferson saw the final draft, he, too, was disappointed at the lack of major religious freedom guarantees; but he found it otherwise acceptable and stated a willingness to trust to the 'good sense and honest intentions of our citizens' to obtain the desired amendments. (Reynolds v. United States 98 U.S. 145 (1878))

"No sooner had local states initiated ratification procedures for the Constitution than the move for a bill of rights was launched. Virginia, New York, and New Hampshire asked for a declaration of religious liberty. As might be expected, James Madison was in the eye of the storm.

"It was Madison who presented a long list of amendments to the First Congress, meeting in 1789. At the top of the list was a religious liberty amendment drawn by Madison himself. His colleagues subjected it to some reworking, but it was one of seventeen proposals sent to the Senate. Twelve amendments were finally sent to the states and ten ultimately ratified.

"When the 'Bill of Rights' was born in 1791, the wall of separation between church and state became the law of the United States of America. 'Congress shall make no law respecting an establishment of religion, or prohibiting the free exercise thereof.'

"Meanwhile the battle for disestablishment in the new state governments got under way. Influential Virginia had pioneered the way. But in the first [state] constitutions during the war period, only two of the thirteen new states, Rhode Island and Virginia, had complete religious freedom and separation. Six required Protestantism, two the Christian religion, and five a nominal establishment; and seven retained other provisions concerning such points as the Bible, the Trinity, and belief in heaven and hell. By the end of the Revolution nearly all the states had accepted the principle of separation of church and state.

"Not until 1833 did Massachusetts abolish some of the last significant remnants of religious establishment—and this state was the last of the original thirteen states to surrender the formal traditions of pseudo-theocracy. Even then, disestablishment was not complete. One symbol of religious establishment, the Sunday blue law, remained on the books of most states." W.L. Johns in Dateline Sunday U.S.A., pp. 24-31.

Sunday blue laws are still on the law books of most states but they are, or should be, prevented from being enforced by Amendments to the Constitution, Article I.

"Congress shall make no law respecting an establishment of religion, or prohibiting the free exercise thereof; or abridging the freedom of speech, or of the press; or the right of the people peaceably to assemble, and to petition the Government for a redress of grievances."

If this amendment is ever removed the freedoms, rights and liberty of conscience which we take for granted would quickly be blown away and replaced with a modern day church-state "image" of the Middle Ages. Indeed, according to Jefferson, eternal vigilance is the price of liberty.

The American Paradox

*T*HE USA OBVIOUSLY REGARDS ITSELF as the international leader in human rights. Any nation seeking mutually friendly relations with America is required to have at least a certain basic standard of human rights acceptable to the USA.

As a nation, America was "conceived in liberty" and boasts a most wonderful amendment to its constitution guaranteeing liberty of conscience, and separation of church and state. Yet America has never quite managed to completely free itself from Sunday blue laws, a legacy from the colonial days of church-state union. Furthermore, America took an inordinately long period of time before giving American blacks, a minority racial group, all the rights and privileges guaranteed under the Constitution.

Throughout the history of America as a Republic, there has been, even up to very recent times, the imposition of criminal sanctions against individuals who "violated" Sunday blue laws.

In order to construct a proper analysis of this paradox we need to understand a number of basic facts, listed as follows:

- Sunday blue laws are state laws.
- The US as a nation, yet, has no federal or national Sunday law.

The Declaration of Independence states very clearly: "We hold these truths to be self-evident, that all men are created equal; that they are endowed by their Creator with certain unalienable rights; that among these are life, liberty, and the pursuit of happiness."

The two crucially important "human-rights" amendments to the US Constitution, for liberty of conscience, are the first and the fourteenth.

Amendments To The Constitution
Article I

Congress shall make no law respecting an establishment of religion, or prohibiting the free exercise thereof; or abridging the freedom of speech, or of the press; or the right of the people peaceably to assemble, and to petition the Government for a redress of grievances.

Article XIV

No state shall make or enforce any law which shall abridge the privileges or immunities of citizens of the United States; nor shall any State deprive any person of life, liberty, or property without due process of law, nor deny to any person within its jurisdiction the equal protection of the laws.

It is an undeniable fact that Sunday laws are religious in their origin as well as in their purpose. Therefore, according to the First Amendment, as applied to the various states through the Fourteenth Amendment, Sunday laws are unconstitutional.

Using these four premises and their inescapable conclusion, we can now proceed to examine the history and the law of the American paradox.

The History Of The 1st And 14th Amendment Applications

The 14th Amendment was added to the U.S. Constitution in 1868. By 1925 the U.S. Supreme Court had decreed that the guarantees of liberty of conscience in the 1st Amendment were applicable to state governments by way of the provisions of the 14th Amendment. [Legal Reference: see Gitlow v New York, 268 U.S. 652 (1925)]

By 1940 the Supreme Court confirmed that the religious freedom guaranteed by the 1st Amendment was applicable to the states through the 14th Amendment. [Legal Reference: see Thornhill v Alabama, 310 U.S. 296 (1940); Cantwell v Connecticut 310 US 296, (1940)]

But while the legal protection of human rights was gradually developing, State Sunday laws were still, frequently, being enforced, with penal sanctions, upon individuals. And many of the cases revealed that the State Sunday-law regulations were arbitrary, capricious and absurd. Here are some examples quoted from Attorney Warren Johns' book *Dateline Sunday, USA*, pp 113,114:

"In Pennsylvania, where the High Court introduced the 'civil regulation' doctrine in 1848, the Pittsburgh Sabbath Association arranged for the arrest of members of the Pittsburgh Symphony Society for 'furnishing music to the public on Sunday' in 1929. Two years later in a Philadelphia suburb 'a policeman arrested a boy for kicking a football on Sunday. When the father protested, the... policeman shot and killed the father.' (Original source of quote, American State Papers, 566, 567).

"A deputy sheriff of Washington County arrested two Seventh-day Adventists for Sunday work, one—a crippled mother who walks on crutches—for washing clothes on her premises, and the other a man who donated and hauled a load of wood to a church to heat it for religious services. (Original source of quote, American State Papers, 567). The place was Virginia, the year, 1932."

"Eight Lincoln, Nebraska, boys were fined \$5 each in 1921 for playing horseshoes in a vacant lot on Sunday. A 1930 Sunday football game in New Jersey was stopped, and in 1924 a New Jersey court invoked a 1798 blue law and found it illegal to play a phonograph or listen to the radio on Sunday because this was 'music for the sake of merriment.'"

"When a Sunday law 'spy' peered into the privacy of a Baltimore home in 1926 and saw a man pressing his pants on Sunday, the act was reported, and a fine resulted. In Georgia, in 1930, the state where the 'police power' doctrine had been aired in the Hennington case, there was arbitrary use of the Sunday law. 'The police in Clayton County protected and helped a traveling circus to land in town and put on a show; they also cooperated with airplanes which took people for rides and made much money; yet they arrested a Bible colporteur for delivering a book explaining the Bible, on Sunday, since the person who ordered the book requested that the book be delivered then because it was the only day he was at home." (Original source of quote, American State Papers, 563).

The Legal Paradox

Let's get to the heart of the problem. After the addition of the First Amendment in the USA there have been differences in legal opinion concerning State Sunday laws and their enforcement.

On one side there have been well-learned, highly respected, and greatly experienced judges who have asserted that Sunday laws are merely civil regulations, and that the enforcement of such laws does not constitute a violation of religious liberty.

On another side there have been equally well-learned, highly respected, and also greatly experienced judges who have asserted, with equal adamancy, that Sunday laws are religious in origin, purpose and intent, and that the enforcement of such laws does in fact constitute a violation of the religious liberty of the individual.

And, thirdly, there have been also well-learned judges of high standing who did not bother to reveal whether they thought the Sunday laws were merely civil or religious, but simply stated that so long as the Sunday law is on the State books, they would impose the penal sanctions affixed to the violation of the laws, until the legislators see fit to change or abolish them.

Let us deal with this third position first. The president and judges of the USA are obliged to preserve, protect and defend the Constitution of the USA. Article III of the US Constitution, Section 2, reads as follows:

> "The judicial power shall extend to all cases, in law and equity, arising under this Constitution, the laws of the United States, and treaties made, or which shall be made, under their authority."

Here it is indicated quite clearly that the Constitution, being the highest law in the land, is primary and fundamental in the application of all other laws.

In other words, it is within the prerogatives and duties of a judge to declare a law which violates liberty of conscience unconstitutional, and therefore to free the defendant of any charges.

There is another important point that should be mentioned here. It is a point concerning a weakness in the democratic process. Suppose the majority of people in a democracy voted to outlaw, let's say, baptism by immersion. Well, the Constitution is supposed to protect the minority from the majority in matters of conscience. John Stuart Mill wrote:

> "If all mankind minus one were of one opinion, mankind would be no more justified in silencing that one person than he, if he had the power, would be justified in silencing mankind." John Stuart Mill, On Liberty, (Indianapolis: Bobbs-Merrill Company, 1956), p. 21.

In the U.S.A., and any other free country, the Supreme Court is supposed to uphold the constitutional rights of the minority against the opposition of the majority, so if there ever occurs a popular demand for something which is unconstitutional, the Supreme Court should uphold the constitution.

This brings us now to the point of this chapter. There has been considerable variation in the interpretation of the constitution. Justices have had the same facts given to them, have read the same constitution, have had the same precedents and yet have come to different, even opposite, conclusions. Let us now turn our attention to the other two judicial opinions of the matter under consideration.

The 'Civil-regulation' Theory

To claim that Sunday laws are merely civil regulations would be tantamount to admitting total ignorance of their history or, worse still, a falsification of the facts to achieve a desired end.

The chief proponents of Sunday legislation have been zealous religious groups demanding respect for the "Lord's Day," or Sunday Sabbath. Furthermore, if Sunday was intended to be merely a civil holiday for the public welfare in the USA, similar to Labor Day or Thanksgiving, why the criminal penalties for violation? There are no penalties for violating other civil holidays.

Moreover, various state courts have repeatedly given a religious reason for supporting Sunday laws, for example, the Massachusetts court in 1923. We quote from Warren Johns' *Dateline Sunday USA*, p. 115:

> "In 1923 the same court ruled against Sunday bread deliveries and explained that the statute which prohibited the performance of labor, business, or work on Sunday 'was enacted to secure respect and reverence for the Lord's Day,' and 'that the day should be not merely a day of rest from labor, but also a day devoted to public and private worship and to religious meditation and repose, undisturbed by secular cares or amusements." (Original quote from *Commonwealth v McCarthy,* 244 Massachusetts 484 (1923).

Yet, notwithstanding these facts, some judges have selected language from various court decisions to support their conclusion that modern Sunday laws are mere civil regulations.

The 1961 U.S. Supreme Court decisions on Sunday law violations followed the 'civil regulation' theory and penalized the defendants for Sunday law violations. The decisions evoked widespread reaction. *Time* magazine of October 25, 1963 declared, "Seldom has an issue of liberty been argued on flabbier grounds."

"U.S. blue laws are riddled with erratic contradictions. In Pennsylvania it is illegal to sell a bicycle on Sunday, but not a tricycle; in Massachusetts it is against the law to dredge for oyster, but not to dig for clams; in Connecticut genuine antiques may lawfully be sold, but not reproductions. The New York blue law code is particularly messy. Bars may open at 1 p.m., but baseball games may not begin until 2 p.m. It is legal to sell fruits but not vegetables, an automobile tire but not a tire jack, tobacco but not a pipe. It is unlawful to sell butter or cooked meat after 10 a.m., except that delicatessens may sell these foods between 4 p.m. and 7:30 p.m."

"The Detroit *Free Press* took a dim view of the decision, noting,

'The machinations of great minds are frequently fascinating, and not easily understood by those who rely on common sense instead of technicalities.' The editor expressed amazement at the court's finding that 'the laws against doing business on Sunday have nothing to do with religion,' and he observed that 'even the justices must have known this is ridiculous.' Then he added:

'How, when the words are written into the law, the justices can pretend they aren't is beyond our comprehension....The clear wording and all past practices indicate that blue laws are intended to enforce religious concepts. Even when providing exceptions such as Michigan's, they can interfere with the right of a minority to a different belief.

'As of this week, they may be considered constitutional, but that does not mean they are reasonable. The court has ruled for the majority and totally ignored the religious rights of minorities.' (Original quote, Detroit Free Press, June 1, 1961).

"The Washington *Post* also criticized the decision and predicted new constitutional tests. 'If, as we fear, the decision spawns a spate of such blue laws, the religious motivation will become so clear that the court will no longer be able to ignore it.'" W.L. Johns, Dateline Sunday, U.S.A., pp. 161, 162-163.

"Gilbert S. Fell, minister of Central Methodist Church in Atlantic City, noted shortly before the landmark 1961 Supreme Court opinions that 'whatever the cause—perhaps the so-called religious revival of the 1950s—there is increasing agitation for more stringent Sabbath observance laws.' While affirming his personal belief in the great religious value of a weekly holy day, he went on record as vigorously opposing 'the recent attempts to reimpose Sabbath laws.' He cited several reasons for his opinion:

'First, these laws run counter to the First Amendment...Since I would not wish to be made to observe Saturday as the Sabbath, I do not see how I can enforce other groups to observe my wish...

'Second, to call such laws "health measures"...is a sham and a fiction. Perhaps at their inception these laws were to some degree intended as health measures—although this interpretation is questionable—but surely in these days we have ample leisure time, so much so that sociologists see its amplitude as a problem.

'Third, these laws violate the Protestant affirmation of personal free choice. Let those who wish the Sabbath observe the Sabbath.

'Fourth, the Sunday laws tend to be discriminatory. In New Jersey it seems likely that a law will pass permitting a man to go out and drink himself under the table on Sunday but preventing him from purchasing a bathing cap or a toothpick on that day." (Original quote—Gilbert S. Fell, Blue Laws—A Minority Opinion, The Christian Century).

"Shortly after the 1961 Supreme Court decisions, the 174th General Assembly of the United Presbyterian Church in the United States heard a report from its Special Committee on Church and State. The report recommended that 'this General Assembly affirms its conviction that the church itself bears sole and vital responsibility for securing from its members a voluntary observance of the Lord's Day. The church should not seek, or even appear to seek, the coercive power of the state in order to facilitate Christians' observance of the Lord's Day.' "
Warren Johns' Dateline Sunday, USA, pp. 218-219.

The 'Religious-law' Theory

While some judges have argued that Sunday laws are merely civil regulations, others have contended that they are, most definitely, religious. And the fact is, they are religious both in their origin and in their purpose.

Perhaps the best modern analysis of the religious nature of Sunday legislation was given by Justice William O. Douglas, who dissented from the majority in the 1961 Supreme Court Sunday law cases. In our next chapter we shall present Justice Douglas' statement in full. It should be carefully read by every student of religious liberty. But before we go to the Douglas Dissent we need to consider yet another judicial opinion on Sunday laws.

In the same 1961 Supreme Court Sunday-law cases, Justice Felix Frankfurter decided that the community interest served by the Sunday laws outweighed the religious freedom of the individual. He reasoned that it was more important to maintain an atmosphere of general repose for the entire community on Sunday, than to allow an individual to carry on work or business on Sunday, even if the individual has another religious persuasion.

This opinion, that the individual must submit his conscientious religious belief to the practice or belief or tradition of the majority, is a dangerous one. It is the very thing that the First Amendment was intended to prevent. Such an opinion is being proposed as one of the reasons for Sunday legislation in the new geopolitical system.

Conclusion

We have seen that there is a considerable variation in legal and judicial interpretation of the U.S. Constitution as it applies to Sunday laws in the USA. The varying opinions are mutually exclusive; they cannot all be accommodated because they cannot all be correct. Yet all of the varying judicial opinions have held sway in U.S. Supreme Court decisions. This is one of the reasons why the USA, notwithstanding the wonderful provisions of its Constitution, could find it easy to pass a federal Sunday law if socio-economic conditions become unstable, and religious zealots push the theory that a Christian nation should enforce Sunday observance, so as to improve societal morals and restore the nation to divine favor.

In the next chapter we present the Douglas Dissent; a wonderful treatise and an incisive analysis of the "Sunday law versus Constitution" debate.

The 1961 Douglas Dissent

By Justice William O. Douglas

(United States Supreme Court Justice William O. Douglas dissented from the majority in the 1961 Sunday-law cases. He believed that the blue laws before the Court constituted a violation of both the "establishment clause" and the "free exercise clause" of the First Amendment. Except for footnotes, Justice Douglas's statement is reproduced here in full, as recorded in McGowan v. Maryland, 366 U.S. 561-581 [1961].) Reproduced from Warren John's *"Dateline Sunday, USA"*

*T*HE QUESTION IS NOT WHETHER ONE DAY OUT OF SEVEN can be imposed by a State as a day of rest. The question is not whether Sunday can by force of custom and habit be retained as a day of rest. The question is whether a State can impose criminal sanctions on those who, unlike the Christian majority that makes up our society, worship on a different day or do not share the religious scruples of the majority.

If the "free exercise" of religion were subject to reasonable regulations, as it is under some constitutions, or if all laws "respecting the establishment of religion" were not proscribed, I could understand how rational men, representing a predominantly Christian civilization, might think these Sunday laws did not unreasonably interfere with anyone's free exercise of religion and took no step toward a burdensome establishment of any religion.

But that is not the premise from which we start, as there is agreement that the fact that a State, and not the Federal Government, has promulgated these Sunday laws does not change the scope of the power asserted. For the classic view is that the First Amendment should be applied to the States with the same firmness as it is enforced against the Federal Government. See *Lovell* v. *City of Griffin*, 303 U.S. 444, 450; *Minersville School District* v. *Gobitis*, 310 U.S. 586, 593; *Murdock* v. *Pennsylvania*, 319 U.S. 105, 108; *Board of Education* v. *Barnette*, 319 U.S. 624, 639; *Staub* v. *City of Baxley*, 355 U.S. 313, 321; *Talley* v. *California*, 362 U.S. 60. The most explicit statement perhaps was in *Board of Education* v. *Barnette*, *supra*, 639.

> "In weighing arguments of the parties it is important to distinguish between the due process clause of the Fourteenth Amendment as an instrument for transmitting the principles of the First Amendment and those cases in which it is applied for its own sake. The test of legislation which collides with the Fourteenth Amendment, because it also collides with the principles of the First, is much more definite than the test when only the Fourteenth is involved. Much of the vagueness of the due process clause disappears when the specific prohibitions of the First become its standard. The right of a State to regulate, for example, a public utility may well include, so far as the due process test is concerned, power to impose all of the restrictions which a legislature may have a 'rational basis' for adopting. But freedoms of speech and of press, of assembly, and of worship may not be infringed on such slender grounds. *They are susceptible of restriction only to prevent grave and immediate danger to interests which the State may lawfully protect.* It is important to note that while it is the Fourteenth Amendment which bears directly upon the State it is the more specific limiting principles of the First Amendment that finally govern this case."

With that as my starting point I do not see how a State can make protesting citizens refrain from doing innocent acts on Sunday because the doing of those acts offends sentiments of their Christian neighbors.

The institutions of our society are founded on the belief that there is an authority higher than the authority of the State; that there is a moral law which the State is powerless to alter; that the individual possesses rights, conferred by the Creator, which government must respect. The Declaration of Independence stated the now familiar theme:

> "We hold these Truths to be self-evident, that all Men are created equal, that they are endowed by their Creator with certain unalienable Rights, that among these are Life, Liberty and the Pursuit of Happiness."

And the body of the Constitution as well as the Bill of Rights enshrined those principles.

The Puritan influence helped shape our constitutional law and our common law as Dean Pound has said: The Puritan "put individual conscience and individual judgment in the first place." The Spirit of the Common Law (1921), p. 42. For those reasons we stated in *Zorach v. Clauson*, 343 U.S. 306, 313, "We are a religious people whose institutions presuppose a Supreme Being."

But those who fashioned the First Amendment decided that if and when God is to be served, His service will not be motivated by coercive measures of government. "Congress shall make no law respecting an establishment of religion, or prohibiting the free exercise thereof" - such is the command of the First Amendment made applicable to the State by reason of the Due Process Clause of the Fourteenth. This means, as I understand it, that if a religious leaven is to be worked into the affairs of our people, it is to be done by individuals and groups, not by the Government. This necessarily means, *first* that the dogma, creed, scruples, or practices of no religious group or sect are to be preferred over those of any others; *second*, that no one shall be interfered with by government for practicing the religion of his choice; *third*, that the State may not require anyone to practice a religion or even any religion; and *fourth*, that the State cannot compel one so to conduct himself as not to offend the religious scruples of another. The idea, as I understand it, was to limit the power of government to act in religious matters *(Board of Education v. Barnette, supra; McCollum v. Board of Education*, 333 U.S. 203), not to limit the freedom of religious men to act religiously nor to restrict the freedom of atheists or agnostics.

The First Amendment commands government to have no interest in theology or ritual; it admonishes government to be interested in allowing religious freedom to flourish - whether the result is to produce Catholics, Jews, or Protestants, or to turn the people toward the path of Buddha, or to end in a predominantly Moslem nation, or to produce in the long run atheists or agnostics. On matters of this kind government must be neutral. This freedom plainly includes freedom from religion with the right to believe, speak, write, publish and advocate antireligious programs. *Board of Education v. Barnette, supra,* 641. Certainly the "free exercise" clause does not require that everyone embrace the theology of some church or of some faith, or observe the religious practices of any majority or minority sect. The First Amendment by its "establishment" clause prevents, of course, the selection by government of an "official" church. Yet the ban plainly extends farther than that. We said in *Everson v. Board of Education,* 330 U.S. 1, 16, that it would be an "establishment" of a religion if the Government financed one church or several churches. For what better way to "establish" an institution than to find the fund that will support it? The "establishment" clause protects citizens also against any law which selects any religious custom, practice, or ritual, puts the force of government behind it, and fines, imprisons, or otherwise penalizes a person for not observing it. The Government plainly could not join forces with one religious group and decree a universal and symbolic circumcision. Nor could it require all children to be baptized or give tax exemptions only to those whose children were baptized.

Could it require a fast from sunrise to sunset throughout the Moslem month of Ramadan? I should think not. Yet why then can it make criminal the doing of other acts, as innocent as eating, during the day that Christians revere?

Sunday is a word heavily overlaid with connotations and traditions deriving from the Christian roots of our civilization that color all judgments concerning it. This is what the philosophers call "word magic."

"For most judges, for most lawyers, for most human beings, we are as unconscious of our value patterns as we are of the oxygen that we breathe." *Cohen, Legal Conscience* (1960), p. 169.

The issue of these cases would therefore be in better focus if we imagined that a state legislature, controlled by orthodox Jews and Seventh-Day Adventists, passed a law making it a crime to keep a shop open on Saturdays. Would a Baptist, Catholic, Methodist, or Presbyterian be compelled to obey that law or go to jail or pay a fine? Or suppose Moslems grew in political strength here and got a law through a state legislature making it a crime to keep a shop open on Fridays. Would the rest of us have to submit under the fear of criminal sanctions?

Dr. John Cogley recently summed up the dominance of the three-religion influence in our affairs:

"For the foreseeable future, it seems, the United States is going to be a three-religion nation. At the present time all three are characteristically 'American,' some think flavorlessly so. For religion in America is almost uniformly 'respectable', bourgeois, and prosperous. In the Protestant world the 'church' mentality has triumphed over the more venturesome spirit of the 'sect.' In the Catholic world, the mystical is muted in favor of booming organization and efficiently administered good works. And in the Jewish world the prophet is too frequently without honor, while the synagogue emphasis is focused on suburban togetherness. There are exceptions to these rules, of course; each of the religious communities continues to cast up its prophets, its rebels and radicals. But a Jeremiah, one fears, would be positively embarrassing to the present position of the Jews; a Francis of Assisi upsetting the complacency of American Catholics would be rudely dismissed as a fanatic; and a Kierkegaard, speaking with an American accent, would be considerably less welcome than Norman Vincent Peale in most Protestant pulpits."

This religious influence has extended far, far back of the First and Fourteenth Amendments. Every Sunday School student knows the Fourth Commandment:

"Remember the sabbath day to keep it holy.

"Six days shalt thou labour, and do all thy work:

"But the seventh day is the sabbath of the LORD thy God: in it thou shalt not do any work, thou, nor thy son, nor thy daughter, thy manservant, nor thy maidservant, nor thy stranger that is within thy gates:

"For in six days the LORD made heaven and earth, the sea, and all that in them is, and rested the seventh day: wherefore the LORD blessed the sabbath day, and hallowed it." Exodus 20:8-11.

This religious mandate for observance of the Seventh Day became, under Emperor Constantine, a mandate for observance of the First Day "in conformity with the practice of the Christian Church." See *Richardson v. Goddard*, 23 How. 28, 41. This religious mandate has had a checkered history; but in general its command, enforced now by the ecclesiastical authorities, now by the civil authorities, and now by both, has held good down through the centuries. The general pattern of these laws in the United States was set in the eighteenth century and derives, most directly, from the seventeenth century English statute, 29 Charles II, c. 7. Judicial comment on the Sunday laws has always been a mixed bag. Some judges have asserted that the statutes have a "purely" civil aim, *i.e.*, limitation of work time and provision for a common and universal leisure. But other judges have recognized the religious significance of Sunday and that the laws existed to enforce the maintenance of that significance. In general, both threads of argument have continued to interweave in the case law on the subject. Prior to the time when the First Amendment was held applicable to the States by reason of the Due Process Clause of the Fourteenth, the Court at least by *obiter dictum* approved State Sunday laws on three occasions: *Soon Hing v. Crowley*, 113 U.S. 703, in 1885; *Hennington v. Georgia*, 163 U.S. 299, in 1896; *Petit v. Minnesota*, 177 U.S. 164, in 1900. And in *Friedman v. New York*, 341 U.S. 907, the Court, by a divided vote, dismissed "for the want of a substantial federal question" an appeal from a New York decision upholding the validity of a Sunday law against an attack based on the First Amendment.

The *Soon Hing, Hennington,* and *Petit* cases all rested on the police power of the State — the right to safeguard the health of the people by requiring the cessation of normal activities one day out of seven. The Court in the *Soon Hing* case rejected the idea that Sunday laws rested on the power of government "to legislate for the promotion of religious observances." 113 U.S. 710. The New York Court of Appeals in the *Friedman* case followed the reasoning of the earlier cases, 302 N.Y. 75, 80, 96 N. E. 2d 184, 186.

The Massachusetts Sunday law involved in one of these appeals was once characterized by the Massachusetts court as merely a civil regulation providing for a "fixed period of rest." *Commonwealth v. Has*, 122 Mass. 40, 42. That decision was, according to the District Court in the *Gallagher* case, "an *ad hoc* improvisation" made "because of the realization that the Sunday law would be more vulnerable to constitutional attack under the state Constitution if the religious motivation of the statute were more explicitly avowed." 176 F. Supp. 466, 473. Certainly prior to the *Has* case, the Massachusetts courts had indicated that the aim of the Sunday law was religious. See *Pearce v.*

Atwood, 13 Mass. 324, 345-346; *Bennett v. Brooks*, 91 Mass. 118, 121. After the *Has* case the Massachusetts court construed the Sunday law as a religious measure. In *Davis v. Somerville*, 128 Mass. 594, 596, 35 Am. Rep. 399, 400, it was said:

> "Our Puritan ancestors intended that the day should be not merely a day of rest from labor, but also a day devoted to public and private worship and to religious meditation and repose, undisturbed by secular cares or amusements. They saw fit to enforce the observance of the day by penal legislation, and the statute regulations which they devised for that purpose have continued in force, without any substantial modification, to the present time."

And see *Commonwealth v. Dextra*, 143 Mass. 28, 8 N. E. 756. In *Commonwealth v. White*, 190 Mass. 578, 581, 77 N. E. 636, 637, the court refused to liberalize its construction of an exception in its Sunday law for works of "necessity." That word, it said, "was originally inserted to secure the observance of the Lord's day in accordance with the views of our ancestors, and it ever since has stood and still stands for the same purpose." In *Commonwealth v. McCarthy*, 244 Mass. 484, 486, 138 N.E. 835, 836, the court reiterated that the aim of the law was "to secure respect and reverence for the Lord's day."

The Pennsylvania Sunday laws before us in Nos. 36 and 67 have received the same construction. "Rest and quiet, on the Sabbath day, with the right and privilege of public and private worship, undisturbed by any mere worldly employment, are exactly what the statute was passed to protect." *Sparhawk v. Union Passenger R. Co.*, 54 Pa. 401, 423. And see *Commonwealth v. Nesbit*, 34 Pa. 398, 405, 406-408. A recent pronouncement by the Pennsylvania Supreme Court is found in *Commonwealth v. American Baseball Club*, 290 Pa. 136, 143, 138 A. 497, 499: "Christianity is part of the common law of Pennsylvania . . . and its people are Christian people. Sunday is the holy day among Christians."

The Maryland court, in sustaining the challenged law in No. 8, relied on *Judefind v. State*, 78 Md. 510, 28 A. 405, and *Levering v. Park Commissioner*, 134 Md. 48, 106 A. 176. In the former the court said:

> "It is undoubtedly true that rest from secular employment on Sunday does have a tendency to foster and encourage the Christian religion, of all sects and denominations that observe

that day, as rest from work and ordinary occupation enables many to engage in public worship who probably would not otherwise do so. But it would scarcely be asked of a court, in what professed to be a Christian land, to declare a law unconstitutional because it requires rest from bodily labor on Sunday, except works of necessity and charity, and thereby promotes the cause of Christianity. If the Christian religion is, incidentally or otherwise, benefited or fostered by having this day of rest, (as it undoubtedly is,) there is all the more reason for the enforcement of laws that help to preserve it." 78 Md., at pages 515-516, 28 A. at page 407.

In the Levering case the court relied on the excerpt from the Jude find decision just quoted. 134 Md. at 54-55, 106 A. at 178.

We have then in each of the four cases Sunday laws that find their source in Exodus, that were brought here by the Virginians and by the Puritans, and that are today maintained, construed, and justified because they respect the views of our dominant religious groups and provide a needed day of rest.

The history was accurately summarized a century ago by Chief Justice Terry of the Supreme Court of California in *Ex Parte Newman*, 9 Cal. 502, 509:

"The truth is, however much it may be disguised, that this one day of rest is a purely religious idea. Derived from the Sabbatical institutions of the ancient Hebrew, it has been adopted into all the creeds of succeeding religious sects throughout the civilized world; and whether it be the Friday of the Mohammedan, the Saturday of the Israelite, or the Sunday of the Christian, it is alike fixed in the affections of its followers, beyond the power of eradication, and in most of the States of our Confederacy, the aid of the law to enforce its observance has been given under the pretense of a civil, municipal, or police regulation."

That case involved the validity of a Sunday law under a provision of the California Constitution guaranteeing the "free exercise" of religion. Calif. Const., 1849, Art. 1, § 4. Justice Burnett stated why he concluded that the Sunday law, there sought to be enforced against a man selling clothing on Sunday, infringed California's constitution:

"Had the act made Monday, instead of Sunday, a day of compulsory rest, the constitutional question would have been the same. The fact that the Christian voluntarily keeps holy the first day of the week, does not authorize the Legislature to make that observance compulsory. The Legislature can not compel the citizen to do that which the Constitution leaves him free to do or omit, at his election. The act violates as much the religious freedom of the Christian as of the Jew. Because the conscientious views of the Christian compel him to keep Sunday as a Sabbath, he has the right to object, when the Legislature invades his freedom of religious worship, and assumes the power to compel him to do that which he has the right to omit if he pleases. The principle is the same, whether the act of the Legislature compels us to do that which we wish to do, or not to do. . . .

"Under the Constitution of this State, the Legislature cannot pass any act, the legitimate effect of which is forcibly to establish any merely religious truth, or enforce any merely religious observances. The Legislature has no power over such a subject. When, therefore, the citizen is sought to be compelled by the Legislature to do any affirmative religious act, or to refrain from doing anything, because it violates simply a religious principle or observance, the act is unconstitutional." *Id.*, at 513-515.

The Court picks and chooses language from various decisions to bolster its conclusion that these Sunday laws in the modern setting are "civil regulations." No matter how much is written, no matter what is said, the parentage of these laws is the Fourth Commandment; and they serve and satisfy the religious predispositions of our Christian communities. After all, the labels a State places on its laws are not binding on us when we are confronted with a constitutional decision. We reach our own conclusion as to the character, effect, and practical operation of the regulation in determining its constitutionality. *Carpenter v. Shaw*, 280 U.S. 363, 367-368; *Dyer v. Sims*, 341 U.S. 22, 29; *Memphis Steam Laundry v. Stone*, 342, U.S. 389, 392; *Society for Savings v. Bowers*, 349 U.S. 143, 151; *Gomillion v. Lightfoot*, 364 U.S. 339, 341-342.

It seems to me plain that by these laws the States compel one, under sanction of law, to refrain from work or recreation on Sunday because of the majority's religious views about that day. The State by law makes Sunday a symbol of respect or adherence. Refraining from work or recreation in deference to the majority's religious feelings about Sunday is within every person's choice. By what authority can government compel it?

Cases are put where acts that are immoral by our standards but not by the standards of other religious groups are made criminal. That category of cases, until today, has been a very restricted one confined to polygamy *(Reynolds v. United States,* 98 U.S. 145) and other extreme situations. The latest example is *Prince v. Massachusetts,* 321 U.S. 158, which upheld a statute making it criminal for a child under twelve to sell papers, periodicals, or merchandise on a street or in any public place. It was sustained in spite of the finding that the child thought it was her religious duty to perform the act. But that was a narrow holding which turned on the effect which street solicitation might have on the child-solicitor:

> "The state's authority over children's activities is broader than over like actions of adults. This is peculiarly true of public activities and in matters of employment. A democratic society rests, for its continuance, upon the healthy, well-rounded growth of young people into full maturity as citizens, with all that implies. It may secure this against impeding restraints and dangers within a broad range of selection. Among evils most appropriate for such action are the crippling effects of child employment, more especially in public places, and the possible harms arising from other activities subject to all the diverse influences of the street. It is too late now to doubt that legislation appropriately designed to reach such evils is within the state's police power, whether against the parent's claim to control of the child or one that religious scruples dictate contrary action." *Id.,* 168-169.

None of the acts involved here implicates minors. None of the actions made constitutionally criminal today involves the doing of any act that any society has deemed to be immoral.

The conduct held constitutionally criminal today embraces the selling of pure, not impure, food; wholesome, not noxious, articles. Adults, not minors, are involved. The innocent acts, now constitutionally classified as criminal, emphasize the drastic break we make with tradition.

These laws are sustained because, it is said, the First Amendment is concerned with religious convictions or opinion, not with conduct. But it is a strange Bill of Rights that makes it possible for the dominant religious group to bring the minority to heel because the minority, in the doing of acts which intrinsically are wholesome and not antisocial, does not defer to the majority's religious beliefs. Some have religious scruples against eating pork. Those scruples, no matter how bizarre they might seem to some, are within the ambit of the First Amendment. See *United States v. Ballard,* 322 U.S. 78, 87. Is it possible that a majority of a state legislature having those religious scruples could make it criminal for the nonbeliever to sell pork? Some have religious scruples against slaughtering cattle. Could a state legislature, dominated by that group, make it criminal to run an abattoir?

The Court balances the need of the people for rest, recreation, late sleeping, family visiting, and the like against the command of the First Amendment that no one need bow to the religious beliefs of another. There is in this realm no room for balancing. I see no place for it in the constitutional scheme. A legislature of Christians can no more make minorities conform to their weekly regime than a legislature of Moslems, or a legislature of Hindus. The religious regime of every group must be respected — unless it crosses the line of criminal conduct. But no one can be forced to come to a halt before it, or refrain from doing things that would offend it. That is my reading of the Establishment Clause and the Free Exercise Clause. Any other reading imports, I fear, an element common in other societies but foreign to us. Thus Nigeria in Article 23 of her Constitution, after guaranteeing religious freedom, adds, "Nothing in this section shall invalidate any law that is reasonably justified in a democratic society in the interest of defence, public safety, public order, public morality, or public health." And see Article 25 of the Indian Constitution. That may be a desirable provision. But when the Court adds it to our First Amendment, as it does today, we make a sharp break with the American ideal of religious liberty as enshrined in the First Amendment.

The State can, of course, require one day of rest a week: one day when every shop or factory is closed. Quite a few States make that requirement. Then the "day of rest" becomes purely and simply a health measure. But the Sunday laws operate differently. They force minorities to obey the majority's religious feelings of what is due and proper for a Christian community; they provide a coercive spur to the "weaker brethren," to those who are indifferent to the claims of a Sabbath through apathy or scruple. Can there be any doubt that Christians, now aligned vigorously in favor of these laws, would be as strongly opposed if they were

prosecuted under a Moslem law that forbade them from engaging in
secular activities on days that violated Moslem scruples?

There is an "establishment" of religion in the constitutional sense
if any practice of any religious group has the sanction of law behind
it. There is an interference with the "free exercise" of religion if what in
conscience one can do or omit doing is required because of the religious
scruples of the community. Hence I would declare each of those laws
unconstitutional as applied to the complaining parties, whether or not
they are members of a sect which observes as its Sabbath a day other
than Sunday.

When these laws are applied to Orthodox Jews, as they are in No. 11
and No. 67, or to Sabbatarians their vice is accentuated. If the Sunday
laws are constitutional, kosher markets are on a five-day week. Thus
those laws put an economic penalty on those who observe Saturday
rather than Sunday as the Sabbath. For the economic pressures on these
minorities, created by the fact that our communities are predominantly
Sunday-minded, there is no recourse. When, however, the State uses
its coercive powers - here the criminal law - to compel minorities to
observe a second Sabbath, not their own, the State undertakes to aid
and "prefer one religion over another" - contrary to the command of the
Constitution. See *Everson v. Board of Education, supra,* 15.

In large measure the history of the religious clause of the First
Amendment was a struggle to be free of economic sanctions for adher-
ence to one's religion. *Everson v. Board of Education, supra,* 330 U.S. 11-14.
A small tax was imposed in Virginia for religious education. Jefferson
and Madison led the fight against the tax, Madison writing his famous
Memorial and Remonstrance against that law. *Id.,* 12. As a result, the tax
measure was defeated and instead Virginia's famous "Bill for Religious
Liberty," written by Jefferson, was enacted. *Id.,* 12. That Act provided:

> "That no man shall be compelled to frequent or support any
> religious worship, place, or ministry whatsoever, nor shall be
> enforced, restrained, molested, or burthened in his body or
> goods, nor shall otherwise suffer on account of his religious
> opinions or belief. . . ."

The reverse side of an "establishment" is a burden on the "free exercise"
of religion. Receipt of funds from the State benefits the established
church directly; laying an extra tax on nonmembers benefits the
established church indirectly. Certainly the present Sunday laws place

Orthodox Jews and Sabbatarians under extra burdens because of their religious opinions or beliefs. Requiring them to abstain from their trade or business on Sunday reduces their workweek to five days, unless they violate their religious scruples. This places them at a competitive disadvantage and penalizes them for adhering to their religious beliefs.

The sanction imposed by the state for "observing a day other than Sunday as holy time" is certainly more serious economically than the "imposition of a license tax for preaching," which we struck down in *Murdock v. Pennsylvania*, 319 U.S. 105, and in *Follett v. McCormick*, 321 U.S. 573. The special protection which Sunday laws give the dominant religious groups and the penalty they place on minorities whose holy day is Saturday constitute, in my view, state interference with the "free exercise" of religion.

I dissent from applying criminal sanctions against any of these complainants since to do so implicates the States in religious matters contrary to the constitutional mandate. Reverend Allan C. Parker, Jr., Pastor of the South Park Presbyterian Church, Seattle, Washington, has stated my views:

> "We forget that, though Sunday-worshiping Christians are in the majority in this country among religious people, we do not have the right to force our practice upon the minority. Only a church which deems itself without error and intolerant of error can justify its intolerance of the minority.
>
> "A Jewish friend of mine runs a small business establishment. Because my friend is a Jew his business is closed each Saturday. He respects my right to worship on Sunday and I respect his right to worship on Saturday. But there is a difference. As a Jew he closes his store voluntarily so that he will be able to worship his God in his fashion. Fine! But, as a Jew living under Christian inspired Sunday closing laws, he is required to close his store on Sunday so that I will be able to worship my God in my fashion.
>
> "Around the corner from my church there is a small Seventh Day Baptist church. I disagree with the Seventh Day Baptists on many points of doctrine. Among the tenets of their faith with which I disagree is the 'seventh-day worship.' But they are good neighbors and fellow Christians, and while we disagree we respect one another. The good people of my congregation

set aside their jobs on the first of the week and gather in God's house for worship. Of course, it is easy for them to set aside their jobs since Sunday-closing laws - inspired by the Church - keep them from their work. At the Seventh Day Baptist church the people set aside their jobs on Saturday to worship God. This takes real sacrifice because Saturday is a good day for business. But that is not all - they are required by law to set aside their jobs on Sunday while more orthodox Christians worship.

"I do not believe that because I have set aside Sunday as a holy day I have the right to force all men to set aside that day also. Why should my faith be favored by the state over any other man's faith?"

With all deference, none of the opinions filed today in support of the Sunday laws has answered that question.

Is The Constitution Right?

*T*HE FIRST AMENDMENT TO THE US CONSTITUTION guarantees liberty of conscience in matters of religion, speech, the press; and the right to peaceably assemble. The Fourteenth Amendment gives the assurance that "no state shall make or enforce any law which abridges the privileges or immunities of citizens of the U.S."

The constitutions of all free western democracies are similar to the constitution of the USA, though, not in all cases as explicit, nor as complete. Religious liberty is guaranteed as one of the inalienable rights of the individual.

In order to understand the basic premises and logic behind the constitution the reader must remember that those early Europeans, mainly English, who, during the seventeenth century, sought refuge in the New World, wanted freedom from the prevailing ecclesiastical and political oppressions of Europe.

Those early settlers were deeply religious, and their struggle for civil and religious liberties developed slowly and painfully at first. Eventually the very principles of the gospel which they believed were used as the foundation of the US Bill of Rights and Amendment XIV.

It is very important, therefore, for one to understand the absolute Biblical basis of liberty of conscience if one is to correctly interpret the first and fourteenth amendments to the US Constitution.

Clear Distinction Between Civil Power and Religious Power

Two statements of Jesus clearly show the distinction between the state and the church. Firstly, John 18:36:

> *"My kingdom is not of this world: if my kingdom were of this world, then would my servants fight, that I should not be delivered to the Jews: but now is my kingdom not from hence."*

In this text Jesus states clearly and categorically that His kingdom is **not** of this world, nor does His kingdom employ the methods of force used by the kingdoms of this world.

Secondly, Matthew 22:21:

> *"Render therefore unto Caesar the things which are Caesar's; and unto God the things that are God's."*

In these words Christ has established a clear distinction between Caesar and God, between that which is Caesar's and that which is God's; that is, between what we owe to the civil authority and what we owe to God. That which is Caesar's is to be rendered to Caesar, and that which is God's is to be rendered to God alone. To say that we are to render to Caesar that which is God's or that we are to render to God, through Caesar, that which is God's, is to pervert the words of Christ and make them meaningless. Such an interpretation would be but to entangle him in his talk, the very thing that the Pharisees sought to do.

Since the word Caesar refers to civil government, it is apparent at once that the duties which we owe to Caesar are civil duties, while the duties we owe to God are wholly moral or religious duties.

Religion may be defined as the recognition of God as an object of worship, love and obedience. It is man's personal relation of faith and obedience to God. It is the duty we owe to God (A.T. Jones).

It is evident, therefore, that religion and religious duties pertain solely to God; and as that which is God's is to be rendered to God and not to Caesar, it follows inevitably that, according to the words of Christ, civil government can never, of right, have anything to do with religion,— with a man's personal relation of faith and obedience to God.

The Distinction Between Civil And Moral Law

Morality may be defined as conformity to the moral law of God. For religionists who believe in the Bible, the moral law of God is known to be expressed in the Ten Commandments (Exodus 20).

The Ten Commandments are divided into the first four, which describe man's "vertical" duties to, and relationships with God; and the last six, which describe man's "horizontal" duties to his fellow men.

Since the first four commandments describe man's responsibilities and duties to God, they are not under the jurisdiction of government. For example, the first commandment states, "Thou shalt have no other gods before me". This is a vertical command defining a specific relationship between man and God according to the man's belief; no government may enforce it or enjoin it. Similarly, the fourth commandment commands to remember to keep holy the Sabbath day; this is also a vertical command involving man's duty to God; and therefore no government may enforce or enjoin any day as a sabbath day or a day of worship.

The last six commandments describe man's duties to his fellowmen and the principles in them are found in the civil codes of Christian and non-Christian nations alike. But it must be made very clear that when these principles are enforced by the government, they are enforced as civil laws, not moral laws or spiritual laws. Civil means pertaining to a city or state, or to a citizen in his relations to his fellow-citizens, or to the state.

God judges morality, the state judges civility. The government must punish crime, but it must not restrain the conscience in matters of man's personal relationship with God. Therefore, the first four commandments must never be interfered with by the government.

The Distinction Between Thoughts And Actions

Morality involves thoughts, words and actions. A man's thoughts can violate the moral law of God. God judges pride and wicked thoughts as immoral. But thoughts are beyond the authority of the government. The state cannot prosecute anyone for merely wicked thoughts.

God judges hatred as murder, but the state cannot touch a man for possessing such thoughts.

All this emphasizes that God alone is the judge of morality while the state is limited in its sphere to deal with civility.

Consider another example. Jesus declared that anyone who looks upon a woman with lust (illicit desire) has already committed adultery in his heart (Matt. 5:28). God judges the lustful desire as immoral but such a judgment is beyond the state.

Nineteenth Century U.S. Constitutional expert A.T. Jones, expressed it this way in his book *Civil Government and Religion:*

"Other illustrations might be given, but these are sufficient to show that obedience to the moral law is morality; that it pertains to the thoughts and the intents of the heart, and therefore, in the very nature of the case, lies beyond the reach or control of the civil power. To hate, is murder; to covet, is idolatry; to think impurely of a woman, is adultery;—these are all equally immoral, and violations of the moral law, but no civil government seeks to punish for them. A man may hate his neighbor all his life; he may covet everything on earth; he may think impurely of every woman that he sees, —he may keep it up all his days; but so long as these things are confined to his thought, the civil power cannot touch him. It would be difficult to conceive of a more immoral person than such a man would be; yet the State cannot punish him. It does not attempt to punish him. This demonstrates again that with morality or immorality the State can have nothing to do.

"But let us carry this further. Only let that man's hatred lead him, either by word or sign, to attempt an injury to his neighbor, and the State will punish him; only let his covetousness lead him to lay hands on what is not his own, in an attempt to steal, and the State will punish him; only let his impure thought lead him to attempt violence to any woman, and the State will punish him. Yet bear in mind that even then the State does not punish him for his immorality, but for his incivility. The immorality lies in the heart, and can be measured by God only. The State punishes no man because he is immoral. If it did, it would have to punish as a murderer the man who hates another, because according to the true standard of morality, hatred is murder. Therefore it is clear that in fact the State punishes no man because he is immoral, but because he is uncivil. It cannot punish immorality; it must punish incivility.

"This distinction is shown in the very term by which is designated State or national government; it is called *civil* government. No person ever thinks of calling it moral government. The government of God is the only moral government. God is the **only** moral governor. The law of God is the only moral law. To God alone pertains the punishment of immorality, which is the transgression of the moral law. Governments of men are civil governments, not moral. Governors of men are civil governors, not moral. The laws of States and nations are civil laws, not moral. To the authorities of civil government pertains the punishment of incivility, that is, the transgression of civil law. It is not theirs to punish immorality. That pertains solely to the Author of the moral law and of the moral sense, who is the sole judge of man's moral relation. All this must be manifest to every one who will think fairly upon the subject, and it is confirmed by the definition of the word *civil*, which is as follows:-

"*Civil:* Pertaining to a city or State, or to a citizen in his relations to his fellow-citizens, or to the State."

"By all these things it is made clear that we owe to Caesar (civil government) only that which is civil, and that we owe to God that which is moral or religious. Other definitions show the same thing. For instance, sin as defined by Webster, is 'any violation of God's will;' and as defined by the Scriptures, is 'the transgression of the law.' That the law here referred to is the moral law—the ten commandments—is shown by Rom. 7:7:

'I had not known sin, but by the law; for I had not known lust, except the law had said, Thou shalt not covet.'

"Thus the Scriptures show that sin is a transgression of the law which says, 'Thou shalt not covet,' and that is the moral law.

"But crime is an offense against the laws of the State. The definition is as follows:

"Crime is strictly a violation of law either human or divine; but in present usage the term is commonly applied to actions contrary to the laws of the State."

"Thus civil statutes define crime, and deal with crime, but not with sin; while the divine statutes define sin, and deal with sin, but not with crime." A.T. Jones, "Civil Government and Religion," pp. 17-19.

The Promotion Of Morality By The Church,
The Promotion Of Civility By The State

Matters of a spiritual, moral or religious nature are matters which belong to God, which are to be rendered only to God and which are to be promoted by God.

Matters of a civil nature are matters which belong to the civil government and which must be rendered only to civil government and be promoted by the civil government.

The Bible admonishes Christians to be both moral and civil. For example, the matter of taxation is a civil matter to be promoted by the state and to be rendered (paid) to the state. God's word commands the Christian to be civil and to pay his or her taxes.

God has committed to the church the work of promoting spirituality and morality; and God has committed to the state the work of promoting civility. When these two spheres of operation are kept distinct, civil and religious liberties flourish and both the church and the state work better than if the state introduces itself into spiritual matters or the church intrudes her doctrines into civil law.

We return to A.T. Jones again in his book *Civil Government and Religion*, published in 1889.

> "As God is the only moral governor, as his is the only moral government, as his law is the only moral law, and as it pertains to him alone to punish immorality, so likewise *the promotion of morality* pertains to him alone. Morality is conformity to the law of God; it is obedience to God. But obedience to God must spring from the heart in sincerity and truth. This it must do, or it is not obedience; for, as we have proved by the word of God, the law of God takes cognizance of the thoughts and intents of the heart. But "all have sinned, and come short of the glory of God." By transgression, all men have made themselves immoral. "Therefore by the deeds of the law [by obedience] there shall no flesh be justified [accounted righteous, or made moral] in his sight." Rom. 3:20. As all men have, by transgression of the law of God, made themselves immoral, therefore no man can, by obedience to the law, become moral; because it is that very law which declares him to be immoral. The demands, therefore, of the moral law, must be satisfied, before he can ever be accepted as moral by either the law or its Author. But the demands of

the moral law can never be satisfied by an immoral person, and this is just what every person has made himself by transgression. Therefore it is certain that men can never become moral by the moral law.

"From this it is equally certain that if ever men shall be made moral, it must be by the Author and Source of all morality. And this is just the provision which God has made. For, "now the righteousness [the morality] of God without the law is manifested, being witnessed by the law and the prophets; even the righteousness [the morality] of God which is *by faith of Jesus Christ* unto all and upon all them that believe; for there is no difference; for all have sinned [made themselves immoral], and come short of the glory of God." Rom. 3:21-23. It is by the morality of Christ alone that men can be made moral. And this morality of Christ is the morality of God, which is imputed to us for Christ's sake; and we receive it by faith in Him who is both the author and finisher of faith. Then by the Spirit of God the moral law is written anew in the heart and in the mind, sanctifying the soul unto obedience - unto morality. Thus, and thus alone, can men ever attain to morality; and that morality is the morality of God which is by faith of Jesus Christ; *and there is no other in this world.* Therefore, as morality springs from God, and is planted in the heart by the Spirit of God, through faith in the Son of God, it is demonstrated by proofs of Holy Writ itself, that *to God alone pertains the promotion of morality.*

"God, then, being the sole promoter of morality, through what instrumentality does He work to promote morality in the world? What body has he made the conservator of morality in the world: the church, or the civil power; which? The church, and the church alone. It is 'the church of the living God.' It is 'the pillar and ground of the truth.' It was to the church that he said, 'Go ye into all the world, and preach the gospel to every creature;' 'And, lo, I am with you alway, even unto the end of the world.' It is by the church, through the preaching of Jesus Christ, that the gospel is "made known to all nations for the obedience of faith." There is no obedience but the obedience of faith; there is no morality but the morality of faith. Therefore it is proved that to the church, and *not* to the State, is committed the conservation of morality in the world. This at once settles the question as to whether the State shall teach morality, or religion. The State *cannot* teach morality or religion. It has not the credentials for it. The Spirit of God and the gospel of Christ are both essential to the teaching of morality, and neither of these is committed to the State, but both to the church.

"But though this work be committed to the church, even then there is not committed to the church the prerogative either to reward morality or to punish immorality. She beseeches, she entreats, she persuades men to be reconciled to God; she trains them in the principles and the practice of morality. It is hers by moral suasion or spiritual censures to preserve the purity and *discipline* of her membership. But hers it is not either to reward morality or to punish immorality. This pertains to God alone, because whether it be morality or immorality, it springs from the secret counsels of the heart; and as God alone knows the heart, he alone can measure either the merit or the guilt involved in any question of morals.

"By this it is demonstrated that to no man, to no assembly or organization of men, does there belong any right whatever to punish immorality. Whoever attempts it, usurps the prerogative of God. The Inquisition is the inevitable logic of any claim of any assembly of men to punish immorality, because to punish immorality, it is necessary in some way to get at the thoughts and intents of the heart. The papacy, asserting the right to compel men to be moral, and to punish them for immorality, had the cruel courage to carry the evil principle to its logical consequence. In carrying out the principle, it was found to be essential to get at the secrets of men's hearts; and it was found that the diligent application of torture would wring from men, in many cases, a full confession of the most secret counsels of their hearts. Hence the Inquisition was established as the means best adapted to secure the desired end. So long as men grant the proposition that it is within the province of civil government to enforce morality, it is to very little purpose that they condemn the Inquisition; for that tribunal is only the logical result of the proposition.

"By all these evidences is established the plain, common-sense principle that to civil government pertains only that which the term itself implies, - that which is civil. The purpose of civil government is civil, and not moral. Its function is to preserve order in society, and to cause all its subjects to rest in assured safety, by guarding them against all incivility. Morality belongs to God; civility, to the State. Morality must be rendered to God; civility, to the State. "Render therefore unto Caesar the things which are Caesar's; and unto God the things that are God's."

"But it may be asked, Does not the civil power enforce the observance of the commandments of God, which say, Thou shalt not steal, thou shalt not kill, thou shalt not commit adultery, and thou shalt not bear false witness? Does not the civil power punish the violation of these commandments of God? *Answer*: The civil power does not enforce these, nor does it punish the violation of them, *as commandments of God*. The State does forbid murder and theft and perjury, and some States forbid adultery, but not as commandments of God. From time immemorial, governments that knew nothing about God, have forbidden these things.

"If the civil power attempted to enforce these as the commandments of God, it would have to punish as a murderer the man who hates another; it would have to punish as a perjurer the man who raises a false report; it would have to punish as an adulterer the person who thinks impurely; it would have to punish as a thief the man who wishes to cheat his neighbor; because all these things are violations of the commandments of God. Therefore if the State is to enforce these things as the commandments of God, it will have to punish the thoughts and intents of the heart; but this is not within the province of any earthly power, and it is clear that any earthly power that should attempt it, would thereby simply put itself in the place of God, and usurp his prerogative.

"More than this, such an effort would be an attempt to punish sin, because transgression of the law of God is sin; but sins will be forgiven upon repentance, and God does not punish the sinner for the violation of his law, when his sins are forgiven.

Now if the civil power undertakes to enforce the observance of the law of God, it cannot justly enforce that law upon the transgressor whom God has forgiven. For instance, suppose a man steals twenty dollars from his neighbor, and is arrested, prosecuted, and found guilty. But suppose that between the time that he is found guilty and the time when sentence is to be passed, the man repents, and is forgiven by the Lord. Now he is counted by the Lord as though he never had violated the law of God. The commandment of God does not stand against him for that transgression. And as it is the law of God that the civil law started out to enforce, the civil power also must forgive him, count him innocent, and let him go free. More than this, the statute of God says, "If thy brother trespass against thee, rebuke him; and if he repent, forgive him. And if he trespass against thee seven times in a day, and seven times in a day turn again to thee, saying, I repent thou shalt forgive him." If civil government is to enforce the law of God, when a man steals, or commits perjury or any form of violence, and is arrested, if he says, "I repent," he must be forgiven if he does it again, is again arrested, and again says, I repent," he must be forgiven; and if he commits it seven times in a day, and seven times in a day says, "I repent," he must be forgiven. It will be seen at once that any such system would be utterly destructive of civil government; and this only demonstrates conclusively that no civil government can ever of right have anything to do with the enforcement of the commandments of God as such, or with making the Bible its code of laws.

"God's government can be sustained by the forgiveness of the sinner to the uttermost, because by the sacrifice of Christ be has made provision 'to save them to the uttermost that come unto God by him; seeing he ever liveth to make intercession for them;' but in civil government, if a man steals, or commits any other crime, and is apprehended and found guilty, it has nothing to do with the case if the Lord does forgive him; he must be punished.

"The following remarks of Prof. W. T. Harris, late superintendent of public schools in the city of St. Louis, are worthy of careful consideration in this connection:-

"A crime, or breach of justice, is a deed of the individual, which the State, by its judicial acts, returns on the individual. The State furnishes a measure for crime, and punishes criminals according to their deserts. The judicial mind is a measuring mind, a retributive mind, because trained in the forms of justice which sees to it that every man's deed shall be returned to him, to bless him or to curse him with pain. Now, a sin is a breach of the law of holiness, a lapse out of the likeness to the divine form, and as such it utterly refuses to be measured. It is infinite death to lapse out of the form of the divine. A sin cannot be atoned for by any finite punishment, but only (as revelation teaches) by a divine act of sacrifice....It would destroy the State to attempt to treat crimes as sins, and to forgive them in case of repentance. It would impose on the judiciary the business of going behind the overt act to the disposition or frame of mind within the depth of personality. But so long as the deed is not uttered in the act, it does not belong to society, but only to the individual and to God. No human institution can go behind the overt act, and attempt to deal absolutely with the substance of man's spiritual freedom...Sin and crime must not be confounded, nor must the same deed be counted as crime and sin by the same authority. Look at it as crime, and it is capable of measured retribution. The law does not pursue the murderer beyond the gallows. He has expiated his crime with his life. But the slightest sin, even if it is no crime at all, as for example the anger of a man against his brother, an anger which does not utter itself in the form of violent deeds, but is pent up in the heart,—such noncriminal sin will banish the soul forever from heaven, unless it is made naught by sincere repentance."

"The points already presented in this chapter are perhaps sufficient in this place to illustrate the principle announced in the word of Christ; and although that principle is plain, and is readily accepted by the sober, common-sense thought of every man, yet through the selfish ambition of men the world has been long in learning and accepting the truth of the lesson. The

United States is the first and only government in history that is based on the principle established by Christ. In Article VI. of the national Constitution, this nation says that 'no religious test shall ever be required as a qualification to any office or public trust under the United States.' By an amendment making more certain the adoption of the principle, it declares in the first amendment to the Constitution, 'Congress shall make no law respecting an establishment of religion, or prohibiting the free exercise there-of.' This first amendment was adopted in 1789, by the first Congress that ever met under the Constitution. In 1796 a treaty was made with Tripoli, in which it was declared (Article II) that 'the Government of the United States of America is not in any sense founded on the Christian religion.' This treaty was framed by an ex-Congregationalist clergyman, and was signed by President Washington. It was not out of disrespect to religion or Christianity that these clauses were placed in the Constitution, and that this one was inserted in that treaty. On the contrary, it was entirely on account of their respect for religion, and the Christian religion in particular, as being beyond the province of civil government, pertaining solely to the conscience, and resting entirely between the individual and God. It was because of this that this nation was Constitutionally established according to the principle of Christ, demanding of men only that they render to Caesar that which is Caesar's, and leaving them entirely free to render to God that which is God's, if they choose, as they choose, and when they choose; or, as expressed by Washington himself, in reply to an address upon the subject of religious legislation:

"Every man who conducts himself as a good citizen, is accountable alone to God for his religious faith, and should be protected in worshiping God according to the dictates of his own conscience."

"We cannot more fitly close this chapter than with the following tribute of George Bancroft to this principle, as embodied in the words of Christ, and in the American Constitution:

"In the earliest States known to history, government and religion were one and indivisible. Each State had its special deity, and often these protectors, one after another, might be overthrown in battle, never to rise again. The Peloponnesian War grew out of a strife about an oracle. Rome, as it sometimes adopted into citizenship those whom it vanquished, introduced in like manner, and with good logic for that day, the worship of their gods. No one thought of vindicating religion for the conscience of the individual, till a voice in Judea, breaking day for the greatest epoch in the life of humanity, by establishing a pure, spiritual, and universal religion for all mankind, enjoined to render to Caesar only that which is Caesar's. The rule was upheld during the infancy of the gospel for all men. No sooner was this religion adopted by the chief of the Roman empire, than it was shorn of its character of universality, and enthralled by an unholy connection with the unholy State; and so it continued till the new nation, - the least defiled with the barren scoffings of the eighteenth century, the most general believer in Christianity of any people of that age, the chief heir of the Reformation in its purest forms, when it came to establish a government for the United States, refused to treat faith as a matter to be regulated by a corporate body, or having a headship in a monarch or a State.

"Vindicating the right of individuality even in religion, and in religion above all, the new nation dared to set the example of accepting in its relations to God the principle first divinely ordained of God in Judea. It left the management of temporal things to the temporal power; but the American Constitution, in harmony with the people of the several States, withheld from the Federal Government the power to invade the home of reason, the citadel of conscience, the sanctuary of the soul; and not from indifference, but that the infinite Spirit of eternal truth might move in its freedom and purity and power." - *History of the Formation of the Constitution*, last chapter.

"Thus the Constitution of the United States as it is, stands as the sole monument of all history representing the principle which Christ established for earthly government. And under it, in liberty, civil and religious, in enlightenment, and in progress, this nation has deservedly stood as the beacon-light of the world, for a hundred years." A.T. Jones, Civil Government and Religion, pp. 19-27.

It ought to be very clear to the reader that the principle of liberty of conscience in matters of faith and worship is an absolute and fundamental right of the individual, which can never be rightly violated.

The Limits of Civil Authority

*I*N OUR LAST CHAPTER WE SAW that the last six of the Ten Commandments deal with man's duty to his fellowman. At least three (and in some societies more) of these six commandments form the basis of the fundamental civil laws protecting the life, property and reputation of the individual.

In order for people to live in any society with safety, security and the protection of their individual rights of life, property and conscience, the civil government or the state must enforce certain fundamental civil laws, which regulate human behavior at the level of human relationships and interactions.

Since society cannot function effectively amid widespread lawlessness, government needs the voluntary obedience of all its citizens to the civil laws and statutes. Those who refuse to obey the civil law are punished by the law enforcement agencies, which include the judicial system and the police force. Here again the Constitution guarantees to all citizens the right to an open and fair trial, including legal representation.

As we clearly saw in our last chapter, the civil law must and should regulate civil matters; but the civil law should not interfere with any matter concerning a man's duty to God in the areas of faith and worship or concerning the first four of the Ten Commandments.

The duties that men owe to God are not to be placed under the control of the state because Christ has commanded to render unto God—not to Caesar, nor by Caesar—that which is God's.

As far as Christians are concerned they are commanded by scripture to obey all just civil laws. Christians, like all others, should be submissive and obedient to government. The Christian should be an exemplary citizen giving due respect and obedience to civil authorities and civil laws. Scripture commands every one to lead a law-abiding, orderly life-style, paying one's taxes, obeying all civil regulations and civil laws. The key Biblical references are found in Romans 13:1-10:

> "Let every soul be subject unto the higher powers. For there is no power but of God: the powers that be are ordained of God. Whosoever therefore resisteth the power, resisteth the ordinance of God: and they that resist shall receive to themselves damnation. For rulers are not a terror to good works, but to the evil. Wilt thou then not be afraid of the power? Do that which is good, and thou shalt have praise of the same: For he is the minister of God to thee for good. But if thou do that which is evil, be afraid; for he beareth not the sword in vain: for he is the minister of God, a revenger to execute wrath upon him that doeth evil. Wherefore ye must needs be subject, not only for wrath, but also for conscience sake. For this cause pay ye tribute also: for they are God's ministers, attending continually upon this very thing. Render therefore to all their dues: tribute to whom tribute is due; custom to whom custom; fear to whom fear; honour to whom honour. Owe no man any thing, but to love one another: for he that loveth another hath fulfilled the law. For this, Thou shalt not commit adultery, Thou shalt not kill, Thou shalt not steal, Thou shalt not bear false witness, Thou shalt not covet; and if there be any other commandment, it is briefly comprehended in this saying, namely, Thou shalt love thy neighbor as thyself. Love worketh no ill to his neighbor: therefore love is the fulfilling of the law."

From 1 Peter 2:13-17.

> "Submit yourselves to every ordinance of man for the Lord's sake: whether it be to the king, as supreme; Or unto governors, as unto them that are sent by him for the punishment of evildoers, and for the praise of them that do well. For so is the will of God, that with well doing ye may put to silence the ignorance of foolish men: As free, and not using your liberty for a cloke of maliciousness, but as the servants of God. Honour all men. Love the brotherhood. Fear God. Honour the king."

Limited Authority

On the other hand, whenever the civil government oversteps its boundaries by making and enforcing laws which interfere with the religious liberty of conscience of the individual, the Christian has the right to disobey such unrighteous and unconstitutional laws and to seek to have them repealed.

The very writers, Paul and Peter, who exhort us to obey the civil government, both were imprisoned and executed for their faith because they refused to obey the Roman civil authorities whose laws forbade the belief in, or preaching of, the Christian message. Earlier, when Jewish authorities arrested Peter and commanded him not to preach Christ, he and the other apostles declared: *"We ought to obey God rather than men"* (Acts 5:29).

Some people quote Romans 13:1 to support a theory that civil government has the right to act or legislate in things pertaining to God. The text says, *"The powers that be are ordained of God."*

Their argument is that since the government is ordained of God it has authority in civil as well as religious matters. But Romans 13 simply endorses the words of Jesus: Render therefore unto Caesar the things which are Caesar's and unto God the things that are God's.

In Romans 13 Paul makes reference only to the last six commandments and to any other command involving a man and his fellowman. A.T. Jones, (19th Century History professor), explains:

> "It is easy to see that this scripture is but an exposition of the words of Christ, 'Render to Caesar the things that are Caesar's.' In the Saviour's command to render unto Caesar the things that are Caesar's, there is plainly a recognition of the rightfulness of civil government, and that civil government has claims upon us which we are in duty bound to recognize, and that there are things which duty requires us to render to the civil government. This scripture in Romans 13 simply states the same thing in other words: 'Let every soul be subject unto the higher powers. For there is no power but of God: the powers that be are ordained of God.'

> "Again, the Saviour's words were called out by a question concerning tribute. They said to him, 'Is it lawful to give tribute unto Caesar, or not?' Rom. 13:6 refers to the same thing, saying, 'For, for this cause pay ye tribute also; for they are God's

ministers, attending continually upon this very thing.' In answer to the question of the Pharisees about the tribute, Christ said, 'Render therefore unto Caesar the things which are Caesar's.' Rom. 13:7, taking up the same thought, says, 'Render therefore to all their dues: tribute to whom tribute is due; custom to whom custom; fear to whom fear; honor to whom honor.' These references make positive that which we have stated,— that this portion of Scripture (Rom. 13:1-9) is a divine commentary upon the words of Christ in Matt. 22:17-21.

"The passage in Romans refers first to civil government, the higher powers, not the highest power, but the powers that be. Next it speaks of rulers, as bearing the sword and attending upon matters of tribute. Then it commands to render tribute to whom tribute is due, and says, 'Owe no man any thing; but to love one another; for he that loveth another hath fulfilled the law.' Then he refers to the sixth, seventh, eighth, ninth, and tenth commandments, and says, 'If there be any other commandment, it is briefly comprehended in this saying, namely, Thou shalt love thy neighbor as thyself.'

"There are other commandments of this same law to which Paul refers. Why, then, did he say, 'If there be any other commandment, it is briefly comprehended in this saying, Thou shalt love thy neighbor as thyself'? There are the four commandments of the first table of this same law,—the commandments which say, 'Thou shalt have no other gods before me; Thou shalt not make any graven image, or any likeness of any thing; Thou shalt not take the name of the Lord thy God in vain; Remember the Sabbath day to keep it holy.' Then there is the other commandment in which is briefly comprehended all these,—'Thou shalt love the Lord thy God with all thy heart, and with all thy soul, and with all thy mind, and with all thy strength.'

"Paul knew full well of these commandments. Why, then, did he say, 'If there be any other commandment, it is briefly comprehended in this saying, Thou shalt love thy neighbor as thyself'? Answer.—Because he was writing concerning the words of the Saviour which relate to our duties to civil government.

"Our duties under civil government pertain solely to the government and to our fellow-men, because the powers of civil government pertain solely to men in their relations one to another, and to the government. But the Saviour's words in the same connection entirely separated that which pertains to God from that which pertains to civil government. The things which pertain to God are not to be rendered to civil government—to the powers that be; therefore Paul, although knowing full well that there were other commandments, said, 'If there be any other commandment, it is briefly comprehended in this saying, Thou shalt love thy neighbor as thyself;' that is, if there be any other commandment which comes into the relation between man and civil government, it is comprehended in this saying, that he shall love his neighbor as himself; thus showing conclusively that the powers that be, though ordained of God, are so ordained simply in things pertaining to the relation of man with his fellow-men, and in those things alone.

"Further, as in this divine record of the duties that men owe to the powers that be, there is no reference whatever to the first table of the law, it therefore follows that the powers that be, although ordained of God, have nothing whatever to do with the relations which men bear toward God.

"As the ten commandments contain the whole duty of man, and as in the scriptural enumeration of the duties that men owe to the powers that be, there is no mention of any of the things contained in the first table of the law, it follows that none of the duties enjoined in the first table of the law of God, do men owe to the powers that be; that is to say, again, that the powers that be, although ordained of God, are not ordained of God in anything pertaining to a single duty enjoined in any one of the first four of the ten commandments. These are duties that men owe to God, and with these the powers that be can of right have nothing to do, because Christ has commanded to render unto God—not to Caesar, nor by Caesar—that which is God's."
A.T. Jones, Civil Government and Religion, pp. 19-32.

Biblical Examples Of The Limits Of Civil Authority

The powers that be are ordained of God. The civil government is ordained by God to regulate civility by enacting and enforcing civil laws. The powers that be, i.e. the civil governments, are not ordained of God in anything pertaining to a man's relationship with God or the first four commandments.

Take for example the Babylonian Empire of Nebuchadnezzar. This empire was "ordained" of God. God even called Nebuchadnezzar His servant and declared that all nations were to serve Nebuchadnezzar, his son and his son's son until Babylon itself be overthrown. (See Jeremiah 27:6-8).

Now, having established that this power was ordained of God, let us see whether it was ordained of God to enforce laws interfering with the relationship between an individual and God in matters of faith or worship or the first four of the Ten Commandments. We quote A.T. Jones again:

> "Now let us see whether this power was ordained of God in things pertaining to God. In the third chapter of Daniel we have the record that Nebuchadnezzar made a great image of gold, set it up in the plain of Dura, and gathered together the princes, the governors, the captains, the judges, the treasurers, the counselors, the sheriffs, and all the rulers of the provinces, to the dedication of the image; and they stood before the image that had been set up. Then a herald from the king cried aloud:
>
> > 'To you it is commanded, O people, nations, and languages, that at what time ye hear the sound of the cornet, flute, harp, sackbut, psaltery, dulcimer, and all kinds of music, ye fall down and worship the golden image that Nebuchadnezzar the king hath set up; and whoso falleth not down and worshipeth shall the same hour be cast into the midst of a burning fiery furnace.'
>
> "In obedience to this command, all the people bowed down and worshiped before the image, except three Jews, Shadrach, Meshach, and Abednego. This disobedience was reported to Nebuchadnezzar, who commanded them to be brought before him, when he asked them if they had disobeyed his order intentionally. He himself then repeated his command to them.

"These men knew that they had been made subject to the king of Babylon by the Lord himself. It had not only been prophesied by Isaiah (chap. 39), but by Jeremiah. At the final siege of Jerusalem by Nebuchadnezzar, the Lord through Jeremiah told the people to submit to the king of Babylon, and that whosoever would do it, it should be well with them; whosoever would not do it, it should be ill with them. Yet these men, knowing all this, made answer to Nebuchadnezzar thus:

> 'O Nebuchadnezzar, we are not careful to answer thee in this matter. If it be so, our God whom we serve is able to deliver us from the burning fiery furnace, and he will deliver us out of thine hand, O king. But if not, be it known unto thee, O king, that we will not serve thy gods, nor worship the golden image which thou hast set up."

"Then these men were cast into the fiery furnace, heated seven times hotter than it was wont to be heated; but suddenly Nebuchadnezzar rose up in haste and astonishment, and said to his counselors, 'Did we not cast three men bound into the midst of the fire?' They answered, 'True, O king.' But he exclaimed, 'Lo, I see four men loose, walking in the midst of the fire, and they have no hurt; and the form of the fourth is like the Son of God.' The men were called forth:

'Then Nebuchadnezzar spake and said, Blessed be the God of Shadrach, Meshach, and Abed-nego, who hath sent his angel and delivered his servants that trusted in him, and have changed the king's word, and yielded their bodies, that they might not serve nor worship any god, except their own God.'

"Here we have demonstrated the following facts : First, God gave power to the kingdom of Babylon; second, he suffered his people to be subjected to that power; third, he defended his people by a wonderful miracle from a certain exercise of that power. Does God contradict or oppose himself?—Far from it. What, then, does this show?—It shows conclusively that this was an undue exercise of the power which God had given. By this it is demonstrated that the power of the kingdom of Babylon, although ordained of God, was not ordained unto any such purpose as that for which it was exercised; and that though ordained of God, it was not ordained to be authority in things pertaining to God, or in things pertaining to men's consciences. And it was written for the instruction of future ages, and for our admonition upon whom the ends of the world are come.

"Another instance: We read above that the power of Babylon was given to Nebuchadnezzar, and his son, and his son's son, and that all nations should serve Babylon until that time, and that then nations and kings should serve themselves of him. Other prophecies show that Babylon was then to be destroyed. Jer. 51: 28 says that the kings of the Medes, and all his land, with the captains and rulers, should be prepared against Babylon to destroy it. Isa. 21:2 shows that Persia (Elam) should accompany Media in the destruction of Babylon. Isa. 45:1-4 names Cyrus as the leader of the forces, more than a hundred years before he was born, and one hundred and seventy-four years before the time. And of Cyrus, the prophet said from the Lord, 'I have raised him up in righteousness, and I will direct all his ways; he shall build my city, and he shall let go my captives, not for price, nor reward, saith the Lord of hosts.' Isa. 45:13. But in the conquest of Babylon, Cyrus was only the leader of the forces. The kingdom and rule were given to Darius the Mede; for, said Daniel to Belshazzar, on the night when Babylon fell, 'Thy kingdom is divided, and given to the Medes and Persians.' Then the record proceeds: 'In that night was Belshazzar the king of the Chaldeans slain. And Darius the Median took the kingdom.' Of him we read in Dan. 11:1, the words of the angel Gabriel to the prophet, 'I, in the first year of Darius the Mede, even I, stood to confirm and to strengthen him.'

"There can be no shadow of doubt, therefore, that the power of Media and Persia was ordained of God. Darius made Daniel prime minister of the empire. But a number of the presidents and princes, envious of the position given to Daniel, attempted to undermine him.

"After earnest efforts to find occasion against him in matters pertaining to the kingdom, they were forced to confess that there was neither error nor fault anywhere in his conduct. Then said these men, 'We shall not find any occasion against this Daniel, except we find it against him concerning the law of his God.' They therefore assembled together to the king, and told him that all the presidents of the kingdom, and the governors, and the princes, and the captains, had consulted together to establish a royal statute, and to make a decree that whoever should ask a petition of any god or man, except the king, for thirty days, should be cast into the den of lions. Darius, not suspecting their object, signed the decree. Daniel knew that the decree had been made, and signed by the king. It was hardly possible for him not to know it, being prime minister. Yet notwithstanding his knowledge of the affair, he went into his chamber, and his windows being opened toward Jerusalem, he kneeled upon his knees three times a day, and prayed and gave thanks before God, as he did aforetime. He did not even close the windows. He paid no attention to the decree that had been made, although it forbade his doing as he did, under the penalty of being thrown to the lions. He well understood that although the power of Media and Persia was ordained of God, it was not ordained to interfere in matters of duty which he owed only to God.

"As was to be expected, the men who had secured the passage of the decree, found him praying and making supplications before his God. They went at once to the king and asked him if he had not signed a decree that every man who should ask a petition of any god or man within thirty days, except of the king, should be cast into the den of lions. The king replied that this was true, and that, according to the law of the Medes and Persians, it could not be altered. Then they told him that Daniel did not regard the king, nor the decree that he had signed, but made his petition three times a day. The king realized in a moment that he had been entrapped; but there was no remedy. Those who were pushing the matter, held before him the law, and said, 'Know, O king, that the law of the Medes and Persians is, That no decree or statute which the king establisheth may be changed.' Nothing could be done; the decree, being law, must be enforced. Daniel was cast to the lions. In the morning the king came to the den and called to Daniel, and Daniel replied, 'O king, live forever; my God hath sent his angel, and hath shut the lions' mouths, that they have not hurt me: forasmuch as before him innocency was found in me; and also before thee, O king, have I done no hurt.'

"Thus again God has shown that although the powers that be are ordained of God, they are not ordained to act in things that pertain to men's relation toward God. Christ's words are a positive declaration to that effect, and Rom. 13:1-9 is a further exposition of the principle." A.T. Jones, Civil Government and Religion, pp. 32-37.

In Society Certain Rights Are To Be Surrendered, But Not The Right To Believe

"When societies are formed, each individual surrenders certain rights, and as an equivalent for that surrender, has secured to him the enjoyment of certain others appertaining to his person and property, without the protection of which society cannot exist."

"I have the right to protect my person and property from all invasions. Every other person has the same right; but if this right is to be personally exercised in all cases by every one, then in the present condition of human nature, every man's hand will be against his neighbor. That is simple anarchy, and in such a condition of affairs society cannot exist. Now suppose a hundred of us are thrown together in a certain place where there is no established order; each one has all the rights of any other one. But if each one is individually to exercise these rights of self-protection, he has the assurance of only that degree of protection which he alone can furnish to himself, which we have seen is exceedingly slight. Therefore all come together, and each surrenders to the whole body that individual right; and in return for this surrender, he receives the power of all for his protection.

"He therefore receives the help of the other ninety-nine to protect himself from the invasion of his rights, and he is thus made many hundred times more secure in his rights of person and property than he is without this surrender.

"But what condition of things can ever be conceived of among men that would justify any man in surrendering his right to believe? What could he receive as an equivalent ? When he has surrendered his right to believe, he has virtually surrendered his right to think. When he surrenders his right to believe, he surrenders everything, and it is impossible for him ever to receive an equivalent; he has surrendered his very soul. Eternal life depends upon believing on the Lord Jesus Christ, and the man who surrenders his right to believe, surrenders eternal life. Says the Scripture, 'With the mind I myself serve the law of God.' A man who surrenders his right to believe, surrenders God. Consequently, no man, no association or organization of men, can ever rightly ask of any man a surrender of his right to believe. Every man has the right, so far as organizations of men are concerned, to believe as he pleases; and that right, so long as he is a Protestant, so long as he is a Christian, yes, so long as he is a man, he never can surrender, and he never will."

How Are 'The Powers That Be' Ordained Of God?

Some Christians do not correctly understand the term "ordained of God". They believe it means that God has directly or personally appointed the particular president or prime minister or royal sovereign. No! The term "ordained of God" refers to God's permission—His permissive will in allowing peoples to determine their own governments. Historian and Religious Liberty Defender, A.T. Jones, gave an important analysis of the meaning of "ordained of God" in 1889 at a critical time of debate on liberty of conscience in the USA:

> "Another important question to consider in this connection is, How are the powers that be, ordained of God? Are they directly and miraculously ordained, or are they providentially so? We have seen by the Scripture that the power of Nebuchadnezzar as king of Babylon, was ordained of God. Did God send a prophet or a priest to anoint him king? or did he send a heavenly messenger, as he did to Moses and Gideon ?—Neither. Nebuchadnezzar was king because he was the son of his father, who had been king. How did his father become king?—In 625 B. C., Babylonia was but a province of the empire of Assyria; Media was another. Both revolted, and at the same time. The king of Assyria gave Nabopolassar command of a large force, and sent him to Babylonia to quell the revolt, while he himself

led other forces into Media, to put down the insurrection there. Nabopolassar did his work so well in Babylonia that the king of Assyria rewarded him with the command of that province, with the title of King of Babylon. Thus we see that Nabopolassar received his power from the king of Assyria. The king of Assyria received his from his father, Asshur-bani-pal; Asshur-bani-pal received his from his father, Esar-haddon; Esar-haddon received his from his father, Sennacherib; Sennacherib received his from his father, Sargon; and Sargon received his from the troops in the field, that is, from the people. Thus we see that the power of the kingdom of Babylon, and of Nebuchadnezzar the king, or of his son, or of his son's son, was simply providential, and came merely from the people.

"Take, for example, Victoria, queen of Great Britain. How did she receive her power? Simply by the fact that she was the first in the line of succession when William the Fourth died. Through one line she traces her royal lineage to William the Conqueror.

"But who was William the Conqueror? He was a Norman chief who led his forces into England in 1066, and established his power there.

"How did he become a chief of the Normans? The Normans made him so, and in that line it is clear that the power of Queen Victoria sprung only from the people.

"Following the other line: The house that now rules Britain, represented in Victoria, is the house of Hanover. Hanover is a province of Germany. How came the house of Hanover to reign in England?—When Queen Anne died, the next in the line of succession was George of Hanover, who became king of England under the title of George the First. How did he receive his princely dignity?—Through his lineage, from Henry the Lion, son of Henry the Proud, who received the duchy of Saxony from Frederick Barbarossa, in 1156. Henry the Lion, son of Henry the Proud, was a prince of the house of Guelph, of Swabia. The father of the house of Guelph was a prince of the Alamanni who invaded the Roman empire, and established their power in what is now Southern Germany, and were the origin of what is now the German nation and empire. But who made this man a prince? The savage tribes of Germany. So in this line also the royal dignity of Queen Victoria sprung from the people.

"And besides all this, the imperial power of Queen Victoria as she now reigns is circumscribed—limited by the people. It has been related, and has appeared in print, and although the story may not be true, it will serve to illustrate the point, that on one occasion, Gladstone, while prime minister and head of the House of Commons, took a certain paper to the queen to be signed. She did not exactly approve of it, and said she would not sign it. Gladstone spoke of the merit of the act, but the queen still declared she would not sign it. Gladstone replied, 'Your Majesty must sign it.' 'Must sign!' exclaimed the queen; 'must sign! Do you know who I am? I am the queen of England.' Gladstone calmly replied, 'Yes, Your Majesty, but I am the PEOPLE of England;' and she had to sign it. The people of England can command the queen of England; the power of the people of England is above that of the queen of England. She, as queen, is simply the representative of their power. And if the people of England should choose to dispense with their expensive luxury of royalty, and turn their form of government into that of a republic, it would be but legitimate exercise of their right, and the government thus formed, the power thus established, would be ordained of God as much as that which now is, or as any could be.

"Personal sovereigns in themselves are not those referred to in the words, 'The powers that be are ordained of God.' It is the governmental power of which the sovereign is the representative, and that sovereign receives his power from the people. Outside of the theocracy of Israel, there never has been a ruler on earth whose authority was not, primarily or ultimately, expressly or permissively, derived from the people. It is not particular sovereigns whose power is ordained of God, nor any particular form of government. It is the genius of government itself. The absence of government is anarchy. Anarchy is only governmental confusion. But says the Scripture, 'God is not the author of confusion.' God is the God of order. He has ordained order, and he has put within man himself that idea of government, of self-protection, which is the first law of nature, and which organizes itself into forms of one kind or another, wherever men dwell on the face of the earth. And it is for men themselves to say what shall be the form of government under which they shall dwell. One people has one form; another has another. This genius of civil order springs from God; its exercise within its legitimate sphere is ordained of God; and the Declaration of Independence simply asserted the eternal truth of God, when it said : 'Governments derive their just powers from the consent of the governed.' It matters not whether it be exercised in one form of government or in another, the governmental power and order thus exercised is ordained of God. If the people choose to change their form of government, it is still the same power; it is to be respected still, because it is still ordained of God in its legitimate exercise,—in things pertaining to men and their relation to their fellow-men; but no power, whether exercised through one form or another, is ordained of God to act in things pertaining to God; nor has it anything whatever to do with men's relations toward God.

"In the previous chapter we have shown that the Constitution of the United States is the only form of government that has ever been on earth which is in harmony with the principle announced by Christ, demanding of men only that which is Caesar's, and refusing to enter in any way into the field of man's relationship to God. This Constitution originated in the principles of the Declaration of Independence, and here we have found that the Declaration of Independence, on this point, simply asserts the truth of God. The American people do not half appreciate the value of the Constitution under which they live. They do not honor in any fair degree the noble men who pledged their lives, their fortunes, and their sacred honor, that these principles might be the heritage of posterity. All honor to these noble men! All integrity to the principles of the Declaration of Independence! All allegiance to the Constitution as it is, which gives to Caesar all his due, and leaves men free to render to God all that he, in his holy word, requires of them!" A.T. Jones, Civil Government and Religion, pp. 39-42.

The Genius of the First Amendment

*T*HE FIRST AMENDMENT CONTAINS TWO CLAUSES dealing with religious liberty: the Establishment Clause, "Congress shall make no law respecting an establishment of religion..." and the Free Exercise Clause, "... or prohibiting the free exercise thereof...."

The Establishment Clause
Any activity or law of the government which establishes a religious practice or sponsors a religion or religious belief or practice or tradition, or favours one religion above others, violates the Establishment Clause of the First Amendment.

The U.S. Supreme Court laid down a three-prong test in 1971 (in the case of *Lemon v Kurtzman*; Ref. 310 US 296) to determine whether a particular government action constitutes an establishment of religion:

- Does the activity have a secular (non-religious) purpose?

- Does the activity primarily advance or inhibit religion?

- Does the activity constitute excessive government involvement with religion?

For example, if government gives a public holiday for rest and recreation there is no violation of the First Amendment. But if government insists that the individual should not do any kind of work or play on that day for religious reasons, or if government insists that people should worship on that day, the Establishment Clause has been violated.

The Free Exercise Clause

The Free Exercise Clause protects the right of the individual to believe, teach and practice his religion according to his own convictions. To show how the two Clauses operate, consider the following:

- If government were to require everyone to attend an Episcopalian (Anglican) church, that would violate the Establishment Clause.

- If government were to prohibit people from attending an Anglican church, that would violate the Free Exercise Clause.

Similarly, if government were to require a particular day to be kept by everyone as the Christian Sabbath or Lord's Day, that would be a violation of the Establishment Clause. If government were to prohibit anyone from keeping a particular day as a special day of worship, that would violate the Free Exercise Clause.

What is Meant by a "Wall Of Separation" Between Church and State?

The term 'wall of separation', which is so often used, comes not from the First Amendment but from the pen of Thomas Jefferson.

The First Amendment was not intended to abolish religious principles or religious thinking in public life. Nor was it intended to prohibit a politician's individual use of religious principles in his public life.

When James Madison offered the First Amendment in its original form to Congress in 1789, and was asked what it meant, his answer was:

> "that Congress should not establish a religion and enforce the legal observation of it by law, nor compel men to worship God in any manner contrary to their conscience."

This then is the true meaning of the 'wall of separation', not that the government should be anti-religious, but that it should not enforce any religious doctrine or practice by law or compel any citizen to obey any religious duty he does not conscientiously believe.

In fact, when a government allows liberty of conscience, it is acting in harmony with New Testament Christianity. But when it does not allow liberty of conscience and enforces or prohibits any religion, thereby violating the consciences of those of a different persuasion, it is an anti-Christian government. The basis for this conclusion is the principle enunciated by Christ, "Render therefore to Caesar the things which are Caesar's, and unto God the things that are God's."

Some people suggest that the term 'wall of separation between church and state' means the establishment of a godless state. No. It simply means that the state allows everyone the freedom to practice one's religion without compelling anyone to practice a religion which one does not believe in.

The state should not oppose religion or show hostility to religion. It should allow the freedom and security for each citizen to practice his conscientious religious beliefs.

There are some who would want the government to establish a secular humanist (atheistic) state by opposing religion but this would also be a violation of constitutional principles of liberty of conscience. The U.S. Supreme Court in the case of Abington Township v Schempp, 374 U.S. 203 (1963), declared that:

> "...the state may not establish a 'religion of secularism' in the sense of affirmatively opposing or showing hostility to religion, thus 'preferring those who believe in no religion over those who do believe."

In summary, then, the term 'wall of separation between church and state', when correctly understood, is a wonderful principle of religious liberty, and is completely in harmony with the principle of Christ: "Render therefore to Caesar the things which are Caesar's, and unto God the things that are God's." James Madison expressed it beautifully when he said, "Religion and government will both exist in greater purity, the less they are mixed."

Protestantism And Republicanism

The US Constitution sets forth a government of the people, by the consent of the people, for the people. It guarantees the right of its citizens to elect the government of their choice through free, fair and open elections. It also guarantees freedom of speech, freedom of the press; freedom of assembly and freedom of peaceful protest. These are the fundamental liberties of democratic republicanism, the freest form of government. The constitutions of free nations of Christendom are all similar.

In addition, the Constitution guarantees religious liberty, or liberty of conscience, in matters of faith, worship and religious duty. It sets forth the very healthy and righteous principles of separation of church and state.

These are the fundamental, inalienable principles of Protestantism.

Republicanism and Protestantism are like the two horns on a lamb's head with the lamb's body representing the benign, gentle and liberty-loving nature of such a government.

A truly Protestant government guarantees full religious liberty. A truly Christian government is one which upholds the rule of civil law and allows full religious liberty and civil rights to its citizens. The moment a government enforces religion or religious duty by law it has departed from the principle of Christ, "Render therefore to Caesar the things which are Caesar's, and unto God the things that are God's," and has become un-Christian even though the religion enforced be some particular form of popular Christianity.

Notwithstanding these clear principles there have been in each generation since the adoption of the First Amendment in 1791, religionists who have sought to have religious matters enforced by the civil legislature. This is especially true with regards to Sunday laws. For example, back in the 1880's and the 1820's there were religious moves to prevent the transportation or handling of mail on Sundays in the USA. The argument was that Congress should enforce the Sunday sabbath by ordering a cessation of public work i.e. a cessation of transportation of mail on Sunday.

But, equally, there have always been those who clearly understood the principles of liberty of conscience contained in the First Amendment, and these have withstood the attempts to enforce religious practices by civil legislation.

As a fitting close to this chapter we insert a portion of the report of a United States Senate Committee on the same subject, 169 years ago — the session of 1828-1829. The arguments are unanswerable, and the principles contained in the report are as worthy now of our most earnest consideration as back then.

Congressional Report — Transportation Of Mail On Sunday

"The Senate proceeded to the consideration of the following report and resolution, presented by Mr. Johnson, with which the Senate concurred:

"The committee to whom were referred the several petitions on the subject of mails on the Sabbath, or first day of the week, report,

"That some respite is required from the ordinary vocations of life, is an established principle, sanctioned by the usages of all nations, whether Christian or pagan. One day in seven has also been determined upon as the proportion of time; and in conformity with the wishes of a great majority of the citizens of this country, the first day of the week, commonly called Sunday, has been set apart to that object.

"The principle has received the sanction of the national legislature, so far as to admit a suspension of all public business on that day, except in cases of absolute necessity, or of great public utility. This principle the committee would not wish to disturb. If kept within its legitimate sphere of action, no injury can result from its observance. It should, however, be kept in mind that the proper object of government is to protect all persons in the enjoyment of their religious as well as civil rights, and not to determine for any whether they shall esteem one day above another, or esteem all days alike holy.

"We are aware that a variety of sentiment exists among the good citizens of this nation, on the subject of the Sabbath day; and our Government is designed for the protection of one as much as another. The Jews, who in this country are as free as Christians, and entitled to the same protection from the laws, derive their obligation to keep the Sabbath day from the fourth commandment of their decalogue, and in conformity with that injunction, pay religious homage to the seventh day of the week, which we call Saturday. One denomination of Christians among us, justly celebrated for their piety, and certainly as good citizens as any other class, agree with the Jews in the moral obligation of the Sabbath, and observe the same day. ...The Jewish Government was a theocracy, which enforced religious observances; and though the committee would hope that no portion of the citizens of our country would willingly introduce a system of religious coercion in our civil institutions, the example of other nations should admonish us to watch carefully against its earliest indication. With these different religious views, the committee are of opinion that Congress cannot interfere. It is not the legitimate province of the legislature to determine what religion is true, or what false.

"Our Government is a civil, and not a religious, institution. Our Constitution recognizes in every person the right to choose his own religion, and to enjoy it freely, without molestation. Whatever may be the religious sentiments of citizens, and however variant, they are alike entitled to protection from the Government, so long as they do not invade the rights of others. The transportation of the mail on the first day of the week, it is believed, does not interfere with the rights of conscience. The petitioners for its discontinuance appear to be actuated by a religious zeal which may be commendable if confined to its proper sphere; but they assume a position better suited to an ecclesiastical than to a civil institution. They appear in many instances to lay it down as an axiom, that the practice is a violation of the law of God. Should Congress in legislative capacity adopt the sentiment, it would establish the principle that the legislature is a proper tribunal to determine what are the laws of God. It would involve a legislative decision on a religious controversy, and on a point in which good citizens may honestly differ in opinion, without disturbing the peace of society or endangering its liberties. If this principle is once introduced, it will be impossible to define its bounds.

"Among all the religious persecutions with which almost every page of modern history is stained, no victim ever suffered but for the violation of what government denominated the law of God. To prevent a similar train of evils in this country, the Constitution has wisely withheld from our Government the power of defining the divine law. It is a right reserved to each citizen; and while he respects the rights of others, he cannot be held amenable to any human tribunal for his conclusions. Extensive religious combinations to effect a political object, are, in the opinion of the committee, always dangerous. This first effort of the kind calls for the establishment of a principle, which, in the opinion of the committee, would lay the foundation for dangerous innovations upon the spirit of the Constitution, and upon the religious rights of the citizens. If admitted, it may be justly apprehended that the future measures of the Government will be strongly marked, if not eventually controlled, by the same influence. All religious despotism commences by combination and influence, and when that influence begins to operate upon the political institutions of a country, the civil power soon bends under it; and the catastrophe of other nations furnishes an awful warning of the consequence.

"While the mail is transported on Saturday, the Jew and the Sabbatarian may abstain from any agency in carrying it, on conscientious scruples. While it is transported on the first day of the week, another class may abstain, from the same religious scruples. The obligation of Government is the same on both these classes; and the committee can discover no principle on which the claims of one should be more respected than those of the other, unless it be admitted that the consciences of the minority are less sacred than those of the majority.

"If the observance of a holy day becomes incorporated in our institutions, shall we not forbid the movement of an army, prohibit an assault in time of war, and lay an injunction upon our naval officers to lie in the wind while upon the ocean on that day? Consistency would seem to require it. Nor is it certain that we should stop here. If the principle is once established that religion, or religious observances, shall be interwoven with our legislative acts, we must pursue it to its ultimatum. We shall, if consistent, provide for the erection of edifices for worship of the Creator, and for the support of Christian ministers, if we believe such measures will promote the interests of Christianity. It is the settled conviction of the committee, that the only method of avoiding these consequences, with their attendant train of evils, is to adhere strictly to the spirit of the Constitution, which regards the general Government in no other light than that of a civil institution, wholly destitute of religious authority. What other nations call religious toleration, we call religious rights.— They are not exercised in virtue of governmental indulgence, but as rights, of which Government cannot deprive any portion of citizens, however small. Despotic power may invade those rights, but justice still confirms them.

"Let the national legislature once perform an act which involves the decision of a religious controversy, and it will have passed its legitimate bounds. The precedent will then be established, and the foundation laid, for that usurpation of the divine prerogative in this country which has been the desolating scourge to the fairest portion of the Old World.

"Our Constitution recognizes no other power than that of persuasion, for enforcing religious observances. Let the professors of Christianity recommend their religion by deeds of benevolence, by Christian meekness, by lives of temperance and holiness. Let them combine their efforts to instruct the ignorant, to relieve the widow and the orphan, to promulgate to the world the gospel of their Saviour, recommending its precepts by their habitual example; Government will find its legitimate object in protecting them. It cannot oppose them, and they will not need its aid. Their moral influence will then do infinitely more to advance the true interests of religion, than any measure which they may call on Congress to enact. The petitioners do not complain of any infringement upon their own rights. They enjoy all that Christians ought to ask at the hands of any Government — protection from all molestation in the exercise of their religious sentiments."

"Resolved, That the committee be discharged from any further consideration of the subject."

That committee really understood the meaning, significance and purpose of the First Amendment. According to A.T. Jones, their arguments are unanswerable and are most worthy of our careful consideration in these days when liberty is taken for granted.

Opposition to the First Amendment

A Brief Historical Review of the
Development of Liberty of Conscience

*T*HE PRINCIPLES OF LIBERTY OF CONSCIENCE enshrined in the constitutions of the democratic nations of Christendom are the outgrowth of the principles enunciated in the Protestant Reformation of the sixteenth century. Let us look again at the principles contained in the Protest of the Reformed German Princes at the Diet of Spires in 1529:

> "The principles contained in this celebrated Protest...constitute the very essence of Protestantism. Now this Protest opposes two abuses of man in matters of faith: the first is the intrusion of the civil magistrate, and the second the arbitrary authority of the church. Instead of these abuses, Protestantism sets the power of conscience above the magistrate, and the authority of the word of God above the visible church. In the first place, it rejects the civil power in divine things, and says with the prophets and apostles, 'We must obey God rather than man.' In presence of the crown of Charles the Fifth, it uplifts the crown of Jesus Christ. But it goes farther: it lays down the principle that all human teaching should be subordinate to the oracles of God."
> D'Aubigné, b. 13, ch. 6.

We have already shown in Chapter 3 that the early Protestant European colonists to the USA did not completely understand the full significance of these principles. They, therefore, established state churches in many of the states and adopted the regulation of permitting only members of the church to vote or to hold office in the civil government. But this led to pernicious results.

This regulation had been accepted as a means of preserving the purity of the state, but it resulted in the corruption of the church. A profession of religion being the condition of suffrage and office holding, many actuated solely by motives of worldly policy, united with the church without a change of heart. Thus the churches came to consist, to a considerable extent, of unconverted persons; and even in the ministry were those who not only held errors of doctrine, but who were ignorant of the renewing power of the Holy Spirit. Thus again was demonstrated the evil results, so often witnessed in the history of the church form the days of Constantine to the present, of attempting to build up the church by the aid of the state, of appealing to the secular power in support of the gospel of Him who declared: *"My kingdom is not of this world."* John 18:36. The union of the church with the state, be the degree ever so slight, while it may appear to bring the world nearer to the church, does in reality but bring the church nearer to the world.

Then came Roger Williams who, according to the great nineteenth century American historian George Bancroft, "was the first person in modern Christendom to establish civil government on the doctrine of liberty of conscience, the equality of opinions before the law" (*George Bancroft, History of the USA Part One, Chapter 15 paragraph 16*). His little state, Rhode Island, increased and prospered until its foundation principles — civil and religious liberty — became the cornerstones of the American Republic. Great advocates for liberty of conscience, Thomas Jefferson, James Madison, George Mason and others, built upon the Roger Williams' foundation until at last the edifice of liberty was completely constructed.

> "The Framers of the Constitution recognized the eternal principle that man's relation with God is above human legislation, and his rights of conscience inalienable. Reasoning was not necessary to establish this truth; we are conscious of it in our own bosoms. It is this consciousness which, in defiance of human laws, has sustained so many martyrs in tortures and flames. They felt that their duty to God was superior to human enactments, and that man could exercise no authority over their consciences. It is an inborn principle which nothing can eradicate." Congressional Documents (USA) No. 200, Document No. 271.

Protestants Oppose Protestantism

Yet, notwithstanding such a wonderful history of the development of liberty, there have always been organizations, and Protestant Christian organizations at that, arising in the very USA seeking to have religious duties enforced by the civil law. Furthermore, in almost all cases the religious duty which they have sought to have enforced is that of Sunday rest and worship.

In the late nineteenth century there arose the National Woman's Christian Temperance Union, the National Reform Association, the Lord's Day Alliance and the Sunday-law Association—all Protestant Christian organizations—which sought the Federal enforcement of strict National Sunday laws in the USA.

The aim of those Protestants at that time (1884 - 1888) was to make America a Christian nation by enforcing Christianity on the population through civil legislation. But in the very act of enforcing religious beliefs and practices by the civil law they would be opposing, or rather rejecting, the very essential principles of Protestantism!

In May 1888, Senator Henry W. Blair introduced a resolution and a bill to Congress. The resolution (May 25, 1888) proposed an amendment to the Constitution of the USA respecting establishment of religion. The bill (May 21, 1888) was introduced to have a National Sunday law enforced.

Senator Blair was in fact expressing the sentiments of those Protestant organizations mentioned earlier. A.T. Jones, American religious liberty defender, successfully opposed the Blair Amendment and Bill.

The National Reform Association's view was published in a periodical called the Christian Statesman. We present now some of Jones' analysis of, and rebuttal to, the attack upon the first Amendment:

The Christian Statesman of Oct. 2, 1884, said, "Give all men to understand that this is a Christian nation, and that, believing that without Christianity we perish, we must maintain by all means our Christian character. Inscribe this character on our Constitution. Enforce upon all who come among us the laws of Christian morality."

Jones replied:

> "To enforce upon men the laws of Christian morality, is nothing
> else than an attempt to compel them to be Christians, and does
> in fact compel them to be hypocrites. It will be seen at once that
> this will be but to invade the rights of conscience, and this, one
> of the vice-presidents of the Association declares, civil power

has the right to do. Rev. David Gregg, D. D., now pastor of Park Street Church, Boston, a vice-president of the National Reform Association, plainly declared in the *Christian Statesman* of June 5, 1884, that the civil power 'has the right to command the consciences of men.'

"Rev. M. A. Gault, a district secretary and a leading worker of the Association, says:

'Our remedy for all these malefic influences, is to have the Government simply set up the moral law and recognize God's authority behind it, and lay its hand on any religion that does not conform to it.'

"Rev. E. B. Graham, also a vice-president of the Association, in an address delivered at York, Neb., and reported in the *Christian Statesman* of May 21, 1885, said:

'We might add in all justice, if the opponents of the Bible do not like our Government and its Christian features, let them go to some wild, desolate land, and in the name of the Devil, and for the sake of the Devil, subdue it, and set up a government of their own on infidel and atheistic ideas; and then if they can stand it, stay there till they die.'

"How much different is that from the Russian despotism? In the *Century* for April, 1888, Mr. Kennan gave a view of the statutes of Russia on the subject of crimes against the faith, quoting statute after statute providing that whoever shall censure the Christian faith or the orthodox church, or the Scriptures, or the holy sacraments, or the saints, or their images, or the Virgin Mary, or the angels, or Christ, or God, shall be deprived of all civil rights, and exiled for life to the most remote parts of Siberia. This is the system in Russia, and it is in the direct line of the wishes of the National Reform Association, with this difference, however, that Russia is content to send dissenters to Siberia, while the National Reformers want to send them to the Devil, straight.

"In a speech in a National Reform convention held in New York City, Feb. 26, 27, 1873, Jonathan Edwards, D.D., said:

'We want State and religion, and we are going to have it. It shall be that so far as the affairs of State require religion, it shall be religion—the religion of Jesus Christ. The Christian oath and Christian morality shall have in this land 'an undeniable legal basis.' We use the word *religion* in its proper sense, as meaning a man's personal relation of faith and obedience to God.'

"Then according to their own definition, the National Reform Association intends that the State shall obtrude itself into every man's personal relation of faith and obedience to God. Mr. Edwards proceeds:

'Now, we are warned that to ingraft this doctrine upon the Constitution will be oppressive; that it will infringe the rights of conscience; and we are told that there are atheists, deists, Jews, and Seventh-day Baptists who would be sufferers under it.'

"He then defines the terms, atheist, deist, Jew, and Seventh-day Baptist, and counts them all atheists, as follows:

'These all are, for the occasion, and so far as our amendment is concerned, one class. They use the same arguments and the same tactics against us. They must be counted together, which we very much regret, but which we cannot help. The first-named is the leader in the discontent and in the outcry—the atheist, to whom nothing is higher or more sacred than man, and nothing survives the tomb. It is his class. Its labors are almost wholly in his interest; its success would be almost wholly his triumph. The rest are adjuncts to him in this contest. They must be named from him; they must be treated as, for this question, one party.'

"What now are the rights of the National Reform classification of atheists? Mr. Edwards asks the question and answers it thus:

'What are the rights of the atheist? I would tolerate him as I would tolerate a poor lunatic; for in my view his mind is scarcely sound. So long as he does not rave, so long as he is not dangerous, I would tolerate him. I would tolerate him as I would a conspirator. The atheist is a dangerous man.'

'Let us inquire for a moment what are the rights of the atheist. So far as earthly governments are concerned, has not any man just as much right to be an atheist as any other man has to be a Christian? If not, why not? We wish somebody would tell. Has not any man just as much right to be an atheist as Jonathan Edwards has to be a Doctor of Divinity? Can you compel him to be anything else? But how long does Mr. Edwards propose to tolerate him?—'So long as he does not rave.' A lunatic may be harmless, and be suffered to go about as he chooses; yet he is kept under constant surveillance, because there is no knowing at what moment the demon in him may carry him beyond himself, and he become dangerous. Thus the National Reformers propose to treat those who disagree with them. So long as dissenters allow themselves to be cowed down like a set of curs, and submit to be domineered over by these self-exalted despots, all may go well; but if a person has the principle of a man, and asserts his convictions as a man ought to, then he is 'raving,' then he becomes 'dangerous,' and must be treated as a raving, dangerous lunatic.

'Next, dissenters are to be tolerated as conspirators are. A political conspirator is one who seeks to destroy the Government itself; he virtually plots against the life of every one in the Government; and in that, he has forfeited all claims to the protection of the Government or the regard of the people. And this is the way dissenters are to be treated by the National Reformers, when they shall have secured the power they want. And these are the men to whom Senator Blair's proposed Constitutional amendment is intensely satisfactory, as that which, if adopted, will assure them, in the end, that which they want.

"Mr. Edwards proceeds:

> 'Yes, to this extent I will tolerate the atheist; but no more. Why should I? The atheist does not tolerate me. He does not smile either in pity or in scorn upon my faith. He hates my faith, and he hates me for my faith.'

"Remember that these men propose to make this a Christian nation. These are they who propose themselves as the supreme expositors of Christian doctrine in this nation. What beautiful harmony there is between these words of Mr. Edwards and those of the Sermon on the Mount! Did the Saviour say, Hate them that hate you; despise them that will not tolerate you; and persecute them that do not smile upon your faith? Is that the Sermon on the Mount?—It is not the Sermon on the Mount. Jesus said, 'Love your enemies; bless them that curse you, do good to them that hate you, and pray for them which despitefully use you, and persecute you; that ye may be the children of your Father which is in heaven.' But this National Reform style of Christianity would have it: 'Hate your enemies; oppress them that hate you; and persecute them who will not smile, either in pity or in scorn, upon your faith, that you may be the true children of the National Reform party' and that is what you will be, if you do it.

"But Mr. Edwards has not yet finished displaying his tolerant ideas; he says:

> 'I can tolerate difference and discussion; I can tolerate heresy and false religion; I can debate the use of the Bible in our common schools, the taxation of church property, the propriety of chaplaincies and the like, but there are some questions past debate. *Tolerate atheism, sir? There is nothing out of hell that I would not tolerate as soon!* The atheist may live, as I have said; but, God helping us, the taint of his destructive creed shall not defile any of the civil institutions of all this fair land!

> 'Let us repeat, atheism and Christianity are contradictory terms. They are incompatible systems. They cannot dwell together on the same continent!'

"Worse than Russia again! Russia will suffer dissenters to dwell on the same continent with her, though it be in the most remote part of Siberia. But these men to whom Senator Blair's religious amendment is so satisfactory, propose to outdo even Russia, and not suffer dissenters to dwell on the same continent with them. In view of these statements of men now living, and actively working for this proposed amendment, is it necessary for us to say that Senator Blair's religious amendment to the Constitution is directly in the line of a religious despotism more merciless than that of Russia, and paralleled only by that of the papacy in the supremacy of its power?

"But as though this were not enough, and as though their tolerant intentions were not sincere enough, they propose in addition to all this to join hands with the Catholic Church and enlist her efforts in their work. The *Christian Statesman* of Dec. 11, 1884, said:

> 'Whenever they [the Roman Catholics] are willing to co-operate in resisting the progress of political atheism, we will gladly join hands with them.'

"What does Pope Leo XIII command all Catholics to do? This: 'All Catholics should do all in their power to cause the constitutions of States, and legislation, to be modeled on the principles of the true church.'

"The National Reformers are doing precisely what the pope has commanded all Catholics to do, and why shouldn't they gladly join hands with them? And we may rest assured that Rome will accept the National Reform proffer just as soon as the influence of that Association becomes of sufficient weight to be profitable to her. Senator Blair's proposed amendment is a direct play into the hands of the papacy.

"Thus it is clearly demonstrated that Senator Blair's proposed Constitutional amendment, if adopted, will only open the way to the establishment of a religious despotism in this dear land, and that this is the very use those who are most in favor of it intend to make of it. And to favor that amendment is to favor a religious despotism."

Protestantism In Reverse

In our modern times of liberty of conscience, freedom of inquiry, and amazing advances in all branches of knowledge, there are still to be found Protestant Christian organizations in the USA seeking to have popular Christian beliefs and practices enforced by the civil law. Organizations such as the 'Christian Coalition' and the 'Christian Right' are increasing phenomenally both in membership and their influence on the average American citizen. Such influence will prove to be critically important as America approaches, reaches and passes the year 2000.

What these modern Protestant groups are working for is the very opposite of what the sixteenth century Protestant Reformation worked so hard to achieve. The Reformation overthrew two abuses of man in matters of faith: first — is the intrusion of the civil magistrate, and the second — the arbitrary authority of the church. Instead of these abuses, Protestantism sets the power of the conscience above the magistrate, and the authority of the word of God above the visible church. In the first place it rejects the civil power in divine things, and says with the prophets and apostles, "We must obey God rather than man."

Yet what these modern Christian groups are seeking to achieve is the intrusion of the civil judiciary into matters of faith and religious duty, i.e. the enforcement of the religion of the majority by the civil law of the state.

It is the duty of the state to protect liberty of conscience, and this is the limit of its authority in matters of religion. Every secular government that attempts to regulate or enforce religious observances by civil authority is sacrificing the very principle for which the true Protestant reformers so nobly struggled.

Isn't it horrifying that, in our age of freedom and enlightenment, modern Protestant Christians should be seeking to return us to the tyranny of the Dark Ages?

Yet these groups are claiming that only through the enforcement of Christianity by the civil law can America achieve moral healing and socioeconomic prosperity.

But history has clearly shown that religious legislation, rather than restraining the lawless, results only in religious intolerance and persecution of upright and good citizens who have a different religious persuasion to the majority.

Papal Opposition To The First Amendment

The principle of liberty of conscience in matters of faith and worship was neither acknowledged nor practised by the Papacy during the more than 1000 years of Roman Catholic supremacy in Europe during the Middle Ages. The Protestant doctrines of civil and religious liberty, and the separation of church and state are regarded as heresy by the Papal hierarchy.

Nineteenth century American historian, Josiah Strong, wrote thus of the attitude of the papal hierarchy as regards freedom of conscience, and of the perils which especially threaten the USA from the success of her policy:

> "There are many who are disposed to attribute any fear of Roman Catholicism in the United States to bigotry or childishness. Such see nothing in the character and attitude of Romanism that is hostile to our free institutions, or find nothing portentous in its growth. Let us, then, first compare some of the fundamental principles of our government with those of the Catholic Church.

> "The Constitution of the United States guarantees liberty of conscience. Nothing is dearer or more fundamental. Pope Pius IX, in his Encyclical Letter of August 15, 1854, said: 'The absurd and erroneous doctrines or ravings in defense of liberty of conscience are a most pestilential error—a pest, of all others, most to be dreaded in a state.' The same pope, in his Encyclical Letter of December 8, 1864, anathematized 'those who assert the liberty of conscience and of religious worship', also 'all such as maintain that the church may not employ force.'

> "The pacific tone of Rome in the United States does not imply a change of heart. She is tolerant where she is helpless. Says Bishop O' Connor: 'Religious liberty is merely endured until the opposite can be carried into effect without peril to the Catholic world'.... The archbishop of St. Louis once said: 'Heresy and unbelief are crimes; and in Christian countries, as in Italy and Spain, for instance, where all the people are Catholics, and where the Catholic religion is an essential part of the law of the land, they are punished as other crimes'...

> "Every cardinal, archbishop, and bishop in the Catholic Church takes an oath of allegiance to the pope, in which occur the

following words: 'Heretics, schismatics, and rebels to our said lord (the pope), or his aforesaid successors, I will to my utmost persecute and oppose.'" Josiah Strong, Our Country, ch. 5, pars. 2-4.

The position of the Papacy in the 1990's is no different. Pope John Paul II asserts that "Just as no system of politics is viable unless it is based on the spirituality of genuine belief in God and Christ, so no religious belief is viable unless it is deeply involved in political systems." Malachi Martin, The Keys of This Blood, p. 492.

Ellen G. White, America's most prolific and famous female Christian author, has left this warning on record:

"The Roman Catholic Church, with all its ramifications throughout the world, forms one vast organization under the control, and designed to serve the interest, of the papal see. Its millions of communicants, in every country on the globe, are instructed to hold themselves as bound in allegiance to the pope. Whatever their nationality or their government, they are to regard the authority of the church as above all other. Though they may take the oath pledging their loyalty to the state, yet back of this lies the vow of obedience to Rome, absolving them from every pledge inimical to her interests.

"Marvelous in her shrewdness and cunning is the Roman Church. She can read what is to be. She bides her time, seeing that the Protestant churches are paying her homage in their acceptance of the Sunday sabbath and that they are preparing to enforce it by the very means which she herself employed in bygone days.

"Let the principle once be established in the United States that the church may employ or control the power of the state; that religious observance may be enforced by secular laws; in short, that the authority of church and state is to dominate the conscience, and the triumph of Rome in America is assured." G.C. 580, 581.

Conclusion

We have always known that the Papacy was, and is, opposed to the principles of the First Amendment. But now we also know that many Protestant organizations are opposed to the First Amendment as well, perhaps not in so many words, but nevertheless they propose the enforcement of religion by the civil law which is a rejection of First Amendment liberties.

Strange things do happen, and this is one. Protestants, whose protest against Old World religious intolerance eventually gave birth to the US First Amendment, have now lost their protest and will ultimately seek to enforce religious dogma by the civil law. They will thereby join hands with Rome in opposing the principle of religious liberty contained in the First Amendment, and this will be the first crucial step in the establishment of America's New World Economic Order.

It is most fitting to close this chapter with the following quotation by Professor W.A. Colcord in his book, "The Rights of Man", written early in the twentieth century.

> "No religion is worth having or worth supporting that needs prisons, racks, inquisitions, fines, fires or fagots to sustain it. No religion is worth embracing that dares not or cannot meet its opposers on the open battlefield of truth, without the myrmidons of the law at its back to enforce its precepts. No religion is worth supporting that needs anything but truth and the Spirit of God to support it. No church ought to be permitted to stand that stands by persecuting others; no church to exist that exists simply by unchurching others. No creed is worth saving from destruction that has to be saved by the destruction of men's rights and liberties; nor is any church worthy of the Christian name that makes nonconformity to its rites and usages a penal offense against the state. It becomes a persecuting church the moment it does so." W.A. Colcord, The Rights of Man, p. 113.

This is in perfect agreement with the words of Jesus in John 16:1-3.

A Morally Renewed America

Will Lead the Nations into the New World Order

*T*HOUGH THE UNITED STATES OF AMERICA has been experiencing progressively increasing levels of lawlessness and crime throughout the 20th century, the increase in crime over the past three decades has been alarming to say the least.

All types of horrible, inhuman, utterly revolting and detestably violent crimes are now being reported from the big cities of the world including some in America. Many of these crimes are related to the trafficking and abuse of illegal, mind-damaging drugs. The USA remains the world's single largest market for illegal drugs.

Modern crime has also become sophisticated and has kept pace with technological developments. Criminals are able to counterfeit almost any financial or security system.

As the level of violent crime continues to rise there will be increasing levels of fear in the minds of law abiding citizens. Such fear will eventually drive America to seek some measure or measures by which to halt or decrease the ever intensifying upsurge of crime and lawlessness. But in America and around the world there is more than crime to worry about.

Fatal accidents and natural calamities are also major problems which generate fear in the popular psyche. Families are falling apart at an alarming rate and an increasing number of teenagers are turning to deviant, non-productive and dangerous lifestyles. More and more Americans are becoming fearful for their children's future.

On the international scene, sexual exploitation of children has become a worldwide problem. *The Economist* recently reported that "every week,

10 million to 12 million men will visit young prostitutes." Indeed, human society is being shaken by a shocking form of child abuse that is of a scope and nature not widely known until recent years. In 1996 representatives of 130 nations met in Stockholm, Sweden, at the first *World Congress Against Commercial Sexual Exploitation of Children*. The information revealed at that Congress was horribly shocking. Consider these reports:

> In Brazil, there are at least a quarter million child prostitutes; in Canada, thousands of teenage girls are being prostituted by organized pimp rings; in China, the figure ranges from 200,000 to 500,000 prostituted children; in Colombia, the number of children sexually exploited on the streets of Bogota has quintupled in the last seven years; in India 400,000 children are involved in the sex industry; in Thailand, 300,000 children are involved; in the USA, official sources speak of more than 100,000 children involved in commercial sexual exploitation. The Congress revealed that sex tourism is a major cause of child exploitation in developing countries.

Pornography is also on the rise and has infiltrated the Internet. Even churches are riddled with perverted sexual behavior and controversies over homosexual marriages.

Is Freedom To Blame?

Many Americans are beginning to wonder if the increase in crime and lawlessness has anything to do with the tremendous freedom which Americans enjoy. Many are inclined to think that the great liberties of the Constitution, especially of the First Amendment, have been progressively abused by every succeeding generation especially since the 1960's.

Religionists and sociologists are suggesting that unrestricted freedom without morality is pushing American society to a dangerous extreme. Furthermore, the recent increase in the number of what are called bizarre cults with mass ceremonial suicides, has led some to begin to doubt the wisdom and relevance of First Amendment religious liberties. Commenting on the fact that First Amendment freedoms are being increasingly questioned, *The Economist* of January 4th, 1997 carried an article entitled *A Slow Retreat From Freedom*. It is reproduced here because it shows how the abuse of freedom can eventually lead to a restriction of freedom:

> "America has the Super Bowl, the hamburger, the baseball cap; America has the first amendment. From the civics classes of their

school days, Americans know that this addition to their constitution, adopted in the first years of the republic as part of the Bill of Rights, guarantees freedom of religion, speech and assembly. For a young country, rebelling against the authoritarianism of the old world, these freedoms amounted to an animating creed. For the mature America of today, they remain a national icon.

"The Freedom Forum, a think-tank, recently distributed 1997 first-amendment calendars: each day a new page offers a quotation (from eminences such as O.J. Simpson, Hillary Clinton, Sophocles) on the preciousness of freedom. A hot new movie, 'The People vs Larry Flynt', celebrates the first amendment too. The film's hero, publisher of Hustler magazine, is set upon by wrong-thinkers who feel pornography should not be allowed. At the high point of the movie, the battle reaches the Supreme Court, and Mr. Flynt's lawyer argues that to condemn pornography on grounds of bad taste would be to violate the first amendment. A legal argument about a constitutional sub-clause becomes the stuff of melodrama: only in America.

"And yet, in diverse ways, America is starting to doubt the wisdom of this exceptionalism. The first amendment has been used to extend free expression beyond the limits tolerated in most advanced societies; the resulting costs are remarked upon increasingly. Freedom, it is now said both on the left and on the right, must be weighed against other goods, such as equity, morality and social order. The first amendment is no longer such a sacred text; where it is invoked, it should be tested.

"Consider, for example, the hottest free-speech issue of the day: the question of whether the first amendment protects campaign spending. In 1976 the Supreme Court threw out post-Watergate limits on election spending, arguing that political advertisements (and, indeed, the spending of money per se) are a form of speech, and so must be unrestricted. The result is that campaign spending has ballooned to a point that most Americans find disgusting. Even before the current scandal concerning the Democrats' fund-raising techniques many thought the Supreme Court's decision wrong. Now a growing band—including Dick Gephardt, the Democratic leader in the House—advocates a constitutional amendment to reverse it.

"The idea of expenditure as speech is a relatively new and tendentious one; but forms of speech long protected by the first amendment are equally under attack. Take indecency. Last February Bill Clinton signed the Communications Decency Act, which aspires to control pornography on the Internet. In November Wal-Mart was found to be cleansing its shelves Of CDs with sexual or violent lyrics, to applause from moralistic politicians. In December political pressure induced television moguls to offer a system of ratings for violent or obscene programmes, modelled on the ones already used in cinemas.

"The first amendment also lays down that 'Congress shall make no law respecting an establishment of religion'; this bars the government from helping any faith, lest rival ones suffer. Again, this principle has grown unpopular. These days Republicans and Democrats agree that religion is such an essential social glue that the state has an interest in promoting it. Many Republicans favour a constitutional amendment to allow prayer in government schools. The Clinton administration has found ways of channeling government money to religious charities, and religious schools are now model partners in government-subsidized voucher schemes.

"In 1964 a Supreme Court ruling based on the first amendment gave America the world's freest press; increasingly, Americans doubt whether this was sensible. The court laid down that, in order to win a libel case, a public figure had to prove that an allegation was not merely inaccurate; it had to be deliberately malicious. As a result, American journalists can print allegations about politicians or tycoons without being required to prove that they are true, a ruinous course in some other countries, especially Britain. This makes it easier to deflate big shots, which is good. But it also makes for uncivil public debate, which stokes public revulsion with the media. Last month a Harris poll found that 84% Of Americans believe government should regulate journalists in order to root out bias; 70% support court-imposed fines for inaccurate or biased reporting.

"In sum, first amendment freedoms are increasingly questioned; and judges who uphold the prevailing wisdom of the courts, no matter how long-established, may find themselves at loggerheads with public opinion, sometimes in the shape of their own juries.

This seems especially true in the case of press freedom. Though judges make it hard to convict journalists for libel, juries vent their wrath against the media by imposing monumental awards on the unlucky few who lose their cases. To inflict maximum pain, they punish individual journalists as well as media firms. Last month ABC television was ordered to pay $10 million in damages to Alan Levan, a financier; the producer of the offending report was ordered to pay $500,000.

"A second case, also involving ABC last month, demonstrates another way in which courts intimidate reporters. Food Lion, a supermarket chain, sued ABC over a documentary that showed employees doctoring spoiled meat and bleaching fish to make it smell better. Food Lion did not claim that the report was wrong, and did not sue for libel. But it successfully sued ABC for fraud: its journalists had lied about themselves in order to get jobs with Food Lion and opportunities to film its unhygienic practices. This legal device—attack reporting techniques rather than the reports themselves—has grown popular in recent years. Despite the first amendment, journalists are on the defensive.

"And so, by various routes, America is reconsidering its famous love of freedom. Some may think this no bad thing. America may be returning to its old balance, correcting the libertarian excesses of first-amendment judgments made in the past couple of generations. It may also be responding sensibly to changed times: and particularly to the view that, since the media has come to saturate American life, protection of free speech in the broadest sense may not be possible without certain limitations.

"Yet the slow retreat from freedom does contain a danger. America has disdained the first amendment before, and the results have not been edifying. In the 1950s Joe McCarthy's Red-baiting was made possible by the courts' refusal to help his victims when they invoked first-amendment rights. This shameful episode partially explains why courts embraced the first amendment with compensating zeal in later years. It would be nice if Americans remembered this history rather than repeated it." The Economist, January 4, 1997.

A Re-awakening Of Religious Life In America

Not only is America reconsidering and questioning the great freedoms of the First Amendment, America is also becoming more religious. Many churches are reporting phenomenal growth in numbers of converts as a result of massive nation-wide religious revivals. After the moderate decline in religious life during the 1960's and 1970's, there has been a progressive resurgence of religion in America during the decades of the eighties and nineties.

An article in *The Economist* of July 1995 reveals some interesting statistics and an incisive analysis into the increasing impact of religion on politics in the USA. Here is the article:

America And Religion

"For proof of God's existence in the American mind, look at opinion polls. Almost all Americans (the figure typically hovers around 95%) say they believe in God. Four out of five believe in miracles, in life after death and in the virgin birth. Belief in the devil has risen sharply, to 65% says a recent poll, and 72% of Americans believe in angels. A survey by the American Bible Society reports that nine out of ten own a bible, and 27% own more than four copies.

"Quite how often or attentively Americans actually read their bibles may be another story (many cannot name any of the four gospels). Nevertheless, their religiosity stands in marked contrast to the rest of the developed world, on the evidence of a World Values Survey conducted in 1990-93. In America, 82% of respondents said they considered themselves 'a religious person', compared with 55% in Britain, 54% in western Germany and 48% in France. In the same survey, 44% of Americans said they attended a religious service at least once a week, against 18% in western Germany, 14% in Britain, 10% in France and a mere 4% in non-worshipping Sweden. There are more places of worship per head in America than anywhere else in the world, with new ones constantly being built.

"How many other places have a National Day of Prayer (the day in May, instituted by a congressional resolution in 1952, that now sees a growing number of events around the country)? Where else are formal or festive occasions so solemnly marked with an 'invocation' before dinner? Whose politicians so liberally deploy the language of the scriptures, from George Bush's enlistment of God in the Gulf war and Bill Clinton's 'new covenant' to the Satanic undertones of Ronald Reagan's 'evil empire'? It seems bizarre that America, of all places, should be viewed as somehow cramping God's style. It would be far more accurate, surely, to talk of a 'culture of belief."

A Culture Of Belief

"People who pray and believe in God,' Mr. Carter writes, 'are encouraged to keep it a secret, and often a shameful one at that.' (Stephen Carter, Yale University, 'Culture of Disbelief', 1993, Anchor Books.) He would like religion to be treated with more respect: for instance, the notion that devout believers are somehow less 'rational' than non-believers deserves to be jettisoned. Although Mr. Carter is a firm supporter of the separation of church and state and the ban on organized prayer in public schools, he objects to what he sees as a trend among politicians and lawyers to treat religious beliefs as arbitrary and unimportant, not really to be taken seriously. Faith, he argues, is being trivialized in modern America.

"Newt Gingrich would agree. Not long before he became speaker of the House of Representatives, Mr. Gingrich gave a lecture on religion and politics to the Heritage Foundation, a right-wing think-tank in Washington. He caricatured the 'secular, anti-religious view of the left' in which religion is fine as a 'tamed hobby' at the weekend. By contrast, Mr. Gingrich's vision is of an America 'in which a belief in the Creator is once again at the centre of defining' what it means to be an American.

"These are big words, and they herald a big debate. The gathering argument over the proper place of religion—whether in private lives, in public places or in politics—may be one of the defining issues of the age.

"The strength of religion should be no surprise in a country many of whose early colonisers were dissident religious enthusiasts. The founding fathers uninhibitedly invoked God in their endeavours—all men, says the Declaration of Independence, are 'endowed by their Creator' with certain inalienable rights—and their suspicion of overbearing government led them to keep church and state separate. The Bill of Rights precludes any law 'respecting an establishment of religion, or prohibiting the free exercise thereof.'

"The combination of freedom and competition proved extraordinarily invigorating. Very early on, the churches proved adept at organizing and marketing themselves; indeed, says Jon Butler, also of Yale, America had 'a national market in religion long before there was a national market in economics.' Now, with no state church, a rich variety of creeds—albeit mostly branches of Christianity—vie for their share of the market. New ones can arise and thrive (the Mormon church, for example, remains one of the fastest-growing); offshoots of old ones can adapt themselves so as to appeal to new audiences.

Pilgrims' Progress

"The ever-perceptive Alexis de Tocqueville observed in 1835: 'Religion in America takes no direct part in the government of society, but it must be regarded as the first of their political institutions.' Americans of all classes and parties, said the French visitor, regarded God as a force for order amid the potentially destructive freedoms of democracy. 'What can be done with people who are their own masters, if they are not submissive to the deity?' (As if Americans needed a reminder, in the 1950s the Pledge of allegiance was amended to read 'one nation under God, indivisible.') Modern European observers cannot fail to be struck by the extent to which America, a nation founded on lofty ideas and forever following a Dream, remains less resistant than cynical old Europe to idealism and faith.

"In America, unlike much of Europe, religious belief has strengthened down the years. Only 17% of adult Americans belonged to a church when the country broke away from Britain. That rose to 37% by the 1861-65 civil war, to 50% in the first decade of the present century and (counting synagogue members, too) to nearly 70% in the 1990s. The rise was remarkably smooth until the rebellious 1960s, when the numbers fell somewhat, prompting a 1966 Time cover story to ask provocatively, and prematurely, 'Is God Dead?'

"A resurrection is now apparent. Baby-boomers with families have returned to church in large numbers. David Roozen, a religion professor at Hartford Seminary in Connecticut, notes that among people born between 1945 and 1954 regular church attendance rose from 33% in 1975 to 41% in 1990.

"The troubles of the American family, and all the social ills associated with family breakdown, have prompted people to turn to religion in search of moral moorings. The approaching millennium is also being invoked as somehow adding to the impetus for spiritual renewal. 'There is a stirring across our land some are calling pre-revival,' says an advertisement for a national clergy conference in 1996. 'Since God has brought revival in every century of our country's history, we are hopeful that He will do so again soon.'

"Examples abound of spectacular growth in the religion business, evidence that a receptive market awaits those who can identify new niches. In his 'state of the union' address to Congress this year, two people Bill Clinton singled out for special mention were the Reverends John and Diana Cherry of Temple Hills, Maryland. From small beginnings in a living-room in the early 1980s, their church has grown to 17,000 members, one of the biggest in the country, and it is still adding 200 members a month. One of its chief aims is to keep families together. "This is the kind of work that citizens are doing in America," said the president, to loud applause. 'We need more of it, and it ought to be lifted up and supported.'

"In the anonymous expanses of American suburbia there is a growing fashion for 'megachurches'. In places where the shopping mall long ago ousted the village centre, places of worship that are more like stadiums or convention centres retail religion carefully tailored to middle-class lifestyles and tastes. These megachurches have lots of convenient amenities and the modern audio-visual technology to reach thousands of worshippers at a time.

"Traditionalists may scoff at this Religion Lite. Enthusiasts see it as moving with the times and, by drawing people in the secular suburbs to religious values, as a way of changing America for the better.

Parties Of God

"This spring and summer (1995), stadiums across America have been filled with Christian men gathering in their thousands to hear how individual virtue can be the starting-point for the transformation of home, community and, ultimately, the country they all belong to. The men pray, bond in small groups and listen en masse as preachers tell them what it means to be 'real men' in today's confusing world. Many return to their local churches having pledged to keep a set of promises, such as following Christ, practising sexual purity, building a strong marriage and forming 'vital relationships' with other Christian men.

"The idea of Promise Keepers, as the organisation behind this movement is called, came to Bill McCartney at the time the University of Colorado's football coach, during a car ride five years ago. Since 4,200 men showed up for the first conference in a Boulder stadium in 1991, Promise Keepers has taken off dramatically. It outgrew Boulder and went national: 280,000 men attended conferences in seven cities last year, and at least double that number are expected this year. A gathering of one million men in Washington, DC, is planned for 1997. When new generations of 'consumers' shop around for religion, some brands will prove more successful than others. Generally, the conservative varieties have been doing best. The total membership of churches that can be loosely categorized as liberal and moderate (such as Episcopalians, Presbyterians and Methodists) shrank somewhat between 1950 and 1990. Over the same period, the number of Roman Catholics in America doubled, as did the membership of conservative Protestant groups, such as Baptists and Lutherans.

"There has long been a close link in America between religion and voting. Roman Catholics and Jews tended to vote for the Democrats, for example; mainline white Protestants formed the backbone of Republican support. But not only has the country's religious composition been changing, so have the traditional party allegiances. Shifts in the voting behavior of America's largest religious groups helped to produce the political earthquake of 1994, when Republicans recaptured control of the Senate and—for the first time in 40 years— the House of Representatives.

"Religion was more powerful than economics in 1994,' concludes a careful analysis of exit polls by four politics professors (Lyman Kellstedt, John Green, James Guth and Corwin Smidt) in the current issue of The Public Perspective, a sociology magazine. White Evangelicals and white Catholics, once core components of the New Deal coalition, have both to varying degrees deserted the Democrats. Together with the lingering Republican loyalty of mainline Protestants, and the general groundswell of concern about the survival of the family, this created the new Republican majority.

"Evangelicals, the sort of Christians who go out clutching a bible to spread the good word, have been moving away from the Democrats since the 1960s. Last November they established themselves as the weightiest chunk (29%) of the Republican coalition. Three out of four people who identify themselves as white Evangelicals voted Republican in the House election. Among white Catholics, the Republican tilt was less pronounced (53% voted Republican) but no less striking, because for so long the Catholic vote had seemed dependably Democratic. Younger Catholics were especially likely to vote Republican. In all, white Catholics constituted a hefty 22% of the Republican coalition last November. The Republicans did particularly well among Evangelicals and Catholics who go to church regularly.

The Advance-guard's Armoury

"A new pattern of politics is emerging, according to the professors' exit-poll analysis, with Republicans 'drawing the more religiously observant voters, at least among whites, and the Democrats attracting the least observant in the major traditions, seculars and various minority groups.'

"Committed people with shared beliefs who gather together frequently in the same place: under the right circumstances regular churchgoers lend themselves splendidly to political mobilization. The Republicans have been mobilizing like mad—none more effectively than Pat Robertson, televangelist, failed presidential candidate and, after his bid for the White House, founder of the

Christian Coalition. In tandem with 33-year-old Ralph Reed, the organization's cherub-faced, Washington-savvy executive director, he has turned the Christian Coalition into a formidable force.

"It boasts 1.6 million members and a dominant voice among Republicans in perhaps 18 states. It has money, grassroots lobby power and, whatever its real ability to sway voters, a lot of influence over Republican politics. It worked hard against Mr. Clinton's health reforms last year, helped to turn out the Republican vote in November, and then spent more than $1 million to support Mr. Gingrich's (mainly economic) legislative programme in the first 100 days of the new Congress.

"Now the Christian Coalition is presenting its bill for these services. Mr. Reed has threatened not to support any Republican presidential candidate or running-mate in 1996 who tolerates abortion. And in May, flanked by top conservative lawmakers, he presented the Coalition's 'Contract with the American Family', a loose outline of a legislative agenda.

"The agenda in part covers some standard conservative themes, such as family tax relief, school choice, stricter prison regimes, a crackdown on pornography. It would seek eventually to abolish the welfare state and replace it by channeling the money, with the help of tax incentives, to private charities (an idea enthusiastically supported by Mr. Gingrich). The Christian Coalition is also asking for a constitutional amendment to allow prayer in public places, and it wants restrictions on late-term abortions.

"Taken in isolation, this programme would not look particularly potent. But the Christian Coalition can count on the backing of a number of other influential family-values groups. It has pledges of help from top Republicans in Congress, and in June some 60 lawmakers formed a Congressional Family Caucus, to restore 'the traditional values of family and faith.' Each item on the agenda was carefully tested in focus groups and found to enjoy at least 60% public support, so the Christian Coalition could present its proposals as mainstream.

"Arch-conservatives such as Pat Buchanan, who is campaigning for the Republican presidential nomination, criticise Mr. Reed's 'contract' as too timid. From the other end of the Republican spectrum, Arlen Specter, who is Jewish and also a would-be president, attacks it as a devious, foot-in-the-door effort intended eventually to get abortion banned outright, to overturn the 1962 Supreme Court ruling that keeps school-sponsored prayer out of public schools, and generally to undermine the separation of church and state.

"Some 80 representatives of a broad spectrum of religious groups responded to the Christian Coalition's 'contract' by signing and delivering to Congress a 'Cry for Renewal', which affirmed the desirability of injecting moral direction into the political process but deplored the Coalition's means. 'The almost total identification of the Religious Right with the new Republican majority in Washington is a dangerous liaison of religion with political power,' they said. 'We testify that there are other visions of faith and politics in the land.'

Belief Has To Stay Free

"This is hardly the first time that religious leaders have ventured controversially into the political breach. They were prominent (on both sides) in the battle over slavery, and in the civil-rights movement. But this time religious values are themselves at the heart of the argument. The argument threatens to be extremely divisive, in the country generally and in the Republican Party in particular. If the Christian right pushes its luck too far, it could lead to a schism in the Republican coalition. Ironically, the rise of religious conservatism may turn out to be as much of a challenge for the Republicans as it has already proved to be for the Democrats.

"The culture of belief is thriving in America, without the help of school prayer. The people who worry aloud about the country's shortage of moral values are part of the process that will probably ensure that the culture continues to thrive. Unless, that is, they go too far and attempt to impose rules based on a certain set of beliefs on everyone. Then the culture of belief clashes with another culture that runs even deeper in America: the culture of freedom." The Economist, July 8th, 1995.

In the past when the "culture of belief" clashed with the "culture of freedom", freedom has emerged victorious though not without intense struggles. In the future freedom will not be so successful. As crime, lawlessness, natural disasters and nasty economic surprises occur, fear rather than reason will control the minds of the people. Then, the idea that America must enforce Christianity by civil law will be much more acceptable.

We have already seen that in every generation of American history there have been religionists who adamantly asserted that the rapid decline in morals was attributable to the desecration of Sunday. As fear tightens its hold on the minds of the people they will eventually be persuaded that the enforcement of Sunday observance by the civil law will greatly improve the morals of American society.

Having passed a National Sunday law America will claim that this moral renewal gives her the right to lead the nations of the world into the new economic religio-political world order in preparation for the coming kingdom of God.

Organizations like the Christian Coalition and the Christian Right will play an important role in persuading the millions of American citizens that without the civil enforcement of strict Sunday laws there can be no improvement in the morals or the socio-economic health of America. A "morally-renewed" America will then do what no other nation can, that is, lead the other nations by persuasion or economic pressure to follow her example in enforcing Sunday worship and rest by law, internationally.

The enforcement of Sunday rest and Sunday worship will be the first step in establishing the new world economic religio-political order.

Doubly UnProtestant

FOR PROTESTANT CHURCHES TO ENFORCE any religious belief or practice by the civil law would be a violation of one of the fundamental tenets of Protestantism and would therefore be unProtestant. This fact has already been clearly established in the previous chapters of this book.

Protestants believe and teach that the only obedience acceptable to God is obedience motivated by love and freely and voluntarily given by virtue of the believer's faith in God. Therefore, to enforce a religious duty by the civil law would only be to compel unbelievers to obey legalistically and without any genuine faith at all. Such a legalistic obedience would not only be unacceptable to God but it would actually be sinful because, according to Romans 14:23, "whatsoever is not of faith is sin."

The reader will remember that the sixteenth century Protestant Reformation opposed "two abuses of man in matters of faith: the first in 'the intrusion of the civil magistrate', and the second, 'the arbitrary authority of the church.' Instead of these abuses, Protestantism sets the power of the conscience above the magistrate, and the authority of the word of God above the visible church. In the first place, it rejects the civil power in divine things, and says with the prophets and apostles, 'we must obey God rather than men'." D'Aubigné, b. 13, ch. 6.

Similarly, in the eighteenth century "the Framers of the American Constitution recognized the eternal principle that man's relation with God is above human legislation, and his rights of conscience inalienable. Reasoning was not necessary to establish this truth; we are conscious of it in our own bosoms. It is this consciousness which, in defiance of human laws, has sustained so many martyrs in tortures and flames. They felt that their duty to God was superior to human enactments, and that man could exercise no authority over their consciences. It is an inborn principle which nothing can eradicate." Congressional Documents (USA) No. 200, Document No. 271.

Therefore, the enforcement of Sunday rest and Sunday worship by the civil law would most definitely be unProtestant and unchristian. But not only would the civil enforcement of Sunday rest be unProtestant, the very Sunday that Protestants keep is, according to the Roman Catholic Church, also unProtestant.

It is a fundamental principle of true Protestantism that the Bible and the Bible alone is the only infallible guide and teacher of the Church and that every doctrine must be established clearly and honestly from the Bible. The Roman Catholic Church declares emphatically that Protestants who keep Sunday as a day of rest and worship are not following the Bible. Rather, they are acknowledging the authority of the Roman Catholic Church because Sunday worship was introduced and progressively developed by the Roman Church and not by scriptural authority.

The following review of Roman Catholic publications on the origin and significance of Sunday observance is indeed revealing.

The Catechismus Romanus was commanded by the Council of Trent and published by the Vatican Press, by order of Pope Pius V, in 1566. This catechism for priests says: "It pleased the church of God, that the religious celebration of the Sabbath day should be transferred to 'the Lord's day.' — Catechism of the Council of Trent (Donovan's translation, 1867), part 3, chap. 4, p. 345. The same, in slightly different wording, is in the McHugh and Callan translation (1937 ed.), p. 402:

> "Q: How prove you that the church hath power to command feasts and holydays?
>
> "A: By the very act of changing the Sabbath into Sunday, which Protestants allow of; and therefore they fondly contradict themselves, by keeping Sunday strictly, and breaking most other feasts commanded by the same Church." — Henry Tuberville, *An Abridgement of the Christian Doctrine.* (1833 approbation), p. 58. (Same statement in *Manual of Christian Doctrine*, ed. by Daniel Ferris [1916 ed.], p. 67)

"Q: Which is the Sabbath day?

"A: Saturday is the Sabbath day.

"Q: Why do we observe Sunday instead of Saturday?

"A: We observe Sunday instead of Saturday because the Catholic church transferred the solemnity from Saturday to Sunday."— Peter Geiermann, The Convert's Catechism of Catholic Doctrine (1946 ed.), p. 50. *Geiermann received the 'apostolic blessing' of Pope Pius X on his labors, Jan. 25, 1910.*

"For ages all Christian nations looked to the Catholic Church, and, as we have seen, the various states enforced by law her ordinances as to worship and cessation of Labor on Sunday. Protestantism, in discarding the authority of the church, has no good reason for its Sunday theory, and ought logically, to keep Saturday as the Sabbath.'

"The State, in passing laws for the due Sanctification of Sunday, is unwittingly acknowledging the authority of the Catholic Church and carrying out more or less faithfully its prescriptions.

"The Sunday, as a day of the week set apart for the obligatory public worship of Almighty God, to be sanctified by a suspension of all servile labor, trade, and worldly avocations and by exercises of devotion, *is purely a creation of the Catholic Church.*"—*The American Catholic Quarterly Review*, January, 1883, pp. 152, 139.

"Nowhere in the Bible is it stated that worship should be changed from Saturday to Sunday. The fact is that the Church was in existence for several centuries before the Bible was given to the world. The Church made the Bible, the Bible did not make the Church.

"Now the Church...instituted by God's authority, Sunday as the day of worship. This same Church, by the same divine authority, taught the doctrine of Purgatory long before the Bible was made. We have, therefore, the same authority for Purgatory as we have for Sunday." Martin J. Scott, Things Catholics Are Asked About (1927 ed.), p. 136.

Cardinal Gibbons, who for many years was the only cardinal and highest authority for the Catholic church in America, in his book, *Faith of Our Fathers*, edition of 1917, pages 72, 73, says:

"You may read the Bible from Genesis to Revelation, and you will not find a single line authorizing the sanctification of Sunday. The Scriptures enforce the religious observance of Saturday, a day which we never sanctify."

We will give just a few more quotations form Catholic authority on this point, although many more could be given. This time we quote from *The Catholic Mirror*, Cardinal Gibbons' official organ, published in the city of Baltimore, in its issue of September 23, 1893:

"The Catholic Church, for over one thousand years before the existence of a Protestant, by virtue of her divine mission, changed the day from Saturday to Sunday . . . .The Christian Sabbath is therefore *to this day* the acknowledged offspring of the Catholic Church as spouse of the Holy Ghost, without a word of remonstrance from the Protestant world."

Also from the issue of September 9, 1893, we take the following:

"Thus, it is impossible to find in the New Testament the slightest interference by the Saviour or His apostles with the original Sabbath, but on the contrary, an entire acquiescence in the original arrangement; nay, a *plenary endorsement* by Him, whilst living; and an unvaried, active participation *in the keeping of that day and no other by the apostles*, for thirty years after His death, as the Acts of the Apostles has abundantly testified to us.

"Hence the conclusion is inevitable; viz. that of those who follow the Bible as their guide, the Israelites and Seventh-day Adventists have the exclusive weight of evidence on their side, whilst the Biblical Protestant has not a word in self-defense for his substitution of Sunday for Saturday."

Again, from the issue of September 23, 1893:

"The most glaring contradiction, involving a deliberate sacrilegious rejection of a most positive precept, is presented to us today in the action of the Biblical Christian world. The Bible and the Sabbath constitute the watchword of Protestantism; but we have demonstrated that it is the *Bible against their Sabbath*. We have shown that no greater contradiction ever existed than their theory and practice. We have proved that neither their Biblical ancestors nor themselves have ever kept one Sabbath in their lives. The Israelites and Seventh-day Adventists are witnesses of their weekly desecration of the day named by God so repeatedly, and whilst they have ignored and condemned their teacher, the Bible, they have adopted a day kept by the Catholic Church.

"What Protestant can, after perusing these articles, with a clear conscience continue to disobey the command of God, enjoining *Saturday to be kept*, which command, his teacher, the Bible, from Genesis to Revelation, records as the will of God? The history of the world cannot present a more stupid, self-stultifying specimen of dereliction of principle than this. The teacher demands emphatically in every page that the law of the Sabbath be observed every week by all recognizing it as 'the only infallible teacher,' whilst the disciples of that teacher have not once, for over three hundred years, observed the divine precept! That immense concourse of Biblical Christians, the Methodists, have declared that the Sabbath has never been abrogated, whilst the followers of the Church of England, together with her daughter, the Episcopal Church of the United States, are committed by the 20th Article of Religion, already quoted, to the ordinance that the church cannot lawfully ordain anything 'contrary to God's written word.' God's written word enjoins His worship to be observed on *Saturday* absolutely, repeatedly, and most emphatically, with a most positive threat of death to him who disobeys. All the Biblical sects occupy the same self-stultifying position which no explanation can modify, much less notify."

So, according to the Roman Catholic Church the observance of Sunday as the Christian sabbath by Protestants is unProtestant because it is unscriptural. Moreover, the Protestant enforcement of Sunday as the Christian sabbath through the civil law is also unProtestant because it violates the fundamental Protestant principle of liberty of conscience.

Therefore, the Protestant enforcement of Sunday rest by the civil law would be doubly unProtestant! In the next chapter, we will answer the question: Is the Roman Catholic charge against Protestants valid?

Is The Charge Valid?

*I*N OUR LAST CHAPTER WE EXAMINED the Roman Catholic charge against Protestant Sunday keeping. The Papacy has consistently argued that if Protestants adhered to the principle of sola scriptura (the Bible alone) they would keep the seventh-day sabbath because there is no scriptural basis for Sunday keeping. Let us see if this Roman Catholic charge against Protestants is true.

Suppose we could find an individual who had no previous religious bias and who was a lover of honest, objective research, and suppose that he was given the Bible as his only source book and asked to determine from the Bible alone which day is the Christian Sabbath. What answer do you think he would come up with?

There is no disagreement among Christians that during the Old Testament era the seventh day was the Sabbath of the Lord.

When we come to the New Testament, however, most Christian people believe that the ancient Sabbath ceases, and that it is superseded by another day. We need to study the New Testament carefully to find out whether this is so or not.

We inquire, What day did Christ and the apostles observe as the Sabbath? Their custom and teaching on this question should put an end to all controversy, and should be followed by all Christians today. The Sabbath is mentioned at least sixty-four times in the New Testament, and in every instance it refers to the seventh day, with no intimation whatever that it had ceased to be of binding obligation. Christ, during

His earthly life, sacredly observed the seventh day, and taught His followers to do the same.

> *"He came to Nazareth, where he had been brought up: and as his custom was, he went into the synagogue on the Sabbath day, and stood up for to read." "He...came down to Capernaum, a city of Galilee, and taught them on the Sabbath days" (Luke 4: 16, 30, 31).*

As this was His *"custom,"* it follows that the Sabbath day found Him habitually in the synagogue, engaged in divine worship. He ever upheld the Sabbath and the Sabbath law. Concerning the law of God, of which the Sabbath commandment is a part, He said:

> *"Verily I say unto you, Till heaven and earth pass, one jot or one tittle shall in no wise pass from the law, till all be fulfilled." (Matthew 5:18).*

And to those who would tamper with any part of this law, He gives the following warning:

> *"Whosoever therefore shall break one of these least commandments, and shall teach men so, he shall be called the least in the kingdom of heaven: but whosoever shall do and teach them, the same shall be called great in the kingdom of heaven." (verse 19).*

There are many who contend that Christ kept the Sabbath because He lived under the old law, and that He observed all the ceremonial ordinances until, by His death, He nailed them to the cross. Such persons, of course, include the Sabbath among the ceremonial ordinances. And then they ask with an air of triumph, "Where are Christians commanded in the New Testament to keep the seventh-day Sabbath after the cross?"

There is a statement which is equivalent to a command given by Christ Himself, and to Christians too. It is this:

> *"Pray ye that your flight be not in the winter, neither on the Sabbath day." (Matthew 24:20).*

In these words Christ identifies the day that would still be the Sabbath forty years after His resurrection. His statement, therefore, virtually constitutes a command. By reading all that has gone before in this twenty-fourth chapter of Matthew, it will be seen that He was foretelling the destruction of the Temple at Jerusalem, when that city should fall into the hands of the Romans; which it did, according to history, in A.D. 70—forty years after the time He made this prediction. Christ, being able to foretell this destruction, and that there would not be left standing one stone upon another in that magnificent building (Matthew 24:2), was equally able to know the exact time it would occur. He knew it would be forty years from the time He was speaking; and knowing this, He instructed His followers (Christians) as if there were no more question about which day would be the Sabbath than which season would be winter.

What stronger evidence could be asked for by anyone desirous of doing the Lord's will than these words of Christ regarding the continuance of the Sabbath in the Christian Era? We thus have both the example and the precept of Christ in this matter.

Christ kept the Sabbath perfectly, because it was part of God's required law, the transgression of which is sin. He did this that He might have the righteousness of perfect Sabbathkeeping to substitute for man's Sabbath-breaking.

Christ never kept Sunday, the first day of the of week, as the Sabbath, nor did He command anyone else to do so; and it follows that it is no sin to labor on the first day of the week. If it were, Christ, having never kept it, would not have the righteousness of Sunday-keeping to substitute for Sunday-breaking. All this proves that the Lord knew that the keeping of the first day of the week would never be a requirement of God upon His children, or He Himself would have set the example and clearly instructed His followers concerning the same; but we have no record in the Gospels anywhere that He ever made mention of the first day of the week.

Since Christ is our example in all things pertaining to righteousness and the Christian life, there is no principle of righteousness required of Christians today that He Himself did not perform. Is it reasonable to believe that if the Lord contemplated a change in the day that should be observed by Christians, He would have maintained absolute silence on so important a matter? And yet He closed His earthly ministry, finished the work of redemption, and ascended to heaven, without giving one scintilla of instruction regarding any other day to be observed than that commanded in the law given on Sinai, which is the seventh day.

The Apostles Kept The Sabbath

Let us now consider the apostles, and find out what their custom and teaching was concerning the Sabbath. Of all the apostles, perhaps none occupied so prominent a place in labors and in the number of epistles written as the apostle Paul, and concerning his custom we read:

> *"Now when they had passed through Amphipolis and Apollonia, they came to Thessalonica, where was a synagogue of the Jews: and Paul, as his manner was, went in unto them, and three sabbath days reasoned with them out of the scriptures" (Acts 17: 1, 2).*

Of Paul in Corinth, where he labored a year and six months, teaching the word of God among the people, it is said:

> *"He reasoned in the synagogue every sabbath, and persuaded the Jews and the Greeks (Acts 18:4).*

Also at Antioch and Philippi he observed the Sabbath, and taught in the synagogues on that day (Acts 13:14; 16:12, 13), Being a tentmaker, Paul labored at his trade during the working days of the week, and these included Sunday, the first day; but the Sabbath day he strictly observed, and was always found at some place of worship, preaching and teaching the Word of God. In practically all the cities where the apostle preached, he raised up Christian churches from among Jews and Gentiles. Most of his epistles were addressed to these churches he had raised up and organized, but in not a single instance does he ever make reference to the first day of the week as being a day that should be observed by Christians as a holy day.

Gentile Sabbathkeepers

It is argued by those who claim that since the resurrection the first day of the week is the day to be observed by Christians, that Paul went to the synagogues on the Sabbath simply because he would there have an opportunity to preach the gospel to the Jews, but that the Gentile Christians observed the first day of the week as the Sabbath. This claim is disproved by the fact that when Paul was at Antioch, he preached the gospel in the synagogue on the Sabbath.

"When the Jews were gone out of the synagogue, the Gentiles besought that these words might be preached to them the next sabbath" (Acts 13:42).

Many of these Gentiles were evidently Christians, for Paul, speaking to them, "persuaded them to continue in the grace of God" (verse 43).

If the foregoing contention in behalf of the first day of the week were true, then these Gentiles would have requested Paul to preach to *them* the next day, which would be the first day of the week. And if Paul was an observer of the first day of the week, he would have said to these Gentiles, "Now we as Christians, since the resurrection of Christ, observe the first day of the week. Why wait until the next Sabbath? I will come and preach to you Gentiles tomorrow."

But no such word was spoken by either Paul or the Gentiles, but they waited until the next Sabbath, and the 44th verse says: *"And the next sabbath day came almost the whole city together to hear the word of God."*

Let us notice further what Paul himself says concerning the things he taught to both Jews ad Gentiles. When he made his defense before Felix, he said:

"This I confess unto thee, that after the way which they call heresy, so worship I the God of my fathers, believing all things which 'are written in the law and in the prophets."(Acts 24:14).

Before Festus he testified that he had offended in nothing "against the law of the Jews" (Acts 25:8).

Before Agrippa he testified that in preaching to both small and great he had taught *"none other things than those which the prophets and Moses did say should come." (Acts 26:22).*

The observance of the Sabbath was one of the things that the Jews of Paul's day most tenaciously contended for; and if the apostle had taught that the Sabbath was no longer binding and that the first day of the week should be observed in its place, the Jews surely would have brought this as a strong accusation against him. The fact that they did not proves that Paul never taught even the Gentile Christians to observe any other day than the original Sabbath.

Weekly And Ceremonial Sabbaths

But someone says: "Did not Paul positively declare in Colossians 2:14-16 that Christ blotted out the 'handwriting of ordinances,' taking it out of the way, nailing it to the cross, and that no man thereafter was to judge them in meat, or in drink, or in respect of a holy day, or of the new moon, or of the sabbath days?"

Paul did make such a statement in Colossians, but in speaking of the sabbath days (plural), he made no reference to the weekly Sabbath, but to those days which were set apart for the performance of certain ceremonies under the Levitical law, and which were called "sabbath days" simply because the people were commanded to do no work on those particular days. These ceremonial sabbaths, which Paul says were nailed to the cross, are spoken of in Leviticus 23. The 24th verse says: *"Speak unto the children of Israel, saying, In the seventh month, in the first day of the month, shall ye have a sabbath, a memorial of blowing of trumpets, a holy convocation."*

Also in the 27th and the 32nd verses, other days are spoken of as ceremonial sabbaths. Then to show the distinction between these and the regular weekly Sabbath, the Lord plainly states in the 38th verse that these were all *"besides the sabbaths of the Lord."*

There is further proof that the apostle Paul referred to these ceremonial sabbaths, and not the regular weekly Sabbath, in Colossians 2:17, when he says that these *"are a shadow of things to come."*

Types and shadows came into existence as a result of sin, but the Sabbath was instituted at creation before sin entered; therefore it cannot be included among the types and shadows referred to by Paul. These ceremonial sabbaths, which were shadows of things to come, pointed forward to Christ; but the seventh-day Sabbath points backward to creation. The Sabbath primarily is not a type or shadow of something to come; it is a memorial of an event that is past. So Paul is perfectly consistent in what he says in Colossians concerning the sabbath days which were a part of the handwriting of ordinances and which were nailed to the cross, and also in his example and teaching concerning the Sabbath commandment. Paul clearly understood the difference between ceremonial shadows and the ten commandment moral law. He wrote to the Corinthians thus: "Circumcision is nothing, and uncircumcision is nothing, but the keeping of the commandments of God." 1 Cor 7:19.

We have referred to Paul and his writings in particular because he was an apostle especially to the Gentiles. So if the contention that the Gentile Christians of apostolic times observed a different day than that enjoined in the fourth commandment had any foundation whatever, Paul would have most likely said something about it. But not only is Paul silent on this point, but the entire New Testament contains no command or instruction, either from Christ or from any of His apostles, for the transfer of the day of worship from the seventh to the first day of the week.

Sunday Has No Claim To Holiness

To prove further the truthfulness of this statement, since the majority of professed Christians today observe the first day of the week as the Sabbath, we will notice every text in the New Testament where the first day of the week is mentioned. By so doing there will be no possible chance for any scriptural evidence for Sunday sacredness to escape us. This will not be a long and difficult task, because the first day of the week is mentioned only eight times in the entire New Testament. The complete list follows:

- Matthew 28:1: *"In the end of the sabbath, as it began to dawn toward the first day of the week, came Mary Magdalene and the other Mary to see the sepulchre."*
- Mark 16:2: *"And very early in the morning the first day of the week, they came unto the sepulchre at the rising of the sun."*
- Mark 16:9: *"Now when Jesus was risen early the first day of the week, he appeared first to Mary Magdalene, out of whom he had cast seven devils."*
- Luke 24:1: *"Now upon the first day of the week, very early in the morning, they came unto the sepulchre, bringing the spices which they had prepared, and certain others with them."*
- John 20:1: *"The first day of the week cometh Mary Magdalene early, when it was yet dark, unto the sepulchre, and seeth the stone taken away from the sepulchre."*
- John 20:19: *"Then the same day at evening, being the first day of the week, when the doors were shut where the disciples were assembled for fear of the Jews, came Jesus and stood in the midst, and saith unto them, Peace be unto you."*
- Acts 20:7: *"And upon the first day of the week, when the disciples came together to break bread, Paul preached unto them, ready to depart on the morrow; and continued his speech until midnight."*
- 1 Corinthians 16:2: *"Upon the first day of the week let every one of you lay by him in store, as God hath prospered him, that there be no gatherings when I come."*

The first five of these texts, as will be seen, merely state the fact that it was on the first day of the week that Christ rose from the dead. Surely there is no evidence here for Sunday observance. The sixth text, John 20:19, cannot possibly be construed to refer to a religious meeting. The text says "the disciples were assembled for fear of the Jews," and not to observe the day in honor of Christ's resurrection. The false rumor had been started by their enemies, that the disciples had stolen the body of Jesus while the guards at the tomb had slept. It was true that Jesus was no longer in the tomb, and the Roman seal with which it had been sealed had been broken. The penalty for breaking this seal might be death, and this was charged against the disciples; so for "fear" they had gone to their own place of abode, and had locked the doors. Furthermore, the disciples did not believe at this time that Jesus had risen from the dead.

> *"Now when Jesus was risen early the first day of the week, he appeared first to Mary Magdalene, out of whom he had cast seven devils. And she went and told them that had been with him, as they mourned and wept. And they, when they had heard that he was alive, and had been seen of her, believed not. After that He appeared in another form unto two of them, as they walked, and went into the country. And they went and told it unto the residue: neither believed they them. Afterward he appeared unto the eleven as they sat at meat, and upbraided them with their unbelief and hardness of heart, because they believed not them which had seen him after he was risen"* (Mark 16:9-14).

This all occurred on the very day on which Christ rose from the dead. How, then, could they be celebrating this day in honor of His resurrection, when they did not believe that He had been raised from the dead? There is positively no evidence here for Sunday sacredness.

Paul's Use Of Sunday

The seventh text mentioning the first day of the week is found in Acts 20:7. We now have before us the only record within the entire New Testament of a religious meeting held on the first day of the week. Upon examination of the text itself and the context, it will be seen that this meeting was not held upon the first day of the week because any sacredness was attached to it by those who held it, but because of the circumstances connected with the occasion. At this meeting, which was held at Troas, Paul preached to the people, *"and continued his speech until midnight. And there were many lights in the upper chamber."* (Acts 20:7, 8).

By this it will be seen that this was a night meeting. It was, therefore, held during the night, or dark part, of the first day of the week, which corresponds to our Saturday night, as the dark part of each day comes first, according to the Bible reckoning of the days of the week, one day ending at sunset and the next day beginning at that point.

"The evening and the morning were the first day." Gen. 1:5.

"From even unto even, shall ye celebrate your sabbath." (Leviticus 23:32).

The Jews, as well as Christ and the apostles, reckoned sunset as the ending of one day and the beginning of another.

"At even, when the sun did set, they brought unto him all that were diseased." (Mark 1:32).

They waited until the Sabbath was past at sundown before bringing their sick to be healed; therefore, the Sabbath ends at sundown Saturday evening, and the first day begins. This meeting at Troas, then, was held on our Saturday night, and lasted until Sunday morning. The occasion of this particular meeting was this:

The apostle Paul was on his way to Jerusalem, after having visited many of the churches, which he had raised up throughout Macedonia and Asia. The Spirit of the Lord had made it plain to Paul that at Jerusalem bonds and afflictions awaited him, and he knew that it would not be his privilege to meet with these believers again, that he would never again see their faces. (Read Acts 20:23, 37, 38.) Naturally, he had many things to say to them, and as a final and fitting farewell he desired to break bread with them; after which they all wept sore, and fell on Paul's neck and kissed him and said good-by, sorrowing most of all for the words he had spoken to them, that they would see his face no more (Acts 21:13, 14).

That the apostle and these early Christians did not regard this first day of the week as holy, is clearly seen from two facts:

First, while Paul was preaching and breaking bread with the disciples at Troas, the other disciples were sailing the ship, which was doubtless a laborious task, around the promontory from Troas to Assos, a distance of about thirty-four miles. This is something they certainly would not have done if they had regarded the day as the Christian Sabbath. (Read Acts 20:13, 14.)

Second, at break of day, which would be the beginning of the light part of the first day of the week, or Sunday morning, Paul himself started on foot on a journey of nineteen miles by land to Assos; which proves that he did not regard the day with the least degree of sacredness, as such a journey would not comport with his idea and custom of Sabbathkeeping. Therefore, there is no evidence in this text for Sunday observance.

An Individual, Not A Congregational, Service

Our next and last text mentioning the first day of the week is in I Corinthians 16:1,2.

> *"Now concerning the collection for the saints, as I have given order to the churches of Galatia, even so do ye. Upon the first day of the week let every one of you lay by him in store, as God hath prospered him, that there be no gatherings when I come."*

It is held by Sunday observers that the churches were accustomed to meet for divine worship on the first day of the week, and that Paul instructed them to take up a public collection at these meetings for the poor saints at Jerusalem; but they assume that which the text does not teach. This scripture gives no such instruction. A regular weekly meeting is not even hinted at, and instead of a public collection, each one was to "lay by him in store"; and many translations of the passage render it "by himself at home." Where was it to be laid by? "By him in store," not placed in the collection basket. There is no proof here whatever that the day was or should be observed as the Sabbath. With this text dies the last hope for evidence of Sunday sacredness in the New Testament.

The Seventh Day Is The Lord's Day

There is one other text, however, which firstday observers use in support of their claim, although it does not mention the first day of the week, and we will notice it for a moment. It is found in Revelation 1:10, where John the revelator says:

> *"I was in the Spirit on the Lord's day, and heard behind me a great voice, as of a trumpet."*

It is claimed that Sunday should more properly be called the Lord's day instead of the Sabbath, and that it was to the first day of the week that John referred in his expression, "Lord's day." But is this so? Did he refer to the first day of the week? This text certainly does not say so. You will have to go to some other scripture than Revelation 1:10 to find out which day is the Lord's day; and the Bible unmistakably points out the day, and the only day, to which such a term as "Lord's day" could apply. In Mark 2:28 Christ says:

> *"The Son of man is Lord also of the sabbath."*

Now if Christ is Lord of the Sabbath day, then candidly, what day is the "Lord's day"? There can be but one answer—The Sabbath.
Again the Lord, through the prophet Isaiah, speaks these words:

> *"If thou turn away thy foot from the sabbath, from doing thy pleasure on my holy day; and call the sabbath a delight, the holy of the Lord, honorable,"* etc. (Isaiah 58:13).

What day does the Lord here call His holy day?—the Sabbath. Then if the Lord calls the Sabbath His holy day, what day is the Lord's day? Again the answer is, The Sabbath, the seventh day of the week. Therefore Revelation 1:10 only proves that the beloved disciple John, banished to the lonely isle of Patmos, almost seventy-five years after the cross, was still a faithful observer of God's holy Sabbath, the seventh day of the week.

Who Changed The Sabbath?

Our study thus far has disclosed the fact that from Genesis to Revelation there is but one Sabbath day brought to view, and that is the seventh day of the week. In not a single place within the covers of the Bible is there one command for the observance of Sunday, the first day of the week. The word "Sunday" is not found in the Bible. Neither is there a particle of evidence to be found, from the first verse of the first chapter of Matthew to the last verse of the last chapter of Revelation, that the first day of the week was regarded as sacred or observed as the Christian Sabbath by the apostles or the early Christians during the time covered by the New Testament record. Someone will ask, "How then has this change come about? If neither Christ nor His apostles transferred the Sabbath from the seventh to the first day of the week, who is responsible?" This is a very natural question, and the Bible furnishes the answer. This phase of the Sabbath question (the attempted change) is a subject of prophecy.

More than five hundred years before the Christian Era, through the prophet Daniel, the Lord foretold a power that should arise that would "think to change" the "times and laws" of God.

It will not be difficult to make the application of the prophecy, for the power thus charged by the high tribunal of God's unalterable Word pleads guilty to the indictment. This prophecy is found in the seventh chapter of the book of Daniel. As recorded in this chapter, Daniel had a vision, in which he saw four great beasts come up from the sea, diverse one from the other. The fourth was a nondescript beast, a monster unlike anything in the animal kingdom, and upon its head were ten horns. Afterward another horn came up, and in order to establish itself, uprooted three of the first horns.

When Daniel sought for a meaning of this vision, an angel appeared and made known to him the interpretation.

Said the angel:

> *"These great beasts, which are four, are four kings, which shall arise out of the earth" (Daniel 7:17).*

These beasts of Daniel's vision were symbols of earthly governments. The interpretation continues:

> *"Thus he said, The fourth beast shall be the fourth kingdom upon earth, which shall be diverse from all kingdoms, and shall devour the whole earth, and shall tread it down, and break it in pieces." (verse 23).*

Every student of history knows that Rome was the fourth great universal empire, (168 B.C. - 476 A.D.), Babylon, Medio-Persia, and Greece being the first three.

> *"And the ten horns out of this kingdom are ten kings that shall arise." (verse 24).*

History also tells us that when the great Roman Empire fell, ten divisions, or kingdoms, sprang up in its territory. The three horns plucked up by the little horn that arose afterward were the Vandals, the Heruli, and the Ostrogoths.

The Change A Subject Of Prophecy

Concerning this little horn, the angel giving the interpretation said:

> *"He shall speak great words against the most High, and shall wear out the saints of the most High, and think to change times and laws: and they shall be given into his hand until a time and times and the dividing of time" (verse 25).*

We have now to inquire, What power arose on the territory of the Roman Empire, that subdued three other powers in order to establish itself; that has spoken great words against the Most High, and that has worn out the saints of the Most High? History, which shows the fulfillment of prophecy, answers that there has been but one power that has fulfilled the work this little horn was to do, and that power is the papacy, or the Roman Catholic Church. It was this power before whom the three Arian kingdoms—the Vandals, the Heruli, and the Ostrogoths—fell, for the reason that these powers believed and held to the doctrines of a certain teacher named Arius, and they stood in the way of the exaltation of the Bishop of Rome to the place of Pontifex Maximus, and denied the arrogant claims made for him. Therefore, before the papacy could be fully and securely established, these opponents had to be removed, and this was accomplished, by A.D. 534, A.D. 493 and A.D. 538, respectively.

Has that power spoken great words against the Most High? It most assuredly has, in the blasphemous titles that have been given to the pope. He has been proclaimed "infallible," and has been termed the "vicar of Christ," another "God on earth," the "ruler of the universe." It is claimed that he has power "to forgive sins" and to "dispense with the very laws of Christ." What more swelling words than these could be spoken against the Most High by mortal man?

Did the papacy "wear out the saints of the most High"? Let history answer. Call the roll of the long Dark Ages when the fires of the Inquisition, the rack, and the gibbet sent to their death the noblest and purest of God's saints, and spread desolation over the fairest portions of earth. The blood of between fifty and one hundred millions of martyrs cries out the answer to the prophecy in the affirmative.

A Frank Confession Of Guilt

Has the Roman Catholic Church tampered with the times and laws of God? We will let her answer for herself. The law of God is summarily contained in the Ten Commandments. The Roman Church has laid impious hands upon the fourth commandment, and substituted the observance of Sunday, the first day of the week, for the observance of the Sabbath, the seventh day, which the fourth commandment strictly enjoins. In this matter the Catholic Church claims sole responsibility for the change, and points to it, as the mark of her ecclesiastical authority. Read the following questions and answers quoted from *The Convert's Catechism of Catholic Doctrine,* by Rev. Peter Geiermann, C. SS. R., published by B. Herder, of St. Louis, Missouri, 1910, pages 49, 50.

(For those who do not know, the Papacy has a shorter version of the original Ten Commandments. The original second commandment has been left out and original third is called the second. Thus the original fourth commandment is call the third.)

> "Q: What is the third commandment?
> "A: The third commandment is: Remember that thou keep holy the Sabbath day.
> "Q: Which is the Sabbath day?
> "A: Saturday is the Sabbath day.
> "Q: Why do we observe Sunday instead of Saturday?
> "A: We observe Sunday instead of Saturday because the Catholic Church, in the Council of Laodicea (A.D. 336), transferred the solemnity from Saturday to Sunday.
> "Q: Why did the Catholic Church substitute Sunday for Saturday?
> "A: The church substituted Sunday for Saturday, because Christ rose from the dead on a Sunday and the Holy Ghost descended upon the Apostles on a Sunday.
> "Q: By what authority did the church substitute Sunday for Saturday?'
> "A: The church substituted Sunday for Saturday by the plenitude of that divine power which Jesus Christ bestowed upon her."

Stand For God And Truth

The foregoing quotations constitute a most glaring confession on the part of the Catholic Church to the charge brought against her by the Word of God. And what a challenge this is to the Protestant who wants to be consistent with the name he bears! Thank God, there are still today faithful followers of the Lord Jesus Christ, who will not bow, in things religious, to the commands of any but their sovereign Lord. The Sabbath question constitutes one of the most serious issues before the Christian world today. This book may perchance fall into the hands of someone who up to this time has been in ignorance of the true Sabbath of God, and who, like the writer, for many years thought he was fulfilling the Word of God in keeping Sunday, the first day of the week. Let me appeal earnestly to all such, now that the light of this question has come, Will you not step over onto the side of God's truth? Unpopular though it may be now, it is sure to triumph at last.

The New Covenant

The faith of Jesus and the obedience of Jesus are of the utmost importance to us. The Bible gives us many reasons why the obedience of Christ is so important, let us consider three of them.

1. The obedience of Christ, the righteousness of Christ, justifies the believer in Christ and makes the believer righteous, we are told so in Romans 5:18,19.

   "Therefore *as* by the offence of one (Adam) judgment came upon *all* men to condemnation; even so by the righteousness of one (Christ) the free gift came upon *all* men unto justification of life. For *as* by one man's disobedience many were made sinners, so *by the obedience of one (Christ) shall many be made righteous.*" Romans 5:18,19.

2. The obedience of Christ is the *perfect example* which the believer *must* follow if he or she wishes to practice *the true* Christianity. We are told so in 1 Peter 2:21, "*For even here unto were ye called: because Christ also suffered for us, leaving us an example, that ye should follow His steps.*"

3. The obedience of Christ is lived out in the believer's life by the indwelling Christ through the Holy Spirit. We are told so in Ephesians 3:17 and Galatians 2:20, "*That Christ may dwell In your hearts by faith; that ye, being rooted and grounded in love, may be able to comprehend with all saints what is the breadth, and length, and depth and height; And to know the love of Christ, which passeth knowledge that ye might be filled with all the fullness of God.*" *Ephesians 3:17-19.*

   "*I am crucified with Christ: nevertheless I live; yet not I, but Christ liveth in me and the life which I now live in the flesh I live by the*

faith of the Son of God, who loved me, and gave himself for me."
Galatians 2:20.

All this brings us to a very important conclusion, and it is this: Any religious practice, popular though it be, which was not part of the obedience of Christ, cannot be any part of the true Christianity. Look around at the various denominations of Christianity in the world today and compare their religious practices with the life of Christ and His teachings. You will be surprised at the many popular religious practices which were not part of the obedience of Christ and therefore cannot be any part of the true Christianity.

Consider the matter of baptism. Christ and His disciples practiced baptism by immersion of believers who were old enough to understand, believe and choose the way of salvation through Christ. Nowhere in the New Testament do we find the slightest hint of baptism of babies by sprinkling or pouring. The practice of infant baptism, (by sprinkling or pouring or putting a little water on the infant's forehead) came from paganism and infiltrated Christianity in the period after the death of the Apostles.

The Apostle Paul had predicted a "falling away" of the early Christian church, read 2 Thessalonians, chapter 2. This "falling away" from the purity of New Testament truth occurred gradually at first, and then more rapidly, eventually resulting in the formation of the Papacy which controlled Europe during the Middle Ages.

Churches which teach non-scriptural practices usually claim that they were included into the New Covenant by the *early church fathers,* after the death of the Apostles. Such claims are untenable.

Jesus Christ established and confirmed the New Covenant or New Testament by His life and death. By His perfect obedience and His sacrificial death He became the author of eternal salvation for the lost race.

The Old Covenant was based upon the people's promises to obey by self-effort. The New Covenant was established upon better promises, the promises of God to forgive, cleanse, and make the believing sinner righteous. Read Hebrews 8:6-13.

In establishing the New Covenant, Jesus put into it all that was necessary for the salvation of mankind. During the three and a half year period between His baptism and death He confirmed the covenant and put in place the practices and ordinances which His church should afterward observe.

The Apostle Paul explained to the Galatians in Galatians 3:15 that after a covenant has been confirmed nothing can be added to, or, subtracted from it!

"Brethren, I speak after the manner of men; Though it be but a man's covenant, yet if it be confirmed, no man disannulleth, or addeth thereto."

Furthermore, Paul told the Hebrews, in Heb. 9:15-17, that the death of the Testator enforces the Covenant or Testament. And so we understand that the death of Christ confirmed, ratified and enforced the New Covenant. *Therefore nothing could be added after His death*! The very first thing Jesus did upon commencing His ministry was to be baptized by immersion in the river Jordan by John the Baptist. He therefore established baptism by immersion as the only true and right type of baptism for the Christian in the New Covenant.

"And for this cause he is the mediator of the new testament, that by means of death, for the redemption of the transgressions that were under the first testament, they which are called might receive the promise of eternal inheritance."

"For where a testament is, there must also of necessity be the death of the testator."

"For a testament is of force after men are dead: other wise it is of no strength at all while the testator liveth." Heb. 9:15-17.

In a similar way we can examine the question of the day of worship for Christians. Sunday keeping was progressively incorporated into Christian practice long after the death of Christ and His disciples. Christ kept the seventh-day sabbath (Luke 4:16, Mark 2:27,28). The disciples, after the death of Christ, kept the seventh-day sabbath. Read Luke 23:52 to 56 and Luke 24: 1; read also Acts 13:42-44; Acts 16:13; Hebrews 4:4,9,10; Matthew 24:20.

Since it is the obedience of Christ which justifies the sinner and establishes the New Covenant; and since Sunday sacredness was *not* part of the obedience of Christ, *then Sunday keeping cannot be part of the new covenant. And it could not have been rightfully added after Christ's death because nothing can be added to the covenant after the death of the testator!*

America In Prophecy

IN THE EARLY TO MIDDLE NINETEENTH CENTURY the fresh atmosphere of religious liberty in the USA encouraged Bible students to search the word of God for new light and clearer understanding of God's will.

During and after 1831 there developed an intense interest in the prophecies of Daniel and Revelation. The study of the prophecies of Daniel led many sincere Christians to believe that the period of history called the time of the end in Daniel 12 had arrived. American Christians of all denominations studied the prophecies with unprecedented zeal and earnestness of purpose. The longest time-prophecy in the Bible—the 2300 day prophecy of Daniel 8:13, 14—became the central prophetic theme. As a result of this study a great religious revival developed in the USA, reaching its highest intensity in the period 1840-1844.

But not only in the USA did this great religious awakening occur: history records that it was a worldwide phenomenon.

The historical account also reveals that many Christians at that time believed that the end of the 2300 day prophecy meant the end of the world. Using the day-year principle, (Numbers 14:34; Eze. 4:6), the 2300 prophetic days were interpreted to mean 2300 years. Bible students understood that the starting point for the prophetic period was 457 B.C. and therefore the end-point would have been 1844, October.

It took more advanced study to show that the termination of the 2300 years pointed to a change in the High Priestly ministration of Christ in Heaven. Clearer study led to the correct understanding that Jesus Christ, the New Covenant Christian High Priest, started the final phase of His High Priestly intercessory work for His people, a work which involves preparing them for His second coming. This advanced knowledge led to a study of the Old Testament sanctuary as a teaching model of the heavenly sanctuary. It was soon seen that just as the earthly sanctuary had two apartments and two ministrations, so too the heavenly sanctuary has two apartments and two ministrations as outlined in Hebrews 9.

In the earthly sanctuary the second apartment, or Most Holy Place, contained the Ten Commandment moral law of God deposited in the ark (or box) of the testament or covenant. (Hebrews 9:14).

Similarly, in the heavenly sanctuary in the Most Holy Place, there is the ark of the testament brought to view in Revelation 11:19.

The discovery of this truth led to a careful reappraisal of the Ten Commandment moral law of God. Those who examined these subjects saw that in the New Covenant the law of God is written in the believer's mind and established by faith (Hebrews 10:16; Romans 8:1-4; Romans 3:31).

God's Law Immutable

The temple of God was opened in heaven, and there was seen in His temple the ark of His testament." Revelation 11:19. The ark of God's testament is in the holy of holies, the second apartment of the sanctuary. In the ministration of the earthly tabernacle, which served "unto the example and shadow of heavenly things," this apartment was opened only upon the great Day of Atonement, (October 22 or the 10th day of the 7th Jewish month), for the cleansing of the sanctuary. Therefore the announcement that the temple of God was opened in heaven and the ark of His testament was seen, points to the opening of the most holy place of the heavenly sanctuary in 1844 as Christ entered there to perform the closing work of the atonement. Those who by faith followed their great High Priest as He entered upon His ministry in the most holy place, beheld the ark of His testament. As they had studied the subject of the sanctuary they had come to understand the Saviour's change of ministration, and they saw that He was now officiating before the ark of God, pleading His blood in behalf of sinners.

The ark in the tabernacle on earth contained the two tables of stone, upon which were inscribed the precepts of the law of God. The ark was merely a receptacle for the tables of the law, and the presence of these divine precepts gave to it its value and sacredness. When the temple of God was opened in heaven, the ark of His testament was seen. Within the holy of holies, in the sanctuary in heaven, the divine law is sacredly enshrined—the law that was spoken by God Himself amid the thunders of Sinai and written with His own finger on the tables of stone.

The law of God in the sanctuary in heaven is the great original, of which the precepts inscribed upon the tables of stone and recorded by Moses in the Pentateuch were an unerring transcript. Those who arrived at an understanding of this important point were thus led to see the sacred, unchanging character of the divine law. They saw, as never before, the force of the Saviour's words: *"Till heaven and earth pass, one jot or one tittle shall in no wise pass from the law."* Matthew 5:18. The law of God, being a revelation of His will, a transcript of His character, must forever endure, *"as a faithful witness in heaven."* Not one command has been annulled; not a jot or tittle has been changed. Says the psalmist: *"Forever, O Lord, Thy word is settled in heaven." "All His commandments are sure. They stand fast for ever and ever."* Psalms 119:89; 111:7, 8.

In the very bosom of the Decalogue is the fourth commandment, as it was first proclaimed: *"Remember the Sabbath day, to keep it holy. Six days shalt thou labor, and do all thy work: but the seventh day is the Sabbath of the Lord thy God: in it thou shalt not do any work, thou, nor thy son, nor thy daughter, thy manservant, nor thy maidservant, nor thy cattle, nor thy stranger that is within thy gates: for in six days the Lord made heaven and earth, the sea, and all that in them is, and rested the seventh day: wherefore the Lord blessed the Sabbath day, and hallowed it."* Exodus 20:8-11.

The Spirit of God impressed the hearts of those students of His word. The conviction was urged upon them that they had ignorantly transgressed this precept by disregarding the Creator's rest day. They began to examine the reasons for observing the first day of the week instead of the day which God had sanctified. They could find no evidence in the Scriptures that the fourth commandment had been abolished, or that the Sabbath had been changed; the blessing which first hallowed the seventh day had never been removed. They had been honestly seeking to know and to do God's will; now, as they saw themselves transgressors of His law, sorrow filled their hearts, and they manifested their loyalty to God by keeping His Sabbath holy.

Those who had accepted the light concerning the mediation of Christ and the perpetuity of the law of God found that these were the truths presented in Revelation 14:6-12. The messages of this chapter constitute a threefold warning which is to prepare the inhabitants of the earth for the Lord's second coming. The announcement, *"The hour of His judgment is come,"* points to the closing work of Christ's ministration for the salvation of men. It heralds a truth which must be proclaimed until the Saviour's intercession shall cease and He shall return to the earth to take His people to Himself. The work of judgment which began in 1844 must continue until the cases of all are decided, both of the living and the dead; hence it will extend to the close of human probation. That men may be prepared to stand in the judgment, the message commands them to *"fear God, and give glory to Him,"* *"and worship Him that made heaven, and earth, and the sea, and the fountains of waters."* The result of an acceptance of these messages is given in the word: *"Here are they that keep the commandments of God, and the faith of Jesus."* In order to be prepared for the judgment, it is necessary that men should keep the law of God. That law will be the standard of character in the judgment. The apostle Paul declares: *"As many as have sinned in the law shall be judged by the law, ... in the day when God shall judge the secrets of men by Jesus Christ."* And he says that *"the doers of the law shall be justified."* Romans 2:12-16. Faith is essential in order to the keeping of the law of God; for *"without faith it is impossible to please Him."* And *"whatsoever is not of faith is sin."* Hebrews 11:6; Romans 14:23.

By the first angel, men are called upon to *"fear God, and give glory to Him"* and to worship Him as the Creator of the heavens and the earth. In order to do this, they must obey His law. Says the wise man: *"Fear God, and keep His commandments: for this is the whole duty of man."* Ecclesiastes 12:13. Without obedience to His commandments no worship can be pleasing to God. *"This is the love of God, that we keep His commandments."* *"He that turneth away his ear from hearing the law, even his prayer shall be abomination."* 1 John 5:3; Proverbs 28:9.

The duty to worship God is based upon the fact that He is the Creator and that to Him all other beings owe their existence. And wherever, in the Bible, His claim to reverence and worship, above the gods of the heathen, is presented, there is cited the evidence of His creative power. *"All the gods of the nations are idols: but the Lord made the heavens."* Psalm 96:5. *"To whom then will ye liken Me, or shall I be equal? saith the Holy One. Lift up your eyes on high, and behold who hath created these things."* *"Thus saith the Lord that created the heavens; God Himself that formed the earth and made it: . . . I am the Lord; and there is none else."* Isaiah 40:25, 26; 45:18. Says the psalmist: *"Know ye that the Lord He is God: it is He that hath made us, and not we ourselves." "O come, let us worship and bow down: let us kneel before the Lord our Maker."* Psalms 100:3; 95:6. And the holy beings who worship God in heaven state, as the reason why their homage is due to Him: *"Thou art worthy, O Lord, to receive glory and honor and power: for Thou hast created all things."* Revelation 4:11.

In Revelation 14, men are called upon to worship the Creator; and the prophecy brings to view a class that, as the result of the threefold message, is keeping the commandments of God. One of these commandments points directly to God as the Creator. The fourth precept declares: *"The seventh day is the Sabbath of the Lord thy God: . . . for in six days the Lord made heaven and earth, the sea, and all that in them is, and rested the seventh day: wherefore the Lord blessed the Sabbath day, and hallowed it."* Exodus 20:10, 11. Concerning the Sabbath, the Lord says, further, that it is *"a sign, . . . that ye may know that I am the Lord your God."* Ezekiel 20:20. And the reason given is: *"For in six days the Lord made heaven and earth, and on the seventh day He rested, and was refreshed."* Exodus 31:17.

> "The importance of the Sabbath as the memorial of creation is that it keeps ever present the true reason why worship is due to God"—because He is the Creator, and we are His creatures. "The Sabbath therefore lies at the very foundation of divine worship, for it teaches this great truth in the most impressive manner, and no other institution does this. The true ground of divine worship, not of that on the seventh day merely, but of all worship, is found in the distinction between the Creator and His creatures. This great fact can never become obsolete, and must never be forgotten."—J. N. Andrews, History of the Sabbath, chapter 27.

It was to keep this truth ever before the minds of men, that God instituted the Sabbath in Eden; and so long as the fact that He is our Creator continues to be a reason why we should worship Him, so long the Sabbath will continue as its sign and memorial. Had the Sabbath been universally kept, man's thoughts and affections would have been led to the Creator as the object of reverence and worship, and there would never have been an idolater, an atheist, or an infidel. The keeping of the Sabbath is a sign of loyalty to the true God, "Him that made heaven, and earth, and the sea, and the fountains of waters." It follows that the message which commands men to worship God and keep His commandments will especially call upon them to keep the fourth commandment.

In contrast to those who keep the commandments of God and have the faith of Jesus, the third angel points to another class, against whose errors a solemn and fearful warning is uttered:

"If any man worship the beast and his image, and receive his mark in his forehead, or in his hand, the same shall drink of the wine of the wrath of God." Revelation 14:9, 10. A correct interpretation of the symbols employed is necessary to an understanding of this message. What is represented by the beast, the image, the mark?

Bible Prophecy Explains

The line of prophecy in which these symbols are found begins with Revelation 12, with the dragon that sought to destroy Christ at His birth. The dragon is said to be Satan (Revelation 12:9); he it was that moved upon Herod to put the Saviour to death. But the chief agent of Satan in making war upon Christ and His people during the first centuries of the Christian Era was the Roman Empire, in which paganism was the prevailing religion. Thus while the dragon, primarily, represents Satan, it is, in a secondary sense, a symbol of pagan Rome.

In chapter 13 (verses 1-10) is described another beast, *"like unto a leopard,"* to which the dragon gave *"his power, and his seat, and great authority."* This symbol, as most Protestants have believed, represents the papacy, which succeeded to the power and seat and authority once held by the ancient Roman empire. Of the leopardlike beast it is declared: *"There was given unto him a mouth speaking great things and blasphemies... And he opened his mouth in blasphemy against God, to blaspheme His name, and His tabernacle, and them that dwell in heaven. And it was given unto him to make war with the saints, and to overcome them: and power was given him over all kindreds, and tongues, and nations."* This prophecy, which is nearly identical with the description of the little horn of Daniel 7, unquestionably points to the papacy.

"Power was given unto him to continue forty and two months." And, says the prophet, *"I saw one of his heads as it were wounded to death."* And again: *"He that leadeth into captivity shall go into captivity: he that killeth with the sword must be killed with the sword."* The forty and two months are the same as the *"time and times and the dividing of time,"* three years and a half, or 1260 days, of Daniel 7—the time during which the papal power was to oppress God's people. This period, as stated in preceding chapters, began with the supremacy of the papacy, A.D. 538, and terminated in 1798. At that time the pope was made captive by the French army, the papal power received

its deadly wound, and the prediction was fulfilled, *"He that leadeth into captivity shall go into captivity."*

The Lamb-like Beast

At this point another symbol is introduced. Says the prophet: "I beheld another beast coming up out of the earth; and he had two horns like a lamb." Verse II. Both the appearance of this beast and the manner of its rise indicate that the nation which it represents is unlike those presented under the preceding symbols. The great kingdoms that have ruled the world were presented to the prophet Daniel as beasts of prey, rising when *"the four winds of the heaven strove upon the great sea."* Daniel 7:2. In Revelation 17 an angel explained that waters represent *"peoples, and multitudes, and nations, and tongues."* Revelation 17:15. Winds are a symbol of strife. Jeremiah 25:32; Revelation 7:1-4. The four winds of heaven striving upon the great sea represent the terrible scenes of conquest and revolution by which kingdoms have attained to power.

But the beast with lamblike horns was seen *"coming up out of the earth."* Instead of overthrowing other powers to establish itself, the nation thus represented must arise in territory previously unoccupied and grow up gradually and peacefully. It could not, then, arise among the crowded and struggling nationalities of the Old World—that turbulent sea of *"peoples, and multitudes, and nations, and tongues."* It must be sought in the Western Continent.

What nation of the New World was in 1798 rising into power, giving promise of strength and greatness, and attracting the attention of the world? The application of the symbol admits of no question. One nation, and only one, meets the specifications of this prophecy; it points unmistakably to the United States of America. Again and again the thought, almost the exact words, of the sacred writer has been unconsciously employed by the orator and the historian in describing the rise and growth of this nation. The beast was seen *"coming up out of the earth;"* and, according to the translators, the word here rendered *"coming up"* literally signifies *"to grow or spring up as a plant."* And, as we have seen, the nation must arise in territory previously unoccupied. A prominent writer, describing the rise of the United States, speaks of "the mystery of her coming forth from vacancy," and says: "Like a silent seed we grew into empire."— G. A. Townsend, The New World Compared With the Old, page 462. A European journal in 1850 spoke of the United States as a wonderful empire, which was "emerging," and "amid the silence of the earth daily adding to its power and pride."—*The Dublin Nation*. Edward Everett, in an oration on the Pilgrim founders of this nation, said:

"Did they look for a retired spot, inoffensive for its obscurity and safe in its remoteness, where the little church of Leyden might enjoy the freedom of conscience? Behold the mighty regions over which, in peaceful conquest, . . . they have borne the banners of the cross!"—Speech delivered at Plymouth, Massachusetts, Dec. 22, 1824, page 11.

"And he had two horns like a lamb." The lamblike horns indicate youth, innocence, and gentleness, fitly representing the character of the United States when presented to the prophet as "coming up" in 1798. Among the Christian exiles who first fled to America and sought an asylum from royal oppression and priestly intolerance were many who determined to establish a government upon the broad foundation of civil and religious liberty. Their views found place in the Declaration of Independence, which sets forth the great truth that "all men are created equal" and endowed with the inalienable right to "life, liberty, and the pursuit of happiness." And the Constitution guarantees to the people the right of self-government, providing that representatives elected by the popular vote shall enact and administer the laws. Freedom of religious faith was also granted, every man being permitted to worship God according to the dictates of his conscience. Republicanism and Protestantism became the fundamental principles of the nation. These principles are the secret of its power and prosperity. The oppressed and downtrodden throughout Christendom have turned to this land with interest and hope. Millions have sought its shores, and the United States has risen to a place among the most powerful nations of the earth.

But the beast with lamblike horns *"spake as a dragon. And he exerciseth all the power of the first beast before him, and causeth the earth and them which dwell therein to worship the first beast, whose deadly wound was healed; . . . saying to them that dwell on the earth, that they should make an image to the beast, which had the wound by a sword, and did live."* Revelation 13:11-14.

The lamblike horns and dragon voice of the symbol point to a striking contradiction between the professions and the practice of the nation thus represented. The "speaking" of the nation is the action of its legislative and judicial authorities. By such action it will give the lie to those liberal and peaceful principles which it has put forth as the foundation of its policy. The prediction that it will speak "as a dragon" and exercise "all the power of the first beast" plainly foretells a development of the spirit of intolerance and persecution that was manifested by the nations represented by the dragon and the leopardlike beast. And the statement that the beast with two horns *"causeth the earth and them which dwell therein to worship the first beast"* indicates that the authority of this nation is to be exercised in enforcing some observance which shall be an act of homage to the papacy.

Such action would be directly contrary to the principles of this government, to the genius of its free institutions, to the direct and solemn avowals of the Declaration of Independence, and to the Constitution. The founders of the nation wisely sought to guard against the employment of secular power on the part of the church, with its inevitable result—intolerance and persecution. The Constitution provides that "Congress shall make no law respecting an establishment of religion, or prohibiting the free exercise thereof," and that "no religious test shall ever be required as a qualification to any office of public trust under the United States." Only in flagrant violation of these safeguards to the nation's liberty, can any religious observance be enforced by civil authority. But the inconsistency of such action is no greater than is represented in the symbol. It is the beast with lamblike horns—in profession pure, gentle, and harmless—that speaks as a dragon.

"Saying to them that dwell on the earth, that they should make an image to the beast." Here is clearly presented a form of government in which the legislative power rests with the people, a most striking evidence that the United States is the nation denoted in the prophecy.

But what is the *"image to the beast"*? and how is it to be formed? The image is made by the two-horned beast, and is an image to the beast. It is also called an image of the beast. Then to learn what the image is like and how it is to be formed we must study the characteristics of the beast itself—the papacy.

When the early church became corrupted by departing from the simplicity of the gospel and accepting heathen rites and customs, she lost the Spirit and power of God; and in order to control the consciences of the people, she sought the support of the secular power. The result was the papacy, a church that controlled the power of the state and employed it to further her own ends, especially for the punishment of "heresy." In order for the United States to form an image of the beast, the religious power must so control the civil government that the authority of the state will also be employed by the church to accomplish her own ends.

Whenever the church has obtained secular power, she has employed it to punish dissent from her doctrines. Protestant churches that have followed in the steps of Rome by forming alliance with worldly powers have manifested a similar desire to restrict liberty of conscience. An example of this is given in the long-continued persecution of dissenters by the Church of England. During the sixteenth and seventeenth centuries, thousands of nonconformist ministers were forced to flee from their churches, and many, both of pastors and people, were subjected to fine, imprisonment, torture, and martyrdom.

It was apostasy that led the early church to seek the aid of the civil government, and this prepared the way for the development of the papacy—the beast. Said Paul: *"There"* shall *"come a falling away, . . . and that man of sin be revealed."* 2 Thessalonians 2:3. So apostasy in the church will prepare the way for the image to the beast.

The Bible declares that before the coming of the Lord there will exist a state of religious declension similar to that in the first centuries. *"In the last days perilous times shall come. For men shall be lovers of their own selves, covetous, boasters, proud, blasphemers, disobedient to parents, unthankful, unholy, without natural affection, trucebreakers, false accusers, incontinent, fierce, despisers of those that are good, traitors, heady, high-minded, lovers of pleasures more than lovers of God; having a form of godliness, but denying the power thereof."* 2 Timothy 3:1-5. *"Now the Spirit speaketh expressly, that in the latter times some shall depart from the faith, giving heed to seducing spirits, and doctrines of devils."* 1 Timothy 4:1. Satan will work "with all power and signs and lying wonders, and with all deceivableness of unrighteousness." And all that *"received not the love of the truth, that they might be saved,"* will be left to accept *"strong delusion, that they should believe a lie."* 2 Thessalonians 2:9-11. When this state of ungodliness shall be reached, the same results will follow as in the first centuries.

The wide diversity of belief in the Protestant churches is regarded by many as decisive proof that no effort to secure a forced uniformity can ever be made. But there has been for years, in churches of the Protestant faith, a strong and growing sentiment in favor of a union based upon common points of doctrine. To secure such a union, the discussion of subjects upon which all were not agreed—however important they might be from a Bible standpoint—must necessarily be waived.

Charles Beecher, in a sermon in the year 1846, declared that the ministry of "the evangelical Protestant denominations" is "not only formed all the way up under a tremendous pressure of merely human fear, but they live, and move, and breathe in a state of things radically corrupt, and appealing every hour to every baser element of their nature to hush up the truth, and bow the knee to the power of apostasy. Was not this the way things went with Rome? Are we not living her life over again? And what do we see just ahead? Another general council! A world's convention! Evangelical alliance, and universal creed!"—Sermon on "The Bible a Sufficient Creed," delivered at Fort Wayne, Indiana, Feb. 22, 1846. When this shall be gained, then, in the effort to secure complete uniformity, it will be only a step to the resort to force.

When the leading churches of the United States, uniting upon such points of doctrine as are held by them in common, shall influence the state to enforce their decrees and to sustain their institutions, then Protestant America will have formed an image of the Roman hierarchy, and the infliction of civil penalties upon dissenters will inevitably result.

The beast with two horns *"causeth [commands] all, both small and great, rich and poor, free and bond, to receive a mark in their right hand, or in their foreheads: and that no man might buy or sell, save he that had the mark, or the name of the beast, or the number of his name."* Revelation 13:16, 17. The third angel's warning is: *"If any man worship the beast and his image, and receive his mark in his forehead, or in his hand, the same shall drink of the wine of the wrath of God."* "The beast" mentioned in this message, whose worship is enforced by the two-horned beast, is the first, or leopardlike beast of Revelation 13—the papacy. The "image to the beast" represents that form of apostate Protestantism which will be developed when the Protestant churches shall seek the aid of the civil power for the enforcement of their dogmas. The "mark of the beast" still remains to be defined.

The Mark of the Beast
After the warning against the worship of the beast and his image the prophecy declares: *"Here are they that keep the commandments of God, and the faith of Jesus."* Since those who keep God's commandments are thus placed in contrast with those that worship the beast and his image and receive his mark, it follows that the keeping of God's law, on the one hand, and its violation, on the other, will make the distinction between the worshipers of God and the worshipers of the beast.

The special characteristic of the beast, and therefore of his image, is the breaking of God's commandments. Says Daniel, of the little horn, the papacy: *"He shall think to change times and the law."* Daniel 7:25,

R.V. And Paul styled the same power the "man of sin," who was to exalt himself above God. One prophecy is a complement of the other. Only by changing God's law could the papacy exalt itself above God; whoever should understandingly keep the law as thus changed would be giving supreme honor to that power by which the change was made. Such an act of obedience to papal laws would be a mark of allegiance to the pope in the place of God.

The papacy has attempted to change the law of God. The second commandment, forbidding image worship, has been dropped from the law, and the fourth commandment has been so changed as to authorize the observance of the first instead of the seventh day as the Sabbath. But papists urge, as a reason for omitting the second commandment, that it is unnecessary, being included in the first, and that they are giving the law exactly as God designed it to be understood. This cannot be the change foretold by the prophet. An intentional, deliberate change is presented: *"He shall think to change the times and the law."* The change in the fourth commandment exactly fulfills the prophecy. For this the only authority claimed is that of the church. Here the papal power openly sets itself above God.

While the worshipers of God will be especially distinguished by their regard for the fourth commandments,—since this is the sign of His creative power and the witness to His claim upon man's reverence and homage,—the worshipers of the beast will be distinguished by their efforts to tear down the Creator's memorial, to exalt the institution of Rome. It was in behalf of the Sunday that popery first asserted its arrogant claims (see Appendix); and its first resort to the power of the state was to compel the observance of Sunday as "the Lord's day." But the Bible points to the seventh day, and not to the first, as the Lord's day. Said Christ:

> *"The Son of man is Lord also of the Sabbath." The fourth commandment declares: "The seventh day is the Sabbath of the Lord." And by the prophet Isaiah the Lord designates it: "My holy day." Mark 2:28; Isaiah 58:13.*

The claim so often put forth that Christ changed the Sabbath is disproved by His own words. In His Sermon on the Mount He said:

> *"Think not that I am come to destroy the law, or the prophets: I am not come to destroy, but to fulfill. For verily I say unto you, Till heaven and earth pass, one jot or one tittle shall in no wise*

pass from the law, till all be fulfilled. Whosoever therefore shall break one of these least commandments, and shall teach men so, he shall be called the least in the kingdom of heaven: but whosoever shall do and teach them, the same shall be called great in the kingdom of heaven," Matthew 5:17-19.

It is a fact generally admitted by Protestants that the Scriptures give no authority for the change of the Sabbath. This is plainly stated in publications issued by the American Tract Society and the American Sunday School Union. One of these works acknowledges "the complete silence of the New Testament so far as any explicit command for the Sabbath [Sunday, the first day of the week] or definite rules for its observance are concerned."—George Elliott, The Abiding Sabbath, page 184.

Another says: "Up to the time of Christ's death, no change had been made in the day;" and, "so far as the record shows, they [the apostles] did not . . . give any explicit command enjoining the abandonment of the seventh-day Sabbath, and its observance on the first day of the week."—A. E. Waffle, The Lord's Day, pages 186-188.

Roman Catholics acknowledge that the change of the Sabbath was made by their church, and declare that Protestants by observing the Sunday are recognizing her power. In the Catholic Catechism of Christian Religion, in answer to a question as to the day to be observed in obedience to the fourth commandment, this statement is made: "During the old law, Saturday was the day sanctified; but the church, instructed by Jesus Christ, and directed by the Spirit of God, has substituted Sunday for Saturday; so now we sanctify the first, not the seventh day. Sunday means, and now is, the day of the Lord."

As the sign of the authority of the Catholic Church, papist writers cite "the very act of changing the Sabbath into Sunday, which Protestants allow of; . . . because by keeping Sunday, they acknowledge the church's power to ordain feasts, and to command them under sin."—Henry Tuberville, An Abridgment of the Christian Doctrine, page 58. What then is the change of the Sabbath, but the sign, or mark, of the authority of the Roman Church—"the mark of the beast"?

The Roman Church has not relinquished her claim to supremacy; and when the world and the Protestant churches accept a sabbath of her creating, while they reject the Bible Sabbath, they virtually admit this assumption. They may claim the authority of tradition and of the Fathers for the change; but in so doing they ignore the very principle which separates them from Rome—that "the Bible, and the Bible only, is the religion of Protestants." The papist can see that they are deceiving themselves, willingly closing their eyes to the facts in the case. As the movement for Sunday enforcement gains favor, he rejoices, feeling assured that it will eventually bring the whole Protestant world under the banner of Rome.

Romanists declare that "the observance of Sunday by the Protestants is an homage they pay, in spite of themselves, to the authority of the [Catholic] Church."—Mgr. Segur, Plain Talk About the Protestantism of Today, page 213. The enforcement of Sunday-keeping on the part of Protestant churches is an enforcement of the worship of the papacy—of the beast. Those who, understanding the claims of the fourth commandment, choose to observe the false instead of the true Sabbath are thereby paying homage to that power by which alone it is commanded. But in the very act of enforcing a religious duty by secular power, the churches would themselves form an image to the beast; hence the enforcement of Sunday-keeping in the United States would be an enforcement of the worship of the beast and his image.

But Christians of past generations observed the Sunday, supposing that in so doing they were keeping the Bible Sabbath; and there are now true Christians in every church, not excepting the Roman Catholic communion, who honestly believe that Sunday is the Sabbath of divine appointment. God accepts their sincerity of purpose and their integrity before Him. But when Sunday observance shall be enforced by law, and the world shall be enlightened concerning the obligation of the true Sabbath, then whoever shall transgress the command of God, to obey a precept which has no higher authority than that of Rome, will thereby honor popery above God. He is paying homage to Rome and to the power which enforces the institution ordained by Rome. He is worshipping the beast and his image. As men then reject the institution which God has declared to be the sign of His authority, and honor in its stead that which Rome has chosen as the token of her supremacy, they will thereby accept the sign of allegiance to Rome—"the mark of the beast." And it is not until the issue is thus plainly set before the people, and they are brought to choose between the commandments of God and the commandments of men, that those who continue in transgression will receive "the mark of the beast."

The prophecy of Revelation 13 declares that the power represented by the beast with lamblike horns shall cause "the earth and them which dwell therein" to worship the papacy —there symbolized by the beast "like unto a leopard." The beast with two horns is also to say "to them that dwell on the earth, that they should make an image to the beast;" and, furthermore, it is to command all, "both small and great, rich and poor, free and bond," to receive the mark of the beast. Revelation 13:11-16. It has been shown that the United States is the power represented by the beast with lamblike horns, and that this prophecy will be fulfilled when the United States shall enforce Sunday observance, which Rome claims as the special acknowledgment of her supremacy. But in this homage to the papacy the United States will not be alone. The influence of Rome in the countries that once acknowledged her dominion is still far from being destroyed. And prophecy foretells a restoration of her power. "I saw one of his heads as it were wounded to death; and his deadly wound was healed: and all the world wondered after the beast." Verse 3. The infliction of the deadly wound points to the downfall of the papacy in 1798. After this, says the prophet, "his deadly wound was healed: and all the world wondered after the beast." Paul states plainly that the "man of sin" will continue until the second advent. 2 Thessalonians 2:3-8. To the very close of time he will carry forward the work of deception. And the revelator declares, also referring to the papacy: "All that dwell upon the earth shall worship him, whose names are not written in the book of life." Revelation 13:8. In both the Old and the New World, the papacy will receive homage in the honor paid to the Sunday institution, that rests solely upon the authority of the Roman Church.

The World Has Been Told
Since the middle of the nineteenth century, students of prophecy in the United States have presented this testimony to the world. In the events now taking place is seen a rapid advance toward the fulfillment of the prediction. With Protestant teachers there is the same claim of divine authority for Sunday-keeping, and the same lack of Scriptural evidence, as with the papal leaders who fabricated miracles to supply the place of a command from God. The assertion that God's judgments are visited upon men for their violation of the Sunday-sabbath, will be repeated; already it is beginning to be urged. And a movement to enforce Sunday observance is fast gaining ground.

The most fearful threatening ever addressed to mortals is contained in the third angel's message. That must be a terrible sin which calls down the wrath of God unmingled with mercy. Men are not to be left in darkness concerning this important matter; the warning against this sin is to be given to the world before the visitation of God's judgments, that all may know why they are to be inflicted, and have opportunity to escape them. Prophecy declares that the first angel would make his announcement to "every nation, and kindred, and tongue, and people." The warning of the third angel, which forms a part of the same threefold message, is to be no less widespread. It is represented in the prophecy as being proclaimed with a loud voice, by an angel flying in the midst of heaven; and it will command the attention of the world.

In the issue of the contest all Christendom will be divided into two great classes—those who keep the commandments of God and the faith of Jesus, and those who worship the beast and his image and receive his mark. Although church and state will unite their power to compel "all, both small and great, rich and poor, free and bond" (Revelation 13:16), to receive "the mark of the beast," yet the people of God will not receive it. The prophet of Patmos beholds "them that had gotten the victory over the beast, and over his image, and over his mark, and over the number of his name, stand on the sea of glass, having the harps of God" and singing the song of Moses and the Lamb. Revelation 15:2, 3. E.G. White, Great Controversy, Chapter 25.

Absolute Principles Involved

FROM THE VERY BEGINNING OF THE GREAT CONTROVERSY in heaven it has been Satan's purpose to overthrow the law of God. It was to accomplish this that he entered upon his rebellion against the Creator, and though he was cast out of heaven he has continued the same warfare upon the earth. To deceive men, and thus lead them to transgress God's law, is the object which he has steadfastly pursued. Whether this be accomplished by casting aside the law altogether, or by rejecting one of its precepts, the result will be ultimately the same. He that offends "in one point," manifests contempt for the whole law; his influence and example are on the side of transgression; he becomes "guilty of all." James 2:10.

In seeking to cast contempt upon the divine statutes, Satan has perverted the doctrines of the Bible, and errors have thus become incorporated into the faith of thousands who profess to believe the Scriptures. The last great conflict between truth and error is but the final struggle of the long-standing controversy concerning the law of God. Upon this battle we are now entering—a battle between the laws of men and the precepts of Jehovah, between the religion of the Bible and the religion of fable and tradition.

The agencies which will unite against truth and righteousness in this contest are now actively at work. God's holy word, which has been handed down to us at such a cost of suffering and blood, is but little valued. The Bible is within the reach of all, but there are few who really accept it as the guide of life. Infidelity prevails to an alarming extent, not in the world merely, but in the church. Many have come to deny doctrines which are the very pillars of the Christian faith. The great facts of creation as presented by the inspired writers, the fall of man, the atonement, and the perpetuity of the law of God, are practically rejected, either wholly or in part, by a large share of the professedly Christian world. Thousands who pride themselves upon their wisdom and independence regard it as an evidence of weakness to place implicit confidence in the Bible; they think it a proof of superior talent and learning to cavil at the Scriptures and to spiritualize and explain away their most important truths. Many ministers are teaching their people, and many professors and teachers are instructing their students, that the law of God has been changed or abrogated; and those who regard its requirements as still valid, to be literally obeyed, are thought to be deserving only of ridicule or contempt.

In rejecting the truth, men reject its Author. In trampling upon the law of God, they deny the authority of the Law-giver. It is as easy to make an idol of false doctrines and theories as to fashion an idol of wood or stone. By misrepresenting the attributes of God, Satan leads men to conceive of Him in a false character. With many, a philosophical idol is enthroned in the place of Jehovah; while the living God, as He is revealed in His word, in Christ, and in the works of creation, is worshiped by but few. Thousands deify nature while they deny the God of nature. Though in a different form, idolatry exists in the Christian world today as verily as it existed among ancient Israel in the days of Elijah. The god of many professedly wise men, of philosophers, poets, politicians, journalists — the god of polished fashionable circles, of many colleges and universities, even of some theological institutions — is little better than Baal, the sun-god of Phoenicia.

No error accepted by the Christian world strikes more boldly against the authority of Heaven, none is more directly opposed to the dictates of reason, none is more pernicious in its results, than the modern doctrine, so rapidly gaining ground, that God's law is no longer binding upon men. Every nation has its laws, which command respect and obedience; no government could exist without them; and can it be conceived that the Creator of the heavens and the earth has no law to govern the beings He has made? Suppose that prominent ministers were publicly to teach that the statutes which govern their land and protect the rights of its citizens were not obligatory — that they restricted the liberties of the people, and therefore ought not to be obeyed; how long would such men be tolerated in the pulpit? But is it a graver offense to disregard the laws of states and nations than to trample upon those divine precepts which are the foundation of all government?

It would be far more consistent for nations to abolish their statutes, and permit the people to do as they please, than for the Ruler of the universe to annul His law, and leave the world without a standard to condemn the guilty or justify the obedient. Would we know the result of making void the law of God? The experiment has been tried. Terrible were the scenes enacted in France when atheism became the controlling power. It was then demonstrated to the world that to throw off the restraints which God has imposed is to accept the rule of the cruelest of tyrants. When the standard of righteousness is set aside, the way is open for the prince of evil to establish his power in the earth.

Wherever the divine precepts are rejected, sin ceases to appear sinful or righteousness desirable. Those who refuse to submit to the government of God are wholly unfitted to govern themselves. Through their pernicious teachings the spirit of insubordination is implanted in the hearts of children and youth, who are naturally impatient of control; and a lawless, licentious state of society results. While scoffing at the credulity of those who obey the requirements of God, the multitudes eagerly accept the delusions of Satan. They give the rein to lust and practice the sins which have called down judgments upon the heathen.

Those who teach the people to regard lightly the commandments of God sow disobedience to reap disobedience. Let the restraint imposed by the divine law be wholly cast aside, and human laws would soon be disregarded. Because God forbids dishonest practices, coveting, lying, and defrauding, men are ready to trample upon His statutes as a hindrance to their worldly prosperity; but the results of banishing these precepts would be such as they do not anticipate. If the law were not binding, why should any fear to transgress? Property would no longer be safe. Men would obtain their neighbor's possessions by violence, and the strongest would become richest. Life itself would not be respected. The marriage vow would no longer stand as a sacred bulwark to protect the family. He who had the power, would, if he desired, take his neighbor's wife by violence. The fifth commandment would be set aside with the fourth. Children would not shrink from taking the life of their parents if by so doing they could obtain the desire of their corrupt hearts. The civilized world would become a horde of robbers and assassins; and peace, rest, and happiness would be banished from the earth.

Already the doctrine that men are released from obedience to God's requirements has weakened the force of moral obligation and opened the floodgates of iniquity upon the world. Lawlessness, dissipation, and corruption are sweeping in upon us like an overwhelming tide. In the family, Satan is at work. His banner waves, even in professedly Christian households. There is envy, evil surmising, hypocrisy, estrangement, emulation, strife, betrayal of sacred trusts, indulgence of lust. The whole system of religious principles and doctrines, which should form the foundation and framework of social life, seems to be a tottering mass, ready to fall to ruin. The vilest of criminals, when thrown into prison for their offenses, are often made the recipients of gifts and attentions as if they had attained an enviable distinction. Great publicity is given to their character and crimes. The press publishes the revolting details of vice, thus initiating others into the practice of fraud, robbery, and murder; and Satan exults in the success of his hellish schemes. The infatuation of vice, the wanton taking of life, the terrible increase of intemperance and iniquity of every order and degree, should arouse all who fear God, to inquire what can be done to stay the tide of evil.

Courts of justice are corrupt. Rulers are actuated by desire for gain and love of sensual pleasure. Intemperance has beclouded the faculties of many so that Satan has almost complete control of them. Jurists are perverted, bribed, deluded. Drunkenness and revelry, passion, envy, dishonesty of every sort, are represented among those who administer the laws. "Justice standeth afar off: for truth is fallen in the street, and equity cannot enter." Isaiah 59:14.

The iniquity and spiritual darkness that prevailed under the supremacy of Rome were the inevitable result of her suppression of the Scriptures; but where is to be found the cause of the widespread infidelity, the rejection of the law of God, and the consequent corruption, under the full blaze of gospel light in an age of religious freedom? Now that Satan can no longer keep the world under his control by withholding the Scriptures, he resorts to other means to accomplish the same object. To destroy faith in the Bible serves his purpose as well as to destroy the Bible itself. By introducing the belief that God's law is not binding, he as effectually leads men to transgress as if they were wholly ignorant of its precepts. And now, as in former ages, he has worked through the church to further his designs. The religious organizations of the day have refused to listen to unpopular truths plainly brought to view in the Scriptures, and in combating them they have adopted interpretations and taken positions which have sown broadcast the seeds of skepticism. Clinging to the papal error of natural immortality and man's consciousness in death, they have rejected the only defense against the delusions of spiritualism. The doctrine of eternal torment has led many to disbelieve the Bible. And as the claims of the fourth commandment are urged upon the people, it is found that the observance of the seventh-day Sabbath is enjoined; and as the only way to free themselves from a duty which they are unwilling to perform, many popular teachers declare that the law of God is no longer binding. Thus they cast away the law and the Sabbath together. As the work of Sabbath reform extends, this rejection of the divine law to avoid the claims of the fourth commandment will become well-nigh universal. The teachings of religious leaders have opened the door to infidelity, to spiritualism, and to contempt for God's holy law; and upon these leaders rests a fearful responsibility for the iniquity that exists in the Christian world.

Yet this very class put forth the claim that the fast-spreading corruption is largely attributable to the desecration of the so-called "Christian sabbath," and that the enforcement of Sunday observance would greatly improve the morals of society. This claim is especially urged in America, where the doctrine of the true Sabbath has been most widely preached. Here the temperance work, one of the most prominent and important of moral reforms, is often combined with the Sunday movement, and the advocates of the latter represent themselves as laboring to promote the highest interest of society; and those who refuse to unite with them are denounced as the enemies of temperance and reform.

But the fact that a movement to establish error is connected with a work which is in itself good is not an argument in favor of the error. We may disguise poison by mingling it with wholesome food, but we do not change its nature. On the contrary, it is rendered more dangerous, as it is more likely to be taken unawares. It is one of Satan's devices to combine with falsehood just enough truth to give it plausibility. The leaders of the Sunday movement may advocate reforms which the people need, principles which are in harmony with the Bible; yet while there is with these a requirement which is contrary to God's law, His servants cannot unite with them. Nothing can justify them in setting aside the commandments of God for the precepts of men.

Through the two great errors, the immortality of the soul and Sunday sacredness, Satan will bring the people under his deceptions. While the former lays the foundation of spiritualism, the latter creates a bond of sympathy with Rome. The Protestants of the United States will be foremost in stretching their hands across the gulf to grasp the hand of spiritualism; they will reach over the abyss to clasp hands with the Roman power; and under the influence of this threefold union, this country will follow in the steps of Rome in trampling on the rights of conscience.

As spiritualism more closely imitates the nominal Christianity of the day, it has greater power to deceive and ensnare. Satan himself is converted, after the modern order of things. He will appear in the character of an angel of light. Through the agency of spiritualism, miracles will be wrought, the sick will be healed, and many undeniable wonders will be performed. And as the spirits will profess faith in the Bible, and manifest respect for the institutions of the church, their work will be accepted as a manifestation of divine power.

The line of distinction between professed Christians and the ungodly is now hardly distinguishable. Church members love what the world loves and are ready to join with them, and Satan determines to unite them in one body and thus strengthen his cause by sweeping all into the ranks of spiritualism. Papists, who boast of miracles as a certain sign of the true church, will be readily deceived by this wonder-working power; and Protestants, having cast away the shield of truth, will also be deluded. Papists, Protestants, and worldlings will alike accept the form of godliness without the power, and they will see in this union a grand movement for the conversion of the world and the ushering in of the long-expected millennium.

Through spiritualism, Satan appears as a benefactor of the race, healing the diseases of the people, and professing to present a new and more exalted system of religious faith; but at the same time he works as a destroyer. His temptations are leading multitudes to ruin. Intemperance dethrones reason; sensual indulgence, strife, and bloodshed follow. Satan delights in war, for it excites the worst passions of the soul and then sweeps into eternity its victims steeped in vice and blood. It is his object to incite the nations to war against one another, for he can thus divert the minds of the people from the work of preparation to stand in the day of God.

Satan works through the elements also to garner his harvest of unprepared souls. He has studied the secrets of the laboratories of nature, and he uses all his power to control the elements as far as God allows. When he was suffered to afflict Job, how quickly flocks and herds, servants, houses, children, were swept away, one trouble succeeding another as in a moment. It is God that shields His creatures and hedges them in from the power of the destroyer. But the Christian world have shown contempt for the law of Jehovah; and the Lord will do just what He has declared that He would—He will withdraw His blessings from the earth and remove His protecting care from those who are rebelling against His law and teaching and forcing others to do the same. Satan has control of all whom God does not especially guard. He will favor and prosper some in order to further his own designs, and he will bring trouble upon others and lead men to believe that it is God who is afflicting them.

While appearing to the children of men as a great physician who can heal all their maladies, he will bring disease and disaster, until populous cities are reduced to ruin and desolation. Even now he is at work. In accidents and calamities by sea and by land, in great conflagrations, in fierce tornadoes and terrific hailstorms, in tempests, floods, cyclones, tidal waves, and earthquakes, in every place and in a thousand forms, Satan is exercising his power. He sweeps away the ripening harvest, and famine and distress follow. He imparts to the air a deadly taint, and thousands perish by the pestilence. These visitations are to become more and more frequent and disastrous. Destruction will be upon both man and beast. *"The earth mourneth and fadeth away," "the haughty people . . . do languish. The earth also is defiled under the inhabitants thereof; because they have transgressed the laws, changed the ordinance, broken the everlasting covenant."* Isaiah 24:4, 5.

And then the great deceiver will persuade men that those who serve God are causing these evils. The class that have provoked the displeasure of Heaven will charge all their troubles upon those whose obedience to God's commandments is a perpetual reproof to transgressors. It will be declared that men are offending God by the violation of the Sunday sabbath; that this sin has brought calamities which will not cease until Sunday observance shall be strictly enforced; and that those who present the claims of the fourth commandment, thus destroying reverence for Sunday, are troublers of the people, preventing their restoration to divine favor and temporal prosperity. Thus the accusation urged of old against the servant of God will be repeated and upon grounds equally well established: "And it came to pass, when Ahab saw Elijah, that Ahab said unto him, Art thou he that troubleth Israel? And he answered, I have not troubled Israel; but thou, and thy father's house, in that ye have forsaken the commandments of the Lord, and thou hast followed

Baalim." 1 Kings 18:17, 18. As the wrath of the people shall be excited by false charges, they will pursue a course toward God's ambassadors very similar to that which apostate Israel pursued toward Elijah.

The miracle-working power manifested through spiritualism will exert its influence against those who choose to obey God rather than men. Communications from the spirits will declare that God has sent them to convince the rejecters of Sunday of their error, affirming that the laws of the land should be obeyed as the law of God. They will lament the great wickedness in the world and second the testimony of religious teachers that the degraded state of morals is caused by the desecration of Sunday. Great will be the indignation excited against all who refuse to accept their testimony.

Satan's policy in this final conflict with God's people is the same that he employed in the opening of the great controversy in heaven. He professed to be seeking to promote the stability of the divine government, while secretly bending every effort to secure its overthrow. And the very work which he was thus endeavoring to accomplish he charged upon the loyal angels. The same policy of deception has marked the history of the Roman Church. It has professed to act as the vicegerent of Heaven, while seeking to exalt itself above God and to change His law. Under the rule of Rome, those who suffered death for their fidelity to the gospel were denounced as evildoers; they were declared to be in league with Satan; and every possible means was employed to cover them with reproach, to cause them to appear in the eyes of the people and even to themselves as the vilest of criminals. So it will be now. While Satan seeks to destroy those who honor God's law, he will cause them to be accused as lawbreakers, as men who are dishonoring God and bringing judgments upon the world.

God never forces the will or the conscience; but Satan's constant resort — to gain control of those whom he cannot otherwise seduce — is compulsion by cruelty. Through fear or force he endeavors to rule the conscience and to secure homage to himself. To accomplish this, he works through both religious and secular authorities, moving them to the enforcement of human laws in defiance of the law of God.

Those who honor the Bible Sabbath will be denounced as enemies of law and order, as breaking down the moral restraints of society, causing anarchy and corruption, and calling down the judgments of God upon the earth. Their conscientious scruples will be pronounced obstinacy, stubbornness, and contempt of authority. They will be accused of disaffection toward the government. Ministers who deny the obligation of the divine law will present from the pulpit the duty of yielding obedience to the civil authorities as ordained of God. In legislative halls and courts of justice, commandment keepers will be misrepresented and condemned. A false coloring will be given to their words; the worst construction will be put upon their motives.

As the Protestant churches reject the clear, Scriptural arguments in defense of God's law, they will long to silence those whose faith they cannot overthrow by the Bible. Though they blind their own eyes to the fact, they are now adopting a course which will lead to the persecution of those who conscientiously refuse to do what the rest of the Christian world are doing, and acknowledge the claims of the papal sabbath.

The dignitaries of church and state will unite to bribe, persuade, or compel all classes to honor the Sunday. The lack of divine authority will be supplied by oppressive enactments. Political corruption is destroying love of justice and regard for truth; and even in free America, rulers and legislators, in order to secure public favor, will yield to the popular demand for a law enforcing Sunday observance. Liberty of conscience, which has cost so great a sacrifice, will no longer be respected. In the soon-coming conflict we shall see exemplified the prophet's words: "The dragon was wroth with the woman, and went to make war with the remnant of her seed, which keep the commandments of God, and have the testimony of Jesus Christ." Revelation 12:17. E.G. White, Great Controversy, chapter 36.

Utopia or Disaster?

*I*T IS A FACT THAT IN OUR WORLD that many changes proceed slowly and uniformly for a long time until a critical point is reached beyond which they proceed with extreme and disastrous velocity. In the physics laboratory the weight attached to a vertically suspended metal wire produces a strain. The weight is progressively increased, producing at first, a slow, uniform, almost imperceptible stretch of the wire. The weight is further increased. Suddenly the wire snaps. From our basic science we know that stress produces strain. The strain develops slowly and uniformly at first but when the critical point is passed it accelerates to the breaking point. Huge dark clouds float across the sky. Vast electric charges build up producing a small unseen leakage — then the dazzling flash of lightning.

Vesuvius, the great mountain which overlooked the ancient cities of Pompeii and Herculaneum, appeared as dormant as it had been for centuries. Of course, there was the occasional rumble. But all would be well. Then, with cataclysmic suddenness on 24 August, 79 A.D., Vesuvius, which had been rumbling for days, underwent a most violent eruption causing utter destruction to the two cities.

The story is the same for Lisbon, suddenly struck by a terrible earthquake on November 1, 1755 with a series of quakes which killed 60,000 people in a few minutes; shocks which were felt over a million square miles.

On 26-28 August, 1883, Krakatoa, after growling steadily for several days, belched out steam and ashes before bursting and throwing a mountain — millions of tons — into the sky. It caused such turbulence in the sea that 36,000 people on Java and Sumatra were drowned and a Dutch warship was hurled two miles inland!

The history of natural calamities on our planet teaches the lesson that great changes come suddenly.

Yet, men do not want to listen to this. They claim that the changes occurring on the earth are relatively small and will take thousands or millions of years before they reach the state of global crisis. They assure us that all things will continue as they are, there is no reason to fear. They will not learn the lesson. On our planet great changes come suddenly.

Let us re-emphasize that global changes develop uniformly, slowly and imperceptibly until a certain critical point is reached, beyond which they proceed with sudden and extreme acceleration towards destruction.

The Bible gives us the mechanism behind global disasters such as the Flood and the destruction of Sodom and Gomorrah. The effect of sin is to separate our planet from God's gracious control of the elements.

The effect of God's mercy is to hold in check the sin-damaged forces of nature. Divine mercy exerts its restraint so long as the level of iniquity remains below a certain critical intensity. During such times global deterioration tends to be uniform, slow and scarcely perceptible, except to those who know how to look and what to look for. When the critical point is reached, mercy gives way to what the Bible calls "wrath". During the ministration of wrath, God withdraws his protective restraint and gives man and his environment over to the consequences of his sinful choices. This critical separation from God by sin triggers the phase of sudden acceleration towards destruction.

There is a passage of scripture in Revelation 7:1 which describe God's merciful restraint on the forces of evil:

> *"And after these things I saw four angels standing on the four corners of the earth, holding the four winds of the earth, that the wind should not blow on the earth, nor on the sea, nor on any tree. And I saw another angel ascending from the east, having the seal of the living God: and he cried with a loud voice to the four angels, to whom it was given to hurt the earth and the sea, Saying, Hurt not the earth, neither the sea, nor the trees, till we have sealed the servants of our God in their foreheads."* Rev. 7:1-3.

When the forces of evil, called the winds of strife in Rev 7:1, are no longer restrained, terrible destruction will envelop our planet.

The mechanism of destruction is clearly revealed in the Bible.

"Let no man say when he is tempted, I am tempted of God: for God cannot be tempted with evil, neither tempteth he any man: But every man is tempted, when he is drawn away of his own lust, and enticed. Then when lust hath conceived, it bringeth forth sin: and sin, when it is finished, bringeth forth death. Do not err, my beloved brethren. Every good gift and every perfect gift is from above, and cometh down from the Father of lights, with whom is no variableness, neither shadow of turning." James 1:13-17

"Behold, the LORD's hand is not shortened, that it cannot save; neither his ear heavy, that it cannot hear: But your iniquities have separated between you and your God, and your sins have hid his face from you, that he will not hear." Isa. 59:1-2

"For a small moment have I forsaken thee; but with great mercies will I gather thee. In a little wrath I hid my face from thee for a moment; but with everlasting kindness will I have mercy on thee, saith the LORD thy Redeemer." Isa. 54:7-8

"Then my anger shall be kindled against them in that day, and I will forsake them, and I will hide my face from them, and they shall be devoured, and many evils and troubles shall befall them; so that they will say in that day, Are not these evils come upon us, because our God is not among us? And I will surely hide my face in that day for all the evils which they shall have wrought, in that they are turned unto other gods." Deut. 31:17-18.

"For the wrath of God is revealed from heaven against all ungodliness and unrighteousness of men, who hold the truth in unrighteousness;

"For this cause God gave them up unto vile affections: for even their women did change the natural use into that which is against nature:

"And even as they did not like to retain God in their knowledge, God gave them over to a reprobate mind, to do those things which are not convenient;" Rom. 1:18, 26, 28.

"We cannot know how much we owe to Christ for the peace and protection which we enjoy. It is the restraining power of God that prevents mankind from passing fully under the control of Satan. The disobedient and unthankful have great reason for gratitude for God's mercy and long-suffering in holding in check the cruel, malignant power of the evil one. But when men pass the limits of divine forbearance, that restraint is removed. God does not stand toward the sinner as an executioner of the sentence against transgression; but he leaves the rejecters of his mercy to themselves, to reap that which they have sown. Every ray of light rejected, every warning despised or unheeded, every passion indulged, every transgression of the law of God, is a seed sown, which yields its unfailing harvest. The Spirit of God, persistently resisted, is at last withdrawn from the sinner, and then there is left no power to control the evil passions of the soul, and no protection from the malice and enmity of Satan." G.C. 36.

The Time Of Trouble

"At that time shall Michael stand up, the great prince which standeth for the children of thy people; and there shall be a time of trouble, such as never was since there was a nation even to that same time; and at that time thy people shall be delivered, every one that shall be found written in the book." [Dan. 12:1.]

"When the third angel's message closes, mercy no longer pleads for the guilty inhabitants of the earth. The people of God have accomplished their work. They have received 'the latter rain,' 'the refreshing from the presence of the Lord,' and they are prepared for the trying hour before them. Angels are hastening to and fro in Heaven. An angel returning from the earth announces that his work is done; the final test has been brought upon the world, and all who have proved themselves loyal to the divine precepts have received 'the seal of the living God.' [Rev. 7:1-4.] Then Jesus ceases his intercession in the sanctuary above. He lifts his hands, and with a loud voice says, 'It is done;' and all the angelic host lay off their crowns as he makes the solemn announcement: 'He that is unjust, let him be unjust still; and he which is filthy, let him be filthy still; and he that is righteous, let him be righteous still; and he that is holy, let him be holy still.' [REV. 22:11.] Every case has been decided for life or death. Christ has made the atonement for his people, and blotted out their sins. The number of his subjects is made up; 'the kingdom and dominion, and the greatness of the kingdom under the whole heaven,' is about to be given to the heirs of salvation, and Jesus is to reign as King of kings, and Lord of lords.

"When he leaves the sanctuary, darkness covers the inhabitants of the earth. In that fearful time the righteous must live in the sight of a holy God without an intercessor. The restraint which has been upon the wicked is removed, and Satan has entire control of the finally impenitent. God's long-suffering has ended. The world has rejected his mercy, despised his love, and trampled upon his law. The wicked have passed the boundary of their probation; the Spirit of God, persistently resisted, has been at last withdrawn. Unsheltered by divine grace, they have no protection from the wicked one. Satan will then plunge the inhabitants of the earth into one great, final trouble. As the angels of God cease to hold in check the fierce winds of human passion, all the elements of strife will be let loose. The whole world will be involved in ruin more terrible than that which came upon Jerusalem of old.

"A single angel destroyed all the first-born of the Egyptians, and filled the land with mourning. When David offended against God by numbering the people, one angel caused that terrible destruction by which his sin was punished. The same destructive power exercised by holy angels when God commands, will be exercised by evil angels when he permits. There are forces now ready, and only waiting the divine permission, to spread desolation everywhere.

"Those who honor the law of God have been accused of bringing judgments upon the world, and they will be regarded as the cause of the fearful convulsions of nature and the strife and bloodshed among men that are filling the earth with woe. The power attending the last warning has enraged the wicked; their anger is kindled against all who have received the message, and Satan will excite to still greater intensity the spirit of hatred and persecution.

"When God's presence was finally withdrawn from the Jewish nation, priests and people knew it not. Though under the control of Satan, and swayed by the most horrible and malignant passions, they still regarded themselves as the chosen of God. The ministration in the temple continued; sacrifices were offered upon its polluted altars, and daily the divine blessing was invoked upon a people guilty of the blood of God's dear Son, and seeking to slay his ministers and apostles. So when the irrevocable decision of the sanctuary has been pronounced, and the destiny of the world has been forever fixed, the inhabitants of the earth will know it not. The forms of religion will be continued by a people from whom the Spirit of God has been finally withdrawn; and the Satanic zeal with which the prince of evil will inspire them for the accomplishment of his malignant designs, will bear the semblance of zeal for God.

"As the Sabbath has become the special point of controversy throughout Christendom, and religious and secular authorities have combined to enforce the observance of the Sunday, the persistent refusal of a small minority to yield to the popular demand, will make them objects of universal execration. It will be urged that the few who stand in opposition to an institution of the church and a law of the State, ought not to be tolerated; that it is better for them to suffer than for whole nations to be thrown into confusion and lawlessness. The same argument over nineteen hundred years ago was brought against Christ by the 'rulers of the people.' 'It is expedient for us,' said the wily Caiaphas, 'that one man should die for the people, and that the whole nation perish not.' [JOHN 11:50.] This argument will appear conclusive; and a decree will finally be issued against those who hallow the Sabbath of the fourth commandment, denouncing them as deserving of the severest punishment, and giving the people liberty, after a certain time, to put them to death. Romanism in the Old World, and apostate Protestantism in the New, will pursue a similar course toward those who honor all the divine precepts." G.C. 613-616.

"As the decree issued by the various rulers of Christendom against commandment-keepers shall withdraw the protection of government, and abandon them to those who desire their destruction, the people of God will flee from the cities and villages, and associate together in companies, dwelling in the most desolate and solitary places. Many will find refuge in the strongholds of the mountains. Like the Christians of the Piedmont valleys, they will make the high places of the earth their sanctuaries, and will thank God for the 'munitions of rocks.' [ISA. 33.16.] But many of all nations, and all classes, high and low, rich and poor, black and white, will be cast into the most unjust and cruel bondage. The beloved of God pass weary days, bound in chains, shut in by prison bars, sentenced to be slain, some apparently left to die of starvation in dark and loathsome dungeons. No human ear is open to hear their moans; no human hand is ready to lend them help." G.C. 626.

The Seven Last Plagues

After the final warning has been given and every individual mind has been made up, Christ's intercession in the heavenly sanctuary will cease. The four winds of strife mentioned in Revelation 7:1 will be let go. Then the seven last plagues will affect the earth. These plagues will be the progressive destructions which will strike the planet as a result of earth's separation from God by sin. The critical sin will have been the enforcement of Sunday worship and the infliction of civil penalties upon the keepers of the true seventh-day Sabbath. These plagues are written down in Revelation, chapter 16.

The First Four Plagues

"And I heard a great voice out of the temple saying to the seven angels, Go your ways, and pour out the vials of the wrath of God upon the earth. And the first went, and poured out his vial upon the earth; and there fell a noisome and grievous sore upon the men which had the mark of the beast, and upon them which worshipped his image. And the second angel poured out his vial upon the sea; and it became as the blood of a dead man: and every living soul died in the sea. And the third angel poured out his vial upon the rivers and fountains of waters; and they became blood. And I heard the angel of the waters say, Thou art righteous, O Lord, which art, and wast, and shalt be, because thou hast judged thus. For they have shed the blood of saints and prophets, and thou hast given them blood to drink; for they are worthy. And I heard another out of the altar say, Even so, Lord

God Almighty, true and righteous are thy judgments. And the fourth angel poured out his vial upon the sun; and power was given unto him to scorch men with fire. And men were scorched with great heat, and blasphemed the name of God, which hath power over these plagues: and they repented not to give him glory. [REV. 16:1-9].

"Says the Revelator, in describing these terrific scourges,
'There fell a noisome and grievous sore upon the men which had the mark of the beast, and upon them which worshiped his image.' The sea 'became as the blood of a dead man, and every living soul died in the sea.' And 'the rivers and fountains of waters became blood.' [REV. 16:2-6, 8, 9.]

Terrible as these inflictions are, God's justice stands fully vindicated. The angel of God declares,
'Thou art righteous, O Lord, . . . because thou hast judged thus. For they have shed the blood of saints and prophets, and thou hast given them blood to drink; for they are worthy.' REV. 16:2-6, 8, 9.

By condemning the people of God to death, they have as truly incurred the guilt of their blood, as if it had been shed by their hands. In like manner, in Matt. 23:34-36, Christ declared the Jews of his time guilty of all the blood of holy men which had been shed since the days of Abel; for they possessed the same spirit, and were seeking to do the same work, with these murderers of the prophets.

"In the plague that follows, power is given to the sun 'to scorch men with fire. And men were scorched with great heat.' [REV. 16:2-6, 8, 9.] The prophets thus describe the condition of the earth at this fearful time: 'The land mourneth;. . . because the harvest of the field is perished.' 'All the trees of the field are withered; because joy is withered away from the sons of men.' 'The seed is rotten under their clods, the garners are laid desolate.' 'How do the beasts groan! the herds of cattle are perplexed, because they have no pasture. . . . The rivers of waters are dried up, and the fire hath devoured the pastures of the wilderness.' 'The songs of the temple shall be howlings in that day, saith the Lord God; there shall be many dead bodies in every place; they shall cast them forth with silence.' [JOEL 1:10-12, 17-20; AMOS 8:3.].

"These plagues are not universal, or the inhabitants of the earth would be wholly cut off. Yet they will be the most awful scourges that have ever been known to mortals. All the judgments upon men, prior to the close of probation, have been mingled with mercy. The pleading blood of Christ has shielded the sinner from receiving the full measure of his guilt; but in the final Judgment, wrath is poured out unmixed with mercy.

"In that day, multitudes will desire the shelter of God's mercy which they have so long despised.

'Behold, the days come, saith the Lord God, that I will send a famine in the land, not a famine of bread, nor a thirst for water, but of hearing the words of the Lord. And they shall wander from sea to sea, and from the north even to the east, they shall run to and fro to seek the word of the Lord, and shall not find it.' [AMOS 8:11, 12.].

'The people of God will not be free from suffering; but while persecuted and distressed, while they endure privation, and suffer for want of food, they will not be left to perish. That God who cared for Elijah will not pass by one of his self-sacrificing children. He who numbers the hairs of their head will care for them, and in time of famine they shall be satisfied. While the wicked are dying from hunger and pestilence, angels will shield the righteous, and supply their wants. To him that 'walketh righteously' is the promise,

'Bread shall be given him; his waters shall be sure.' 'When the poor and needy seek water, and there is none, and their tongue faileth for thirst, I the Lord will hear them, I the God of Israel will not forsake them.' [ISA. 33:16; 41:17.].

"Although the fig-tree shall not blossom, neither shall fruit be in the vines; the labor of the olive shall fail, and the fields shall yield no meat; the flock shall be cut off from the fold, and there shall be no herd in the stalls;' yet shall they that fear him 'rejoice in the Lord,' and joy in the God of their salvation. [HAB. 3:17, 18.].

"The Lord is thy keeper; the Lord is thy shade upon thy right hand. The sun shall not smite thee by day, nor the moon by night. The

Lord shall preserve thee from all evil; he shall preserve thy soul.' 'He shall deliver thee from the snare of the fowler, and from the noisome pestilence. He shall cover thee with his feathers, and under his wings shalt thou trust; his truth shall be thy shield and buckler. Thou shalt not be afraid for the terror by night; nor for the arrow that flieth by day; nor for the pestilence that walketh in darkness; nor for the destruction that wasteth at noonday. A thousand shall fall at thy side, and ten thousand at thy right hand; but it shall not come nigh thee. Only with thine eyes shalt thou behold and see the reward of the wicked. Because thou hast made the Lord, which is my refuge, even the Most High, thy habitation; there shall no evil befall thee, neither shall any plague come nigh thy dwelling.' [PS. 121:5-7; 91:3-10.].

"Yet to human sight it will appear that the people of God must soon seal their testimony with their blood, as did the martyrs before them. They themselves begin to fear that the Lord has left them to fall by the hand of their enemies. It is a time of fearful agony. Day and night they cry unto God for deliverance. The wicked exult, and the jeering cry is heard. 'Where now is your faith? Why does not God deliver you out of our hands if you are indeed his people?' But the waiting ones remember Jesus dying upon Calvary's cross, and the chief priests and rulers shouting in mockery, 'He saved others; himself he cannot save. If he be the King of Israel, let him now come down from the cross, and we will believe him.' [MATT. 27:42.] Like Jacob, all are wrestling with God. Their countenances express their internal struggle. Paleness sits upon every face. Yet they cease not their earnest intercession.

'Could men see with heavenly vision, they would behold companies of angels that excel in strength stationed about those who have kept the word of Christ's patience. With sympathizing tenderness, angels have witnessed their distress, and have heard their prayers. They are waiting the word of their Commander to snatch them from their peril. But they must wait yet a little longer. The people of God must drink of the cup, and be baptized with the baptism. The very delay, so painful to them, is the best answer to their petitions. As they endeavor to wait trustingly for the Lord to work, they are led to exercise faith, hope, and patience, which have been too little exercised during their religious experience. Yet for the elect's sake, the time of trouble will be shortened.

'Shall not God avenge his own elect, which cry day and night unto him? . . . I tell you that he will avenge them speedily.' *[LUKE 18:7, 8.]*

The end will come more quickly than men expect. The wheat will be gathered and bound in sheaves for the garner of God; the tares will be bound as fagots for the fires of destruction.

"The heavenly sentinels, faithful to their trust, continue their watch. Though a general decree has fixed the time when commandment-keepers may be put to death, their enemies will in some cases anticipate the decree, and, before the time specified, will endeavor to take their lives. But none can pass the mighty guardians stationed about every faithful soul. Some are assailed in their flight from the cities and villages; but the swords raised against them break and fall as powerless as a straw. Others are defended by angels in the form of men of war." G.C. 628-631.

The Last Three Plagues
The Bible calls false Christianity Babylon, and its popular support, the river Euphrates. Revelation 17:1,15. Under the fifth plague darkness covers the earth. Revelation 16:10. Under the sixth plague the people who had been deceived into supporting the mark of the beast system will realise their mistake and withdraw their support from the system. Moreover, they will vent their revenge and anger upon the religious leaders who misled them. There will be unprecedented bloodshed.

During the seventh plague, a great earthquake and falling hailstones will produce total destruction of civilization. But God's voice will deliver His faithful believers. Rev. 16:17-21.

"When the protection of human laws shall be withdrawn from those who honor the law of God, there will be, in different lands, a simultaneous movement for their destruction. As the time appointed in the decree draws near, the people will conspire to root out the hated sect. It will be determined to strike in one night a decisive blow, which shall utterly silence the voice of dissent and reproof.

"The people of God—some in prison cells, some hidden in solitary retreats in the forests and the mountains—still plead for divine protection, while in every quarter companies of armed men, urged on by hosts of evil angels, are preparing for the work of death. It is now, in the hour of utmost extremity, that the God of Israel will interpose for the deliverance of his chosen. Saith the Lord: 'Ye shall have a song, as in the night when a holy solemnity is kept; and gladness of heart, as when one goeth . . . to come into the mountain of Jehovah, to the Mighty One of Israel. And the Lord shall cause his glorious voice to be heard, and shall show the lighting down of his arm, with the indignation of his anger, and with the flame of a devouring fire, with scattering, and tempest, and hailstones.' ISA. 30:29, 30..

"With shouts of triumph, jeering, and imprecation, throngs of evil men are about to rush upon their prey, when lo, a dense blackness, deeper than the darkness of the night, falls upon the earth. Then a rainbow, shining with the glory from the throne of God, spans the heavens, and seems to encircle each praying company. The angry multitudes are suddenly arrested. Their mocking cries die away. The objects of their murderous rage are forgotten. With fearful forebodings they gaze upon the symbol of God's covenant, and long to be shielded from its overpowering brightness.

"By the people of God a voice, clear and melodious, is heard, saying, 'Look up,' and, lifting their eyes to the heavens, they behold the bow of promise. The black, angry clouds that covered the firmament are parted, and like Stephen they look up steadfastly into Heaven, and see the glory of God, and the Son of man seated upon his throne. In his divine form they discern the marks of his humiliation; and from his lips they hear the request, presented before his Father and the holy angels,

'I will that they also, whom thou hast given me, be with me where I am.' [1 JOHN 17:24.]

Again a voice, musical and triumphant, is heard, saying, 'They come! they come! holy, harmless, and undefiled. They have kept the word of my patience; they shall walk among the angels;' and the pale, quivering lips of those who have held fast their faith, utter a shout of victory.

"It is at midnight that God manifests his power for the deliverance of his people. The sun appears, shining in its strength. Signs and wonders follow in quick succession. The wicked look with terror and amazement upon the scene, while the righteous behold with solemn joy the tokens of their deliverance. Everything in nature seems turned out of its course. The streams cease to flow. Dark, heavy clouds come up, and clash against each other. In the midst of the angry heavens is one clear space of indescribable glory, whence comes the voice of God like the sound of many waters, saying,

'It is done.' [REV. 16:17, 18.].

"That voice shakes the heavens and the earth. There is a mighty earthquake, 'such as was not since men were upon the earth, so mighty an earthquake and so great.' [REV. 16:17, 18.] The firmament appears to open and shut. The glory from the throne of God seems flashing through. The mountains shake like a reed in the wind, and ragged rocks are scattered on every side. There is a roar as of a coming tempest. The sea is lashed into fury. There is heard the shriek of the hurricane, like the voice of demons upon a mission of destruction. The whole earth heaves and swells like the waves of the sea. Its surface is breaking up. Its very foundations seem to be giving way. Mountain chains are sinking. Inhabited islands disappear. The seaports that have become like Sodom for wickedness, are swallowed up by the angry waters. Babylon the Great hath come in remembrance before God, 'to give unto her the cup of the wine of the fierceness of his wrath.' [REV. 16: 19, 21.] Great hailstones, every one 'about the weight of a talent,' are doing their work of destruction. The proudest cities of the earth are laid low. The lordly palaces, upon which the world's great men have lavished their wealth in order to glorify themselves, are crumbling to ruin before their eyes. Prison walls are rent asunder, and God's people, who have been held in bondage for their faith, are set free." G.C. 635-637.

"When the voice of God turns the captivity of His people, there is a terrible awakening of those who have lost all in the great conflict of life. While probation continued they were blinded by Satan's deceptions, and they justified their course of sin. The rich prided themselves upon their superiority to those who were less favored; but they had obtained their riches by violation of the law of God. They had neglected to feed the hungry, to clothe the naked, to deal justly, and to love mercy. They had sought to exalt themselves and to obtain the homage of their fellow creatures. Now they are stripped of all that made them great and are left destitute and defenseless. They look with terror upon the destruction of the idols which they preferred before their Maker. They have sold their souls for earthly riches and enjoyments, and have not sought to become rich toward God. The result is, their lives are a failure; their pleasures are now turned to gall, their treasures to corruption. The gain of a lifetime is swept away in a moment. The rich bemoan the destruction of their grand houses, the scattering of their gold and silver. But their lamentations are silenced by the fear that they themselves are to perish with their idols.

"The wicked are filled with regret, not because of their sinful neglect of God and their fellow-men, but because God has conquered. They lament that the result is what it is; but they do not repent of their wickedness. They would leave no means untried to conquer if they could.

"The world see the very class whom they have mocked and derided, and desired to exterminate, pass unharmed through pestilence, tempest, and earthquake. He who is to the transgressors of his law a devouring fire, is to his people a safe pavilion.

"The minister who has sacrificed truth to gain the favor of men, now discerns the character and influence of his teachings. It is apparent that an omniscient eye was following him as he stood in the desk, as he walked the streets, as he mingled with men in the various scenes of life. Every emotion of the soul, every line written, every word uttered, every act that led men to rest in a refuge of falsehood, has been scattering seed; and now, in the wretched, lost souls around him, he beholds the harvest.

"Saith the Lord: 'They have healed the hurt of the daughter of my people slightly, saying, Peace, peace; when there is no peace.' 'With lies ye have made the heart of the righteous sad, whom I have not made sad; and strengthened the hands of the wicked, that he should not return from his wicked way, by promising him life.' JER. 8:11; EZE. 13:22.

"Woe be unto the pastors that destroy and scatter the sheep of my pasture! . . . Behold, I will visit upon you the evil of your doings.' 'Howl, ye shepherds, and cry; and wallow yourselves in the ashes, ye principal of the flock; for your days for slaughter and your dispersions are accomplished;...and the shepherds shall have no way to flee, nor the principal of the flock to escape.' JER. 23:1, 2; 25:34, 35 (MARGIN).

"Ministers and people see that they have not sustained the right relation to God. They see that they have rebelled against the Author of all just and righteous law. The setting aside of the divine precepts gave rise to thousands of springs of evil, discord, hatred, iniquity, until the earth became one vast field of strife, one sink of corruption. This is the view that now appears to those who rejected truth and chose to cherish error. No language can express the longing which the disobedient and disloyal feel for that which they have lost forever,—eternal life. Men whom the world has worshiped for their talents and eloquence now see these things in their true light. They realize what they have forfeited by transgression, and they fall at the feet of those whose fidelity they have despised and derided, and confess that God has loved them.

"The people see that they have been deluded. They accuse one another of having led them to destruction; but all unite in heaping their bitterest condemnation upon the ministers. Unfaithful pastors have prophesied smooth things; they have led their hearers to make void the law of God and to persecute those who would keep it holy. Now, in their despair, these teachers confess before the world their work of deception. The multitudes are filled with fury. 'We are lost!' they cry, 'and you are the cause of our ruin;' and they turn upon the false shepherds. The very ones that once admired them most, will pronounce the most dreadful curses upon them. The very hands that once crowned them with laurels will be raised for their destruction. The swords which were to slay God's people are now employed to destroy their enemies. Everywhere there is strife and bloodshed.

"A noise shall come even to the ends of the earth; for the Lord hath a controversy with the nations: he will plead with all flesh; he will give them that are wicked to the sword.' [JER. 25:31.] For six thousand years the great controversy has been in progress; the Son of God and his heavenly messengers have been in conflict with the power of the evil one, to warn, enlighten, and save the children of men. Now all have made their decision; the wicked have fully united with Satan in his warfare against God. The time has come for God to vindicate the authority of his downtrodden law. Now the controversy is not alone with Satan, but with men. 'The Lord hath a controversy with the nations;' 'he will give them that are wicked to the sword.'

"The mark of deliverance has been set upon those 'that sigh and that cry for all the abominations that be done.' Now the angel of death goes forth, represented in Ezekiel's vision by the men with the slaughtering weapons, to whom the command is given: 'Slay utterly old and young, both maids, and little children, and women; but come not near any man upon whom is the mark; and begin at my sanctuary.' Says the prophet, 'They began at the ancient men which were before the house.' [EZE. 9:1-6.] The work of destruction begins among those who have professed to be the spiritual guardians of the people. The false watchmen are the first to fall. There are none to pity or to spare. Men, women, maidens, and little children perish together.

"The Lord cometh out of his place to punish the inhabitants of the earth for their iniquity; the earth also shall disclose her blood, and shall no more cover her slain.' [ISA. 26:21.] 'And this shall be the plague wherewith the Lord will smite all the people that have fought against Jerusalem: Their flesh shall consume away while they stand upon their feet, and their eyes shall consume away in their holes, and their tongue shall consume away in their mouth. And it shall come to pass in that day that a great tumult from the Lord shall be among them; and they shall lay hold every one on the hand of his neighbor, and his hand shall rise up against the hand of his neighbor.' ZECH. 14:12, 13. In the mad strife of their own fierce passions, and by the awful outpouring of God's unmingled wrath, fall the wicked inhabitants of the earth,—priests, rulers, and people, rich and poor, high and low. 'And the slain of the Lord shall be at that day from one end of the earth even unto the other end of the earth; they shall not be lamented, neither gathered, nor buried." JER. 25:33. G. C. 654-657.

The Second Coming Of Christ

After the seven last plagues have finished their destructive work, Christ will return to the earth. He will come in blazing glory. Every eye will see Him, but especially will the faithful ones behold Him with indescribable joy.

At the second coming of Christ the righteous dead will be resurrected, the righteous living will be changed, and all the righteous will be caught up to meet Him in the air, to begin their long but quick journey to heaven where the 1000 year millennium will be spent.

> *"For the Lord himself shall descend from heaven with a shout, with the voice of the archangel, and with the trump of God: and the dead in Christ shall rise first: Then we which are alive and remain shall be caught up together with them in the clouds, to meet the Lord in the air: and so shall we ever be with the Lord."* 1Thess. 4:16-17.

> *"And when he had spoken these things, while they beheld, he was taken up; and a cloud received him out of their sight. And while they looked stedfastly toward heaven as he went up, behold, two men stood by them in white apparel; Which also said, Ye men of Galilee, why stand ye gazing up into heaven? this same Jesus, which is taken up from you into heaven, shall so come in like manner as ye have seen him go into heaven."* Acts 1:9-11.

> *"Behold, he cometh with clouds; and every eye shall see him, and they also which pierced him: and all kindreds of the earth shall wail because of him. Even so, Amen."* Rev. 1:7.

> *"And the heaven departed as a scroll when it is rolled together; and every mountain and island were moved out of their places. And the kings of the earth, and the great men, and the rich men, and the chief captains, and the mighty men, and every bondman,*

and every free man, hid themselves in the dens and in the rocks of the mountains; And said to the mountains and rocks, Fall on us, and hide us from the face of him that sitteth on the throne, and from the wrath of the Lamb: For the great day of his wrath is come; and who shall be able to stand?" Rev. 6:14-17.

"Behold, I shew you a mystery; We shall not all sleep, but we shall all be changed, In a moment, in the twinkling of an eye, at the last trump: for the trumpet shall sound, and the dead shall be raised incorruptible, and we shall be changed. For this corruptible must put on incorruption, and this mortal must put on immortality. So when this corruptible shall have put on incorruption, and this mortal shall have put on immortality, then shall be brought to pass the saying that is written, Death is swallowed up in victory. O death, where is thy sting? O grave, where is thy victory? The sting of death is sin; and the strength of sin is the law. But thanks be to God, which giveth us the victory through our Lord Jesus Christ. Therefore, my beloved brethren, be ye stedfast, unmoveable, always abounding in the work of the Lord, forasmuch as ye know that your labour is not in vain in the Lord." 1Cor. 15:51-58.

"And then shall appear the sign of the Son of man in heaven: and then shall all the tribes of the earth mourn, and they shall see the Son of man coming in the clouds of heaven with power and great glory. And he shall send his angels with a great sound of a trumpet, and they shall gather together his elect from the four winds, from one end of heaven to the other." Matt. 24:30-31.

"Let not your heart be troubled: ye believe in God, believe also in me. In my Father's house are many mansions: if it were not so, I would have told you. I go to prepare a place for you. And if I go and prepare a place for you, I will come again, and receive you unto myself; that where I am, there ye may be also." John 14:1-3.

"And I saw thrones, and they sat upon them, and judgment was given unto them: and I saw the souls of them that were beheaded for the witness of Jesus, and for the word of God, and which had not worshipped the beast, neither his image, neither had received his mark upon their foreheads, or in their hands; and they lived and reigned with Christ a thousand years." Rev. 20:4.

The Survivors

SUDDEN, OVERWHELMING AND CATACLYSMIC DESTRUCTION will be the end result of the proposed New World Economic Order. There will be such massive destruction of human life that it is unimaginable. What will be even more amazing is the fact that the world would have been warned, yet the vast majority would have refused to believe the warning. Solomon wrote about this strange phenomenon whereby unbelief leads the transgressor on to total destruction.

> "Because I have called, and ye refused; I have stretched out my hand, and no man regarded; But ye have set at nought all my counsel, and would none of my reproof: I also will laugh at your calamity; I will mock when your fear cometh; When your fear cometh as desolation, and your destruction cometh as a whirlwind; when distress and anguish cometh upon you. Then shall they call upon me, but I will not answer; they shall seek me early, but they shall not find me: For that they hated knowledge, and did not choose the fear of the LORD: They would none of my counsel: they despised all my reproof. Therefore shall they eat of the fruit of their own way, and be filled with their own devices." Prov. 1:24-31.

In the global catastrophe of the Flood, there were eight survivors. In the holocaust of Sodom and Gomorrah there were three survivors. So too, in the final destruction there will be survivors. Similarly, there will be those who will be loyal to God, His truth, His law and His true Sabbath, when the whole world will unite to enforce Sunday worship by the civil law.

It is fitting to end this study with a description of the characteristics of the survivors, for indeed, such characteristics are essential for survival.

Their Names Will Be Written In The Book Of Life

"And at that time shall Michael stand up, the great prince which standeth for the children of thy people: and there shall be a time of trouble, such as never was since there was a nation even to that same time: and at that time thy people shall be delivered, every one that shall be found written in the book." Dan. 12:1.

"And all that dwell upon the earth shall worship him (the beast), whose names are not written in the book of life of the Lamb slain from the foundation of the world." Rev. 13:8.

A person's name is entered in the Book of Life at conversion.

"Jesus answered and said unto him, Verily, verily, I say unto thee, Except a man be born again, he cannot see the kingdom of God....Jesus answered, Verily, verily, I say unto thee, Except a man be born of water and of the Spirit, he cannot enter into the kingdom of God." John 3:3, 5.

"And this is the record, that God hath given to us eternal life, and this life is in his Son. He that hath the Son hath life; and he that hath not the Son of God hath not life." 1 John 5:11-12.

There is an interesting text in Revelation which reveals the truth that the final generation of the true people of God must overcome in order to have their names retained in the Book of Life.

"He that overcometh, the same shall be clothed in white raiment; and I will not blot out his name out of the book of life, but I will confess his name before my Father, and before his angels." Rev. 3:5.

"Repent ye therefore, and be converted, that your sins may be blotted out, when the times of refreshing shall come from the presence of the Lord;" Acts 3:19.

Those who survive earth's final crisis must have been genuinely initially converted and must overcome sin as Jesus overcame.

"To him that overcometh will I grant to sit with me in my throne, even as I also overcame, and am set down with my Father in his throne." Rev. 3:21.

They Will Overcome As Jesus Overcame

When the Son of God became man He took on sinful fallen human flesh and blood, and He overcame by faith in, and absolute surrender to, His Father. His victory over the sinful urges of human nature and over the fear of death is the victory that enables His faithful believers to overcome. Jesus was really tempted in all points as we are tempted yet He remained sinless. He overcame in order to enable us to overcome.

> *"Forasmuch then as the children are partakers of flesh and blood, he also himself likewise took part of the same; that through death he might destroy him that had the power of death, that is, the devil; And deliver them who through fear of death were all their lifetime subject to bondage. For verily he took not on him the nature of angels; but he took on him the seed of Abraham. Wherefore in all things it behoved him to be made like unto his brethren, that he might be a merciful and faithful high priest in things pertaining to God, to make reconciliation for the sins of the people. For in that he himself hath suffered being tempted, he is able to succour them that are tempted."* Heb. 2:14-18.

> *"For we have not an high priest which cannot be touched with the feeling of our infirmities; but was in all points tempted like as we are, yet without sin. Let us therefore come boldly unto the throne of grace, that we may obtain mercy, and find grace to help in time of need."* Heb. 4:15-16.

> *"These things I have spoken unto you, that in me ye might have peace. In the world ye shall have tribulation: but be of good cheer; I have overcome the world."* John 16:33.

By abiding in Christ through faith and surrender, the final generation of true believers will overcome all sin and will remain loyal to God in the face of death.

They Will Be Sealed With The Seal Of The Living God

God's end-time people will have fully received the righteousness of Christ and will therefore keep the commandments of God and the faith of Jesus. The fourth commandment is the commandment of true Sabbath rest. This rest is found only in Christ.

> *"Come unto me, all ye that labour and are heavy laden, and I will give you rest. Take my yoke upon you, and learn of me; for I am meek and lowly in heart: and ye shall find rest unto your souls. For my yoke is easy, and my burden is light."* Matt. 11:28-30.

> *"There remaineth therefore a rest to the people of God. For he that is entered into his rest, he also hath ceased from his own works, as God did from his. For he spake in a certain place of the seventh day on this wise, And God did rest the seventh day from all his works."* Heb. 4:9, 10, 4.

> *The keeping of the true Sabbath will be the special sign or seal of those who will survive the final crisis of history.*

> *"Moreover also I gave them my sabbaths, to be a sign between me and them, that they might know that I am the LORD that sanctify them. And hallow my sabbaths; and they shall be a sign between me and you, that ye may know that I am the LORD your God."* Eze. 20:12, 20.

They Will Be Sanctified By The Truth

> *"Sanctify them through thy truth: thy word is truth."* John 17:17.

> "Those who endeavor to obey all the commandments of God will be opposed and derided. They can stand only in God. In order to endure the trial before them, they must understand the will of God as revealed in his Word; they can honor him only as they have a right conception of his character, government, and purposes, and act in accordance with them. None but those who have fortified the mind with the truths of the Bible will stand through the last great conflict. To every soul will come the searching test, Shall I obey God rather than men? The decisive hour is even now at hand. Are our feet planted on the rock of God's immutable Word? Are we prepared to stand firm in defense of the commandments of God and the faith of Jesus? G.C. 593-594.

> "When God sends to men warnings so important that they are represented as proclaimed by holy angels flying in the midst

of heaven, he requires every person endowed with reasoning powers to heed the message. The fearful judgments denounced against the worship of the beast and his image, [REV. 14:9-11.] should lead all to a diligent study of the prophecies to learn what the mark of the beast is, and how they are to avoid receiving it. But the masses of the people turn away their ears from hearing the truth, and are turned unto fables. The apostle Paul declared, looking down to the last days, 'The time will come when they will not endure sound doctrine.' [2 TIM. 4:3.] That time has fully come. The multitudes do not want Bible truth, because it interferes with the desires of the sinful, world-loving heart; and Satan supplies the deceptions which they love.

"But God will have a people upon the earth to maintain the Bible, and the Bible only, as the standard of all doctrines, and the basis of all reforms. The opinions of learned men, the deductions of science, the creeds or decisions of ecclesiastical councils, as numerous and discordant as are the churches which they represent, the voice of the majority,— not one or all of these should be regarded as evidence for or against any point of religious faith. Before accepting any doctrine or precept, we should demand a plain 'Thus saith the Lord' in its support.

"Satan is constantly endeavoring to attract attention to man in the place of God. He leads the people to look to bishops, to pastors, to professors of theology, as their guides, instead of searching the Scriptures to learn their duty for themselves. Then, by controlling the minds of these leaders, he can influence the multitudes according to his will." G.C. 594-595.

"Only those who have been diligent students of the Scriptures and who have received the love of the truth will be shielded from the powerful delusion that takes the world captive. By the Bible testimony these will detect the deceiver in his disguise. To all the testing time will come. By the sifting of temptation the genuine Christian will be revealed. Are the people of God now so firmly established upon His word that they would not yield to the evidence of their senses? Would they, in such a crisis, cling to the Bible and the Bible only? Satan will, if possible, prevent them from obtaining a preparation to stand in that day. He will so arrange affairs as to hedge up their way, entangle them with earthly treasures, cause them to carry a heavy, wearisome burden, that their hearts may be overcharged with the cares of this life and the day of trial may come upon them as a thief." G.C. 625.

They Will Be Men And Women Of Faith And Prayer

"Here is the patience of the saints: here are they that keep the commandments of God, and the faith of Jesus." Rev. 14:12.

"The season of distress and anguish before us will require a faith that can endure weariness, delay, and hunger,—a faith that will not faint, though severely tried. The period of probation is granted to all to prepare for that time. Jacob prevailed because he was persevering and determined. His victory is an evidence of the power of importunate prayer. All who will lay hold of God's promises, as he did, and be as earnest and persevering as he was, will succeed as he succeeded. Those who are unwilling to deny self, to agonize before God, to pray long and earnestly for his blessing, will not obtain it. Wrestling with God—how few know what it is! How few have ever had their souls drawn out after God with intensity of desire until every power is on the stretch. When waves of despair which no language can express sweep over the suppliant, how few cling with unyielding faith to the promises of God.

"Those who exercise but little faith now, are in the greatest danger of falling under the power of Satanic delusions and the decree to compel the conscience. And even if they endure the test, they will be plunged into deeper distress and anguish in the time of trouble, because they have never made it a habit to trust in God. The lessons of faith which they have neglected, they will be forced to learn under a terrible pressure of discouragement.

"We should now acquaint ourselves with God by proving his promises. Angels record every prayer that is earnest and sincere. We should rather dispense with selfish gratifications than neglect communion with God. The deepest poverty, the greatest self-denial, with his approval, is better than riches, honors, ease, and friendship without it. We must take time to pray. If we allow our minds to be absorbed by worldly interests, the Lord may give us time by removing from us our idols of gold, of houses, or of fertile lands.

"The young would not be seduced into sin if they would refuse to enter any path, save that upon which they could ask God's blessing. If the messengers who bear the last solemn warning to the world would pray for the blessing of God, not in a cold, listless, lazy manner, but fervently and in faith, as did Jacob, they would find many places where they could say, 'I have seen God face to face, and my life is preserved.' [Gen. 32:30.] They would be accounted of Heaven as princes, having power to prevail with God and with men.

"The 'time of trouble such as never was,' is soon to open upon us; and we shall need an experience which we do not now possess, and which many are too indolent to obtain. It is often the case that trouble is greater in anticipation than in reality; but this is not true of the crisis before us. The most vivid presentation cannot reach the magnitude of the ordeal. In that time of trial, every soul must stand for himself before God. Though Noah, Daniel, and Job were in the land, 'as I live, saith the Lord God, they shall deliver neither son nor daughter; they shall but deliver their own souls by their righteousness.' Eze. 14:20.

"Now, while our great High Priest is making the atonement for us, we should seek to become perfect in Christ. Not even by a thought could our Saviour be brought to yield to the power of temptation. Satan finds in human hearts some point where he can gain a foot-hold; some sinful desire is cherished, by means of which his temptations assert their power. But Christ declared of himself, 'The prince of this world cometh, and hath nothing in me.' [JOHN 14:30.] Satan could find nothing in the Son of God that would enable him to gain the victory. He had kept his Father's commandments, and there was no sin in him that Satan could use to his advantage. This is the condition in which those must be found who shall stand in the time of trouble.

"It is in this life that we are to separate sin from us, through faith in the atoning blood of Christ. Our precious Saviour invites us to join ourselves to him, to unite our weakness to his strength, our ignorance to his wisdom, our unworthiness to his merits. God's providence is the school in which we are to learn the meekness and lowliness of Jesus. The Lord is ever setting before us, not the way we would choose, which seems easier and pleasanter to us, but the true aims of life. It rests with us to co-operate with the agencies which Heaven employs, in the work of conforming our characters to the divine model. None can neglect or defer this work but at the most fearful peril to their souls." G.C. 621-623.

They Will Be Without Fault Before The Throne Of God

"And in their mouth was found no guile: for they are without fault before the throne of God." Rev. 14:5.

"Now unto him that is able to keep you from falling, and to present you faultless before the presence of his glory with exceeding joy, To the only wise God our Saviour, be glory and majesty, dominion and power, both now and ever. Amen." Jude 24, 25.

They will fully reflect the character of Christ. Even though the whole world will be against them, they will exhibit the forgiving, loving, non-retaliating Spirit of Christ. They will reflect the patience, perseverance and endurance of Christ. All of their sins will have been blotted out, and they will be filled with the victory of Christ.

They Will Have The Father's Name Written In Their Foreheads

"And I looked, and, lo, a Lamb stood on the mount Sion, and with him an hundred forty and four thousand, having his Father's name written in their foreheads." Rev. 14:1.

The survivors of earth's last crisis will have such a knowledge of God, intellectually and spiritually, that their minds will be sustained by the assurance of His infinite wisdom, infinite power and infinite love. They will have such a clear understanding of His character that they will patiently endure the terrors of the final crisis knowing that sin has to be allowed to ripen into self-destruction before God intervenes to deliver them. They will therefore give to the world an exhibition of God's loving character, an exhibition that will be similar to the one Christ gave when He was here on earth.

A Final Word To The Reader

We are living in the time of the end. The fast-fulfilling signs of the times declare that the coming of Christ is near at hand. The days in which we live are solemn and important. The Spirit of God is gradually but surely being withdrawn from the earth. Plagues and judgments are already falling upon the despisers of the grace of God. The calamities by land and sea, the unsettled state of society, the alarms of war, are portentous. They forecast approaching events of the greatest magnitude. The agencies of evil are combining their forces, and consolidating. They are strengthening for the last great crisis. Great changes are soon to take place in our world, and the final movements will be rapid ones.

This book has furnished you with the basic knowledge needed to make the right decision and to be among the survivors of Earth's final crisis.

Publications Available from
Truth For the Final Generation

The Powerful Message of the Two Covenants in the Doctrine of Righteousness by Faith

This book seeks to show the difference between the Old and New Covenants, but more importantly to show how loving, compassionate, merciful, and sweet is our gracious God who is not only able but eager to fulfill His promises in our lives.

Elect According to the Foreknowledge of God

Election, predestination and free choice are subjects that have agitated the minds of God's people down through the centuries of the Christian era. If God has foreknown all things are we really free to choose? Is there a true doctrine of predestination? Christians want to make their calling and election sure. Who are the elect? This book seeks to give the Biblical answers to these questions.

The Sealing Work in the Final Generation

The sealing work begins at conversion when the believer's name is entered into the Book of Life. For the final generation, the sealing ends with the believer's name being retained in the Book of Life, after he has passed the great final test and has demonstrated that his mind is fully fixed in loyalty to God.

God's Character—The Best News in the Universe

A study of the character of God from the Bible alone, allowing scripture to interpret scripture. It is dedicated to the ongoing search for truth and the shining light that results from such scriptural research.

The Power of God's Word in the Science of Faith

Many Christians drift along in a superficial experience without appreciating the power of God's word. In this series of studies we discover the victorious power in God's word, and learn to receive and employ that power in the work of overcoming sin.

The Proclamation of the Acceptable Year of the Lord

Discussions include studies of the Harvest principle and the Generation concept. They examine the reasons for the long delay of the Second Advent and what must be our responsibilities if we are to hasten the day of the Lord and finish the work early in this new generation.